Praise for _The Game of Life_

Beautiful work. This is the way people should adopt the _Ramayana_ in their lives. Very practical and goes with every age.

– Anup Jalota, Padma Shri award winner for Indian Classical Music

The book's strength lies in its simplicity and lucid writing, which takes us through Rama's unique birth and early life. Finally, here's a book that connects us to the original scriptures and gives us a first-hand insight into the real story and mindset of Rama!

– Mahesh Jethmalani, Eminent Lawyer and Political Leader

There can't be a finer effort than this to make the country's proud culture and century-old literary treasure available to the new generation in palatable form with so much of authenticity and conviction.

– Bhuwanesh Jain, Deputy Editor of _Rajasthan Patrika_

This adroit retelling of the Ramayana unravels its all too human struggles and power strategies, as well as the subtle and enduring wisdom of the epic.

– Namita Gokhale, Founder-Director of Jaipur Literature Festival

Shubha Vilas has laid out the story of the _Ramayana_ in colourful and poetic detail. The book truly mirrors the game of life... its ups and downs, follies and foibles and above all, the deep lessons and learnings that emerge as we probe deeper into the events and stories in our life.

It is hoped that the reader will come Home to the Ram within, our own Eternal and Infinite Self – the Source and Home of all stories. I wish the book and the series all success.

– Arun Wakhlu, Executive Chairman, Pragati Leadership

Thoroughly enjoyed reading this immensely insightful book. There is so much in the pages that I am able to apply to my life every day.

– Gayatri Ruia, Director, Phoenix Mills

I have read [other] versions of the *Ramayana* earlier, but Prabhu Shubh Vilas' version is the first that combines an engaging narrative with strategically placed insights that allowed me to get a much deeper understanding of this holy book. This volume will appeal to newcomers to Hindu spirituality and seasoned scholars alike.

– Akhil Shahani, Director of Thadomal Shahani Centre for Management

How to transform values into action? How to make tough decisions? This is a lovely read that is strikingly effective in answering such variegated predicaments of life and persuades you to raise your performance bar, whether you are a corporate executive or simply interested in leading a meaningful life.

– Shrinivas Dempo, Chairman, Dempo Group of Companies

RAMAYANA
—THE—
GAME
OF LIFE

Shattered Dreams

BOOK 2

SHUBHA VILAS

JAICO PUBLISHING HOUSE
Ahmedabad Bangalore Bhopal Bhubaneswar Chennai
Delhi Hyderabad Kolkata Lucknow Mumbai

Published by Jaico Publishing House
A-2 Jash Chambers, 7-A Sir Phirozshah Mehta Road
Fort, Mumbai - 400 001
jaicopub@jaicobooks.com
www.jaicobooks.com

RAMAYANA: THE GAME OF LIFE
Shattered Dreams – Book 2
ISBN 978-81-8495-531-6

First Jaico Impression: 2015

Printed by
Snehesh Printers
320-A, Shah & Nahar Ind. Est. A-1
Lower Parel, Mumbai - 400 013

To my grandmother, whose eloquent narrations of the Ramayana *at bedtime, eventually became the seed that expanded into the fruit of my love for this timeless epic.*

ACKNOWLEDGEMENTS

Walking through life, I have always seen myself as a student, surrounded by teachers who have touched and enhanced my life immensely. I would like to express my heartfelt gratitude for all that I have been fortunate enough to learn from them.

To name all of them here would be impossible; however, some of the most prominent teachers in my life have been: H.D.G. A.C. Bhaktivedanta Swami Srila Prabhupada, the founder of the Hare Krsna Movement, and H.H. Radhanath Swami, the author of the international bestseller *The Journey Home – Autobiography of an American Swami*.

I am indebted to Valmiki *muni*, the author of the *Ramayana*. And Kamba *muni*, who further enriched the flavor of the original with his amazing poetry. I am also grateful to the ocean of love that I experienced while reading the *Ramacharitramanas* of Tulsidas. I have learnt a lot about the intricacies of the *Ramayana* from Sri Velukkudi Krishnan Swami and K.S. Narayanacharya, C. Sita Ramamurti and Sri S. Appalacharyulu. I would also like to appreciate all those who have worked on the website – www.valmikiramayan.net – to make the epic accessible to the world.

My special gratitude to Dr. Shrilekha Hada, for her tireless zeal and invaluable inputs in developing every aspect of the book. My thanks also to Mrs. Natasha Vasudev, for her kind help in further editing the book.

I personally owe a million thanks to Meera Menon, whose meticulousness shows through in every sentence of this book, whose thought-provoking enquiries have helped me go deeper into the *Ramayana*.

And of course, my warm thanks to the entire team of Jaico, especially Mr. Akash Shah, Sandhya Iyer, Sabine Algur, Nita Satikuwar and Vijay Thakur – their intense efforts and sincere dedication are visible on every page of the book. This journey with them has not only been about working on a book but also bonding deeply with the Jaico family.

AUTHOR'S NOTE

Have you ever wondered if the age-old epics hold any immediate relevance to our lives? Why great historical figures like Shivaji felt their education incomplete without a study of such epics as the *Ramayana*? Are you confident about your knowledge and understanding of the *Ramayana*? Or perhaps you are waiting for it to be presented as a gripping new-age thriller without any twists?

If your answers to the questions above are yes, then I bring to you **Ramayana – The Game of Life**, a series that will gracefully remedy your doubts with faith and guidance.

The latest authentic rendition of the *Ramayana*, this series is also a genuine exploration of the epic's many dimensions. It is spine-tingling and soul-stirring, the sort of narrative every bookworm craves, yet carrying a gentle revelation of the *Ramayana's* wisdom at every turn of its story.

While Valmiki's *Ramayana* is its guiding light, the beauty and poetry of the *Kamba Ramayana* and Tulsi Das's *Ramacharitramanas* also find their place in its volumes. In addition, the series brings in folktales (*LokaPramana*) that are in philosophical alignment with Valmiki's original.

The first book in **Ramayana – The Game of Life**, titled *Rise of the Sun Prince*, matched the first chapter (the *Bal Kanda*) of the original work, which starts before the birth of Lord Rama and ends with his glorious marriage to Sita. Twelve joyful years have passed in Ayodhya since the end of Book 1.

This second book, *Shattered Dreams*, begins with a bewildering dilemma and ends with a riddle. It promises to keep you turning the pages through its fascinating narrative, though you may also want to sit back and ponder the teachings embedded in its footnotes.

The book begins with Dasaratha's desperate attempt to change his and Ayodhya's ordained destiny. It also gives a quick peek into the haughty life of the grand anti-hero, Ravana, and his international conquests. Then the drama intensifies as the sinister plot of Manthara is successfully executed.

The steadfastness of Rama in the face of his people's shattered dreams, the extraordinary husband-wife dynamics that Rama and Sita demonstrate, and the contrasting attitudes of Lakshmana and Urmila all add to the charm and drama of this book.

Here too is Bharata, unhappily misunderstood by his own people, yet teaching us six solutions to overcoming obstacles to our ambitions and goals. His meeting with Rama in the forest of Chitrakoota is the heartrending crescendo of the book. Rama offers two gifts to Bharata, convincing him to return to Ayodhya – his footwear to adorn the imperial throne, and a set of five management mantras that are the foundation of the vision-based leadership that leads to Rama Rajya.

The book teaches us how to handle reversals positively. Each situation is a reflection of our own modern dilemmas and illustrates the best way forward, free from clouded minds and thoughtless actions. At its core, *Shattered Dreams* reveals profound rules of human relationships and conduct – what works, what fails to work and how to navigate through this amazing labyrinth.

Shubha Vilas

CONTENTS

Contents

CHAPTER 1

IN HOPE AND IN DESPAIR

a restless night

Dasaratha was breathless from all the running. He had been running with all his might; he was panting and his tired, aging legs were aching for this chase to end. His ashen face and horror-seared eyes longed for a familiar face. Frantic and terrified, he was fleeing from this dark, menacing monster. The monster had been chasing him around *his* Ayodhya, the city he had ruled for so long and knew every lane and bylane and every nook and cranny of. Yet he seemed to find no place to hide or no one to turn to. He was hoping to trick the monster off his back and escape into this familiar city, but with every step, the chase got worse. He seemed to be running past every memory, every incident and every event of his life as he tried to stay off the evil creature's reach. As every little detail of his life flashed by with each step that he took, he heard a blood-curdling, chilling shriek. Could it be the monster? Alas no! It was his past! How could his life let out such a spine-wrecking scream?

Between his delusions and his consciousness, Dasaratha realized that he was in fact fighting two monsters – the monster within and the monster outside. Everything had become a big blur. Which of the two monsters was he fleeing from?[1]

Dasaratha ran on until he reached the door of one of his ministers. His desperate knocks seemed to die silent deaths. None opened the door. The dark creature's thumping footsteps became louder and clearer. It felt as though it was marching to the sound of Dasaratha's loud heartbeat. Petrified at the thought of being captured, Dasaratha began running again. He looked around. Dead calm. The streets that he loved so much for their hustle and bustle now lay empty. Not a soul seemed to have ever walked or lived in Ayodhya. No citizens, no guards, no animal even. Where did they all go? This isn't the time to rationalize. Just run, Dasaratha told himself.

time seizes dasaratha

Just when Dasaratha was about to make it round the bend and manage to fox the creature, a huge furry hand gripped him. Time had "ceased" him. It was all over now. There was nowhere to run, no more to run. He had just run into Time. Dasaratha tried to wrestle out of Time's tight grasp. The harder he tried, the tighter it gripped him. No matter how much he fluttered and flapped like a bird in a snare, flipped and flopped like a fish in a net or scratched

---

[1] The present on the canvas of life is the result of a multitude of past strokes. Rather than brooding over those erroneous past strokes that can no longer be undone, learn from them and apply those strokes of wisdom today to paint a beautiful future. As in a relay race, your past chases you to the present and the present runs toward the future. The baton to success always lies in the hands of the present.

and scrambled like a rat in a trap, he just could not escape this unyielding grasp.

By now, the sweat beads on his forehead burst and began pouring along his temples. Dasaratha twisted and turned in his sleep and his legs flapped helplessly, as if they were not his own. He wanted to shout for help, but fear had robbed him of his voice. Or, perhaps he had come to terms with his destiny. Dasaratha tried to make that one last attempt to escape the monster's grasp. He threw his mighty arms up to grab the monster's neck... Kaboom!

The deafening explosion jolted Dasaratha back to consciousness. He looked around. He was on his soft white bed, although still trembling and sweating profusely. A knocked-over heavy urn lay vacillating on the floor. Dasaratha was half relieved. "I am still in my room! It was just the urn! I must have knocked it down in my sleep. There's no monster here." But what was that? It was a nightmare he wished would never come true. His heart hadn't stopped pounding, and seemed like it never would. It was a recurring nightmare that had left Dasaratha sleepless till the end.

The crashing urn brought ten guards rushing to the king's bedside. Dasaratha had half an urge to send them off to arrest the monster that had so traumatized him. Alas, a nightmare monster cannot be captured. He waved his bewildered guards away. The worried look on their king's face was indication enough to leave him alone. The guards returned to their stations.

The pensive king stepped off his luxurious bed and began pacing the room. Every bit of opulent furnishing in his room seemed lackluster. Everything around him had lost its sheen. Even the mirror in the corner of his room wore a sad look. Dasaratha walked up to the mirror and saw the angst that had traveled from his heart to his face. He had flashed endless happy smiles and worn the mask of calmness for the entire world, but the mirror reflected the truth: He was standing there forlorn, miserable, helpless. All the happy vibes he sent out at daytime were but lies that buried the truth of his nighttime horrors. These were dark dreams and dark fears he could not risk sharing with anyone. This was a battle he had to wage alone. How many more such dreams to endure? What do they all portend? Dasaratha was no fool. He had a premonition that something terrible was coming his way. How terrible? Dasaratha had no clue.[2]

How does one prepare for a danger one knows nothing about? Dasaratha looked hard at the mirror. Did it have any answers? Wait… did he just see… ? The king abandoned his nightmare analysis to face a far more worrying reality: a strand of gray on his head! He looked again. Goodness! His head was teeming with gray! His duties as king had kept him too busy to even realize that he was graying, and growing older. Perhaps the monarch's white umbrella camouflaged the grays. There was no escaping the truth now: he was aging, and aging fast. He had been king for far longer than any other from the Ikshvaku line.[3]

moonbeam of hope

Just then a happy thought crossed Dasaratha's sad mind. As he broke into a smile, his worry wrinkles disappeared. He had spotted the

---

[2] How long can one go on with smiling faces and crying hearts? Either till the smile of the face goes to the heart or the cry of the heart reaches the face.

[3] The easiest way to forget your limitations is to shift the focus from self-absorption to active-facilitation. Dasaratha had not realized his shortcomings because of his absorption in his responsibilities.

moonbeam that would chase away his darkness. For two decades and a half, Dasaratha must have smiled countless times at the thought of this moonbeam – the bright spot in his life, the solution to all his ills. His moonbeam was Rama Himself – Dasaratha's life, his breath, his real wealth and luckily, also his eldest son.

Dasratha had always thought of himself as a man with four arms, because his sons were his arms. He loved all his arms equally, but always gravitated toward the strongest. He loved all his sons dearly, but he had an instinctive attraction for and an innate connection with Rama.

Dasaratha began pacing the room again. Only this time, it was not out of worry but out of hope. Dasaratha was restless. He wanted the sun to rise because sleep had become a nemesis. He could not return to that monster. He knew that it would sneak up on him the moment he shut his eyes, almost as if it lay hidden under his lids. Dasaratha kept staring toward the east through what was left of the horrible night. Half the night had been damned by despair and the other half buoyed by hope. Wasn't this what life was all about?[4]

At long last, the sun rose to rid Dasaratha of the anxiety of how long it would take for sunrise. His other worries were his own, and he had to deal with them all by himself. He dressed to go to his courtroom. As he slipped into his robes and tightened his waist belt, he gritted his teeth in firm resolve: His twin problems would have to be resolved today.

Dasaratha rode on his royal elephant across the citizen-lined streets of Ayodhya. Hundreds stood waiting to greet and admire their

---

[4] Life is a combination of hope and despair, the one that dominates you carves your personality.

powerful king and bask under his protective glances. But an array of weak thoughts furrowed the mind of their powerful king. Who would protect him from these thoughts?[5]

Dasaratha's mind kept raking up his nightmares again and again, almost as if some evil force was trying hard to stop him from making the optimistic decision he was about to make. Suddenly, he winced. He wanted to shake his thought off the black serpent that been the villain of the worst nightmare he had in days. The serpent had nearly strangled him to death. Just thinking about the horrid reptile left Dasaratha cold and perspiring. His thoughts somehow raced back to that time in his youth when he had made a weird promise. That promise was like a sword dangling over his head, waiting to pierce through it. That memory rattled him as did the thought of the all the meteors that had hurtled toward Earth over the past few weeks. As the thoughts in his head grew louder with the sound of the gurgling pot in the river and the haunting wail of a dying human, the applause and cat whistles of his subjects grew fainter. In his head, he could clearly visualize his glistening sonic arrow whiz past, hit its target and let out a shriek. These haunting visions kept draining him. The majestic king who surveyed his subjects was secretly hoping some higher power would have some mercy on him and save him.

No! Dasaratha tried to talked himself out of his fear. "No! I will put an end to all this inauspiciousness in my life by doing the most auspicious thing. O mind! Disturb me not from carrying out my desires."

---

[5] Every protector needs protection. Being constantly reminded of such a need keeps the protector humble. Everyone in this world has a role to play and a role to depend on. The absence of a role to play causes despair and the absence of a role to depend on (higher powers) causes hauteur.

Dasaratha decided to take a detour. Instead of going to the courtroom, he made his way to the "hope center" of Ayodhya. This was the center that had always stood like a beacon of hope for him as it had for all his ancestors, especially in trying times. All his dark thoughts and negativity seemed to plunge as the elephant took the turn toward the center. It was as if the dark powers had backed off, realizing that they could haunt him no more. Dasaratha jumped off his faithful elephant of many years to enter the safe haven. His folded palms in a *namaste mudra*,[6] the king stepped into the temple of Lord Ranganatha, the nine-foot long form of Lord Vishnu lying on his celebrated snake bed. Dasaratha lay prostrate in front of that deity and prayed for protection from all evil and for empowerment to make the right decisions. Dasaratha now felt truly blessed.[7]

the king's assembly

Dasaratha always entered the courtroom to blaring trumpets, booming drums, reverberating conches and hundreds of bowing heads. A regular day would have Dasaratha saunter in, with a nod here and a nod there, savoring the adulation of his citizens as he trundled to his throne. Something was different today. The king was in earlier than usual, his detour notwithstanding. Who would keep time on a day such as this? Certainly not Dasaratha! He walked briskly toward his throne like a horse with blinders. He had

---

[6] An age-old yogic posture that indicates shelter-seeking.

[7] Prayer peppered with a feeling of helplessness is a tool to attract grace. But grace really descends when this prayer is unobstructed by the transparent wall of pride in one's abilities.

determination and a sense of urgency. As he looked straight ahead to the throne he had occupied for years and years, he seemed to be conversing with it. He had to do it here and now. The throne needed more security than he could offer.

The court was soon brimming with hundreds of citizens, sages and ministers. Today was not an ordinary court day, for the king had called in a special convention. Dasaratha had earlier invited all subordinate princes, chieftains and officers of the various cities and villages of his kingdom, army chiefs, public leaders, important state functionaries, his Big M (Dristi, Jayantha, Vijaya, Suraashtra, Raashtravardhana, Akopa, Dharmapaala and Sumantra) and his two spiritual *gurus* (Vasistha and Vamadeva) to this epic meeting. He had held his decision close to his chest till every important person of his kingdom had gathered to hear him. He had called the most important people of his kingdom, but not the most important people of his life. He had deliberately not invited Mithila ruler King Janaka, Sita's father, and Yuthajit, his wife Keikeyi's brother and Bharata's maternal uncle, keeping in mind the time it would take for them to reach Ayodhya. Dasaratha could not afford that time. Not for this decision he was about to make. Was the omission merely because of the distance his relatives had to cover? That the invitations had gone out to those living farther away seemed to suggest there was more to it. For now though, all but two of the most important people in Dasaratha's rule were before him.[8]

As Dasaratha walked briskly toward the throne, his invitees followed him, and it seemed as though an elephant king was leading his herd to the lake of joy. Only this king was wounded. Dasaratha

---

[8] A complex mindset is indicative of the complexities of the past. An exception made on the basis of some excuse provides a glimpse of those complexities.

reached the throne, turned around and surveyed the audience. Such intoxicating respect, he thought. Dasaratha seemed in control despite the tumult in his mind. As he sat on his throne, every king, minister, every courtier and every citizen settled on their seats.

Dasaratha regarded every member in the audience. These were the loyal people who had helped him achieve and maintain supremacy over the entire world for such a long time. He was grateful to them all. Everyone had so many divine qualities that each person seemed perfect; they were knowledgeable, ready to sacrifice their lives, selfless, free from wrath even in the most provoking of circumstances; in fact calamities brought the best in them.[9] They were spiritual, far-sighted, wise, tradition-loving heritage-bearers who passed down every ounce of their virtues to the next generation. Everywhere Dasaratha turned, he saw loyal and caring faces. He could feel their effusive love for him. Often he had seen them maintain such calm and balance handling situations, keeping in mind the time, the place, the circumstances, the injunctions of ancient texts, the opinions of wise saints, the advice of loyal people and the sentiments of the citizens. Dasaratha's faith was reaffirmed. He was certain that seated before him were the right people to endorse his decision today.[10]

---

[9] Calamity in friendship is absence of a person during sad times; calamity in governance is absence of courage in emergencies; calamity in culture is absence of determination during temptations; calamity in agriculture is absence of rain during cultivation; calamity in parenting is absence of time during development.

[10] Decision-making is akin to breathing. Just as in breathing there is careful balance between inhalation and exhalation, decision-making must be a careful balance between personal benefits (taking in or inhalation) and communal harmony (giving out or exhalation).

Dasaratha thought of this assembly of loyals as physicians gathered to calm his restless mind. Although they were many in number, these people were so inspiringly cohesive that they became one body and one mind when it came to serving the interests of their king and their kingdom.[11]

Each member of that audience loved Dasaratha and respected Vasistha. Dasaratha had always been like a father figure to them, treating them as his children and caring for their needs. Today, when everyone had gathered before him, Dasaratha gestured to his help to shower innumerable valuable gifts upon all gathered in his assembly. He felt the joy a father would as he saw them receive their gifts.

"Hail King Dasaratha! Long live King Dasaratha, our protector!" A chorus of appreciation reverberated through the court. As the din continued, the adulation echoed inside Dasaratha's ears. Dasaratha! Dasaratha! Dasaratha! He had heard this several times, but none sounded as special as the first. With the chorus of his name echoing through the courtroom, Dasaratha traveled far away from the now to the then: a distinct distant memory.

the ten-chariot hero

"Dasaratha! Dasaratha! Dasaratha!" the demigods were shouting out in joy now. But it wasn't long ago that an attractive messenger from the land of the demigods (universal administrators) had

---

[11] Unity without loyalty to a common goal is like cement without water to seal bricks.

crashed into the courtroom of the young King Nemi. "Help! The heavens are in trouble and the gods need your help in saving them from a never-before-experienced calamity named Sambara!"

The youthful and ever-ready-for-a-fight Nemi ventured into the heavenly realm, beaming with pride that even the demigods depended on his valor. He was itching for the fight to begin, but the demigods thought it prudent to inform him about the complexity of the job at hand. The commander in chief of the demigod's army painstakingly expounded the illusory power of Sambarasura and about his abilities to use all kinds of weapons to perfection. Nemi was nonchalant; he had squashed far too many powerful and multiple weapon-wielding opponents with his mighty arms. The chief of the demigods noticed Nemi's arrogance and smirked. As he walked away, he warned: "Be ready for the surprise of your life when you face ten Sambaras."[12]

What did he just say? Ten Sambaras?! What would that mean? Who cares? Nothing is really difficult, thought Nemi.

Nemi's war-anointed, scar-seared left arm gripped his mighty bow, which he had mounted on the chariot floor. He was all set to attack the jeering Sambarasura he had spotted a little distance away. Nemi then stole a quick glance at his petite charioteer for this battle outing – his own favorite queen, the beautiful Keikeyi! The king was searching for traces of fear, but instead, steering the chariot in the direction of the heckling monster was the gallant

---

[12] A foolhardy person seems enthusiastic to the ignorant, but he seems ignorant to the wise. The fine delineation between overconfidence and self-confidence is determined by the reaction to good advice. When the water of good advice is poured, an overconfident person's already-filled jug rejects it, whereas a self-confident person's sponge absorbs it.

Keikeyi with a glint in her eyes – the glint of anticipation of an adrenaline-pumping battle.[13]

During the terrible fight that followed, Sambarasura realized that Nemi was not the usual puny human, the kind he had swallowed by the dozen so often in the past. Sensing a tough battle with the mighty-armed Nemi, the demon unleashed his powerful illusory tricks. Nemi dodged each of those tricks and began shooting his sharp arrows at Sambara. It took a while for Nemi to realize that arrows from behind him had begun penetrating his armor. He turned around and was startled to see a Sambarasura clone standing right there! How? Yet another arrow pierced him from another side. He turned to fight another Samabarasura. Three of them! Soon a bewildered Nemi was being pelted with arrows from seven directions. Nemi was right in the middle of a foray of darting arrows, and all his energy was expended in just trying saving himself, leave alone attacking Sambarasura. The brave queen Keikeyi realized that her husband was in deep trouble. She urged him to hold on to the mast of the chariot and suddenly veered the chariot toward the sky and whisked the wounded king to safety.

Keikeyi patiently attended to her semiconscious husband and nursed him back to health. The ever-grateful Nemi thanked her for saving his life and decided to end the battle that he had left halfway. Once again, bow in hand and arrows sharpened, Nemi charged at the demon with full vigor. Soon, the seven Sambaras lay grievously wounded. But then three more appeared and locked Nemi in yet another high-pitch battle. By this time, the seven Samabaras recovered and Nemi was left fending off ten attacking

---

[13] Confidence is contagious; so is fear. Both act inversely. Confidence increases our capacity and fear decreases it.

Sambaras from ten different directions. Nemi's chariot kept circling in all directions – at times flying, at times veering sideways, at times charging headlong, at times moving backward but rarely surging ahead. Nemi himself seemed to be dancing as he dodged the whizzing arrows, rattling spears, pacey clubs and scores of other weapons that were being hurled at him simultaneously. It seemed like the dance of death.

Just as Nemi seemed to have an edge, an arrow hit a slot on his chariot wheel, almost dislodging it. The chariot began to wobble and Keikeyi knew she had to think and act fast. She stooped and inserted her finger into the slot to keep the wheel from coming off. The entire weight of the chariot rested on the brave queen's fragile finger. Nemi's eyes welled up with tears at the sight of his wife enduring excruciating pain just to save him. The king trembled with a rage that seemed to have transferred on to his sharp arrows. As Keikeyi fixed the chariot, Nemi shot arrow after arrow at the ten-cloned Sambara. Every arrow hit its mark, and soon Sambarasura was slain and had become yet another of the many glorious conquests of the valiant Nemi.[14]

"Dasaratha! Dasaratha! Dasaratha!" the elated and relieved demigods had cried. They had been watching the battle from afar. Nemi was now Dasaratha, the man whose chariot could move in ten directions!

---

[14] If service is like a flower and genuine service attitude is like fragrance, then gratitude is like a bee that hovers over it. Relationships thrive when genuine service is acknowledged by active gratitude. Keikeyi was happy to serve and Nemi was grateful to receive. She provided assistance and he gave appreciation.

a king steps down

"Dasaratha! Dasaratha! Dasaratha! Hail, King Dasaratha!"
The loud adorations dragged Dasaratha back to the present – a grim
present. Past glories were now history, and reminiscing served no
purpose. The king had to refocus on the present, so he straightened
himself.[15]

All formalities had been completed, and the most important
people had assembled and settled down. Dasratha began to speak;
his voice was an elegant blend of power and sweetness: deep as
the thundering cloud but sweet as the whistling flute. Dasaratha
spoke with the charisma of the king of the world, with clarity and
from his heart.[16]

"The magnanimous city of Ayodhya thrives on the principle of
sacrifice – a student lives not for himself but to serve his teacher;
a husband lives to serve his wife; a king to serve his kingdom; the
kingdom to serve the country and the country to serve *dharma*. The
'I' generation is a dangerous one, where everyone is only worried
about 'I, me and mine.' When the mentality is who is going to serve
me, it will keep a person dissatisfied. Even to breathe, one has to
let out and let in air. This is nothing but giving and taking. One
cannot be naïve and say, 'I will only let in and not let out, because
I don't like giving.'

---

[15] One should not ruminate about glories of the past to act as the salve to
ease the pain of the gloom of the present.

[16] Superficial speech is shallow and sensible speech deep. Depth in speech
is indicative of a person of substance. Harsh speech is bitter, sweet speech
is pleasant. Pleasantness in speech is indicative of a person of kindness. A
charismatic leader is a blend of substance and kindness.

"The satisfaction of Ayodhya's citizens has been my life's sole purpose. Administrative schemes were laid out with sharp acumen, protective measures taken with great vigor and limitless charity granted with humble benevolence, all keeping this goal in mind. And all of this has not been my doing alone. To the degree a blind man depends on his stick, I have depended on the collective wisdom of all of you gathered here to make this kingdom what it is – a heaven on earth."[17]

Dasaratha drew a deep breath and continued in a tone that reflected his present predicament, "I am now weary, old age has decayed my strength and rendered me unfit to fulfill the demands of the royal crown. If the royal white umbrella above my head could speak, it would tell you a hundred tales of my valor and my ceaseless efforts to keep my people safe. But now, under the same umbrella, time has taken its toll on me and I am shriveling up as does a flower under the summer sun. The burden of righteousness is indeed heavy. I have been carrying it around on my never-resting shoulders across so many seasons. An aging man cannot do justice to the weight of a zillion expectations. I long for rest and wish to hand over this burden now. Like the bull that after years of slogging for its master needs care and rest, I, too, crave for some repose.[18]

---

[17] Being a genius is not so much about knowing everything as much as it is about knowing when to admit to the self that 'I don't know' and seek guidance.

[18] The burden of responsibility brings to the ground the one floating in the clouds of self-interest. Expecting responsibility to be fun is no different from a weightlifter expecting his weights to be as light as a mushroom. Treating people like chewing gum is akin to hedonism in a relationship. Use-and-throw works fine for chewing gum but not for people. Dasaratha, like many leaders, led a life of service to others, and the last thing such leaders expect is to be overthrown by being branded useless.

Hear my friends and well-wishers, Dasaratha, your king wants to pour out his heart. When time comes for a season to change, none can stop it. Only a fool would even think of attempting to stop the change. Coping with change and seeing nature's wisdom in the change is a sign of mature intelligence. Just as my ancestors of the Ikshvaku line had ruled this kingdom with paternal care, I, too, have trod the path of the glorious dead and served my kingdom with endless zeal. And just as the glorious kings of this dynasty, in time, had handed over the reins to able hands and focused on the next aspect of their lives, I, too, wish to do the same. I have been witness to some disturbing ill omens, which calls for a change of guard.[19]

I was named Dasaratha because my chariot was trained to move in ten directions and conquer ten nemeses. A king is called *maharaja* and so is a renunciant. Why? Because a renunciant too is a *maharaja* in the way he has fought and triumphed over his six inner demons that embody the six directions within every person that pull him apart. I am a king only externally but a prisoner internally. I now want to focus on battling my six inner demons. Six aspects of nature teach us how to conquer these six inner enemies."

---

[19] Resistance to inevitable change is a result of nature's painful unpredictability of the consequences of change. The tendency of controlling minutely leads to the fear of losing control as a result of change. Change management is about gracefully changing the way we perceive change.

Six *Anarthas* to Conquer

Lust: As long as fire is confined to a fireplace, it provides warmth. As soon as it surges and spreads, it unleashes disaster. Lust, like fire, should stay confined by self-control.

Rage: Water sprayed on the face from a sprinkler feels cool, but water gushing uncontrollably from a dam destroys villages sometimes. Rage, like gushing water, should be curbed to avoid devastation.

Ego: A frog, overestimating the harmony of its voice, croaks on and on only to attract a hungry snake. Ego and self-praise attract the snakes of time. The mouth needs to be sealed with the nectar of humility.

Greed: Accumulating water in a pot holds for as long as the pot has no holes. Greed, which is the hole from which leaks the fluid of intense attachment to accumulation and leaves one thirsty for peace, needs to be plugged with satisfaction.

Illusion: A camel feeding on thorny cactus mistakes blood oozing from its tongue for nectar; a victim of illusion considers miseries to be cradles of happiness. Illusion can be curbed by acquiring real vision, which ensures clear action.

Envy: A man unconvinced about the poisonous effect of the *datura* plant may test it on himself before using it on his enemy. Would he live to see its effect on his target? Envy when harbored destroys the bearer even before impairing the target. It has to be nipped in the bud because when it grows, like a *datura*, it could fill the world with the fruits of evil and seeds of destruction.

Fire when not confined, water when not controlled, frog when not silent, the pot when not holed, camel when not prudent and the *datura* when not nipped in the bud can all have disastrous consequences. So the flaws in fire, water, frog, pot, camel and *datura* plant are teachers in that they teach us how to subjugate the six inner enemies of lust, anger, ego, greed, illusion and envy.

Dasaratha's eyes darted from person to person in the courtroom to see the effect of his speech. He scanned everyone's expressions. He had just laid bare his life before everyone. What were they thinking? He could not read anything from their baffled blank expressions. Perhaps he needed to communicate his thoughts more clearly.

"I want my eldest son Rama to take over from me, and I want to retire to focus on the deeper aspects of my own life. I have served you all for so long and now I request that you all grant me some time to serve myself, while there is still some vivacity left in me. Rama is already married to Sita, now I want to marry Rama to this planet Earth. I trust your decision more than I trust mine. So dear friends, please be forthright with your opinions about my decision so that a consensus can be reached at the earliest."[20]

Dasaratha stopped talking. There was silence; perhaps a pin would drop and be heard loud as thunder. The king was palpitating; mixed emotions ran through him. This deafening silence was killing him.

---

[20] Just as pressure between two powerful stones grinds grains to fine powder, consensus between neutral people results in well-rounded and impartial decisions.

The dark thoughts in his mind began to grow louder than ever now. He had pushed all of those aside to bravely declare what he wanted to. But why were they all so silent? Was everyone wondering why would Dasaratha, who had ruled so well for so many years, now hand over his kingdom to a novice, a young inexperienced boy, when everything was perfect in Ayodhya? What if all of them decided to reject this proposal? What if they felt Rama was not qualified enough to be king? God, please let them not think this way! Dasaratha decided to accept and abide by whatever conclusion everyone arrived at together. After all, wasn't this the kind of cooperation and mutual trust that had made Ayodhya invincible? But why was everyone silent? Say something, this silence is stifling![21]

Suddenly Dasaratha's court erupted and everyone spoke in unison, and they said exactly the same thing: '*Icchaamah, mahaabahum, Raghuveeram.*' A tumultuous uproar went up in the air, the vibrations of which reached every corner of Ayodhya. It seemed as if the palace walls would crack. Though deafening, the sound was like music, like the cry of a muster of peacocks on seeing the first rainclouds. It was indeed a cry of joy!

"We desire (*icchaamah*) the mighty armed one (*mahaabahum*) Rama (*raghuveeram*)." A member of the assembly rose and spoke on behalf of everyone: "You have indeed ruled for a long time, you should now step down and allow the royal white umbrella to shield Rama."

---

[21] Decision-making in the kingdom of Ayodhya followed a circular system. Which point in a circle could be considered the most important? The center, naturally. In a circular system, the king was also one of the points on the circle but not the center. At the center was the welfare of the kingdom. The king was not a lawmaker, instead he was a lawkeeper. The king expressed ideas, all citizens laid down their opinions, and the churning of ideas and opinions resulted in a collective decision.

Everyone in the audience smiled, but Dasaratha became sullen. Ironic! He should have been happy. It was his proposal after all. A downcast Dasaratha told them that it was wonderful that they had accepted Rama as their next king, but their enthusiasm left him wondering if they had always wanted him to relinquish his throne and give it away to Rama. Dasaratha began to have this unnerving feeling that he had been an unjust and unqualified king and that his subjects were patiently waiting for this day. He clarified his doubt with them so that he did not have to step down feeling rejected. A chieftain stood and said: "Your only disqualification is that you have someone as worthy as Rama for a son."

Another got up and said: "Rama has so many good qualities that the moment we think of Him, we cannot imagine anyone else leading us." Yet another rose to say: "Our situation is similar to that of a cow that delivers twin calves, confused about which of the two calves to give more love and attention to because she loves them both equally. Similarly, we love you and Rama equally, so we are not sure whom to choose to be our king."

Now that his doubts were set aside, Dasaratha was beaming with each comment. The pride of a father had replaced the insecurity of a king. Words of glory for his son were sweeter than honey. He knew these weren't just platitudes but showers of genuine appreciation toward Rama.[22]

---

[22] Empty flattery soothes the mind, whereas copious appreciation touches the heart. Flattery engages only the tongue, while appreciation employs the eyes to observe, the ears to listen, the intelligence to analyze, the tongue to speak and the heart to feel. When eaten, the flattery fruit intoxicates and weakens, whereas the appreciation fruit gives strength and encouragement.

Triple Virtues

Ayodhya's citizens considered Rama as the greatest of all Ikshvaku kings. A great person is labeled prodigious only if he is a combination of three virtues – magnificent talent, right attitude and spotless character. Rama embodied all these virtues.

Talent

Talent is like a sword, not to be merely admired but to be actually used. Just as Rama's quiver is equipped with multiple arrows, His personality is equipped with multifarious talents.

Rama not only knew all the Vedas by rote, he also knew how to apply them. His skillful use of all celestial weapons was not an arrogant display of power but a premeditated show of care.

His excellence in singing was not superficial melody but a love-awakening and hope-giving euphony. His oratory wasn't a long-winding river of discourse but eloquent drops of nectar. His grasp of public administration was abetted by a wary balance of reward to the virtuous and reprimand to the wicked, avoiding excesses on either side.

Attitude

Talent without the right attitude is like sweet rice without sugar. Talent brings one to the brink of the bridge to success and right attitude helps one cross it.

The symptom of the disease of vanity is the desire to be approached by others rather than to approach others; the sweet-smiling Rama vaccinated Himself from this disease and initiated discussions using the elixir of humility. The symptom of the disease of intellectual snobbery is utmost self-reliance; Rama was immune to this disease because he gulped down the amalgam of submissive inquiry from three sources, the experienced (*vayo vriddha* – those possessing the wealth of age), the wise (*jnana vriddha* – those possessing the wealth of knowledge) and the cultured (*shila vriddha* – those possessing the wealth of character). The symptom of the disease of insensitivity is extreme self-concern and sheer indifference toward others; Rama was untouched by this disease because of the tonic of empathy he had obtained by partaking in the joys and sufferings of his people. Rama kept His mind healthy with the vitamin of gratitude for all those who did Him good, even if only once, and eliminated the toxins of lapses toward Him.

Character

Talent and attitude take one to success, but character helps one maintain it. Spotless character is a tripod of self-control, honesty and integrity.

Nature puts an ordinary piece of coal through extreme pressure to transform it into the most precious jewel. When an ordinary human happily subjects himself to the pressure of self-control, he transforms himself to a man of spotless character.

An elephant has two sets of teeth – a useless set of (tusks) just for show because these could not be used for eating and another to actually chew food. Just like an elephant, a man who lacks integrity has two sets of value systems – one for preaching (high standards) and another for practice (compromised standards). Rama's life was an open book. He chose to embrace invaluable principles and demonstrate integrity rather than make a compromise for self-interest and personal convenience. Rama's connection with the truth was the same as a cuckoo's connection to its sweet song, pleasant and constant.

One of the kings present in the assembly compared Rama to the moon when it came to making people happy, to the earth when it came to forgiveness, to the sun when it came to His radiance, to Brihaspati (the *guru* of the gods in heaven) when it came to wisdom and to Indra (the king of gods) when it came to courage.

Everyone took this opportunity to shower praises on Rama. An elderly minister rose, tears of affection in his eyes, and said that the entire kingdom was praying for Rama – across every stately mansion, every little hamlet, the young and the old were praying for Rama through the day. This observation touched Dasaratha. So many blessings for his son![23]

All those praises from all those eminent people and the buoyant mood of everyone in the assembly was incentive enough for a beaming Vasistha, the spiritual *guru* of Dasaratha and the entire Ikshvaku dynasty, to get up and speak: "Dasaratha, rest assured that your decision to step down and hand over the reins to Rama is not only acceptable to everyone but also highly desired by all. We are waiting to see Rama seated under the white umbrella, ride on the

---

[23] The blessing of the strong is to facilitate the weak. The blessing of the weak is to strengthen the strong. Blessing is an intangible currency that helps one buy the ingredients for success.

royal elephant across the streets of Ayodhya. In fact, we wish to see this lion of Ayodhya astride an elephant! Historic!"

Vasistha's assurance filled Dasaratha with immense hope and happiness. He quickly tried to make a rough calculation to compare the amount of joy he experienced now with that of the happiest moments of his life – this was twice the joy of hearing about Rama's birth, thrice the joy of Rama's marriage, four times the joy of Rama breaking Lord Shiva's bow and five times the joy of Parashurama's defeat.

Phew! Such relief! A huge burden was taken off Dasaratha's head. He suddenly felt giddy with happiness because his mind stopped tormenting him as soon as the court seconded his decision. He thanked everyone profusely for obliging and concurring with his decision. Let the celebrations begin! No more delays. Let the coronation take place the very next day, Dasaratha declared and walked off with Sumantra, his confidant, charioteer and minister, following closely behind.

Vasistha plunged into action. Right away, an executive organizing committee was formed; the finest quality of rice, milk and yogurt were packed for distribution to a hundred thousand brahmanas; a host of things, including gold, diamonds, worship paraphernalia, hundreds of natural herbs, floral garlands, corn, honey, clarified butter, new clothes, chariots, all kinds of weapons, four divisions of army, an elephant with special auspicious signs, a white fan, a flag staff, a white umbrella, a hundred shiny golden pots, a bull with gilded horns, were listed for procurement before dawn; all doorways in the kingdom including that of the royal palace were to be swathed in sandalwood paste, decorated with floral garlands and smoked with fragrant incense; prayers and oblations were to be carried out in every temple in Ayodhya with great pomp and reverence;

musicians and dancers were to perform in all corners of Ayodhya starting right away and make it to the royal palace by dawn... the list was endless! Despite his age, the enthusiastic Vasistha went on and on, poring over every tiny detail with great gusto. This was no ordinary occasion. For many, it was a once-in-a-lifetime event.[24]

While Vasistha was busy making arrangements for the following day's ceremony, Dasaratha entered his private quarters with Sumantra. At last, he was free to speak his mind and express his emotions without the pressure of being watched by all. With tears of joy in his eyes, Dasaratha ordered Sumantra to beckon his life, Rama, to his presence.

a king steps in

About 200 yards from him, Dasaratha could see a greenish beacon, effulgent like the sun flickering atop a golden frame. It took a while for the frail and world-weary eyes of king to realize that the gold–green light was actually the radiant body of his oldest son, Rama, dismounting gracefully from his golden chariot with the help of Sumantra. Such beauty! How could anyone take their eyes off this boy? Two and a half decades had passed by just looking at Him, but now time stood still upon seeing Rama. Dasaratha had the most beautiful queens of this world for wives and the most beautiful objects to behold, yet all those beauties could not hold

---

[24] The joy of giving is higher than the joy of the occasion of giving. But this joy of benevolence can be only perceived when the giver gives with gratitude. If the giver gives with arrogance, his act of giving will be perceived by a receiver as being punched by a boxer.

his attention.[25] But it was different with Rama, he never tired of looking at his beautiful son. As the world-famous hero Rama was getting off the chariot holding its mast, Dasaratha's eyes went up to the flag fluttering on top of the chariot. Soon that flag would bear the royal emblem.

The moment Rama stepped on to the ground, it seemed to light up. His walk resembled the vigorous gait of an elephant. His long arms draped in silk reached His knees. His enchanting face resembled the moon and was held high, as if challenging the moon that was now hiding. Carefully protected within the *bimba*-fruit red lips was a row of teeth, shiny as pearls.

Am I touching silk or is it butter? wondered Sumantra as Rama held him while dismounting from His chariot. How could these soft, delicate hands have broken Lord Shiva's mighty bow? As Rama alighted the steps toward Dasaratha's palace, Sumantra followed Him with folded hands, gazing meditatively at His delicate feet which seemed to dance as They climbed the royal steps.[26] Rama's lotus feet took Sumantra back in time by half an hour.

Rama, Sita and Lakshmana were talking to each other, smiling. Sumantra had literally barged into Rama's palace and interrupted this happy discussion. But the three of them immediately rose from

---

[25] Just as snow vanishes with the warmth of the sun, the beauty of the objects of this world diminishes with passing time. Both the Sun and Time rise of their own accord.

[26] The stern posture of the eagle indicates confidence, the twitchy posture of the sparrow indicates fear and the callous posture of the vulture indicates meanness. Similarly, the folded hands of Sumantra suggested his loyalty and downward gaze revealed his modesty. The science of gestures indexes the traits of the mind and the moods of the individual.

their seats and offered their respects to the elderly and wise minister, Sumantra. His presence heralded an instruction from the king. Soon, Sumantra was Rama's charioteer. Sumantra was more elated to hear that Rama would be king than he would have been had he himself been made king of the universe. Sumantra's joy increased manifold when he saw the effect Rama's chariot trip to Dasaratha's palace had on the citizens of Ayodhya.

Drum beats and loud music ushered the chariot along every street. People seemed to say that they were now in safe hands, protected from all misery. Sumantra noticed the scintillating effect Rama's charm had on Ayodhya's damsels, who shed their shyness and ran like deer to keep pace with Rama's chariot so that they could see His lotus face for a little while longer. Their eyes were like darts piercing Rama's shining body and lotus-like face. Rama's looks were driving everyone crazy. The minds of the girls were swept away by overflowing love that tore down discipline and etiquette just as a gushing river breaks the embankments. Their shamelessness surprised them. Even the men were reeling under the effect of Rama's personality. He was robbing the eyes and minds of all of Ayodhya with His beauty, His generosity and His virtues. Ayodhya's men behaved like cows separated from their calves and chased Rama's chariot just as they had chased butterflies in their childhood.[27] Sumantra thought it was comical: so many royals running like crazy people. As Rama passed by, a wave of calm swept across the minds of people, in the way a cool breeze would bring relief to people scorched by the summer heat.

From atop tall buildings and palaces, flowers rained down from the

---

[27] The simplest joys of nature cannot be replaced by the complex creations of man.

hair of girls leaning over their windows trying to catch a glimpse of Rama. Some even swooned seeing Rama's broad chest adorned with a beautiful garland of fresh lotus flowers. Sumantra noticed the streets of Ayodhya were strewn with flowers. It seemed as though even the gods had showered some rain praise on Rama.

dasaratha's lament

"Accept my respects, O Lord of Ayodhya!" The sweet-voiced Rama's voice boomed across the room as He bowed down in veneration in front of His father with folded hands. The melodious voice brought Sumantra back to the present.[28]

Dasaratha lifted Rama up and pulled him close to his bosom. The loving embrace suddenly turned into a test – the mighty-armed Dasaratha tightened his grip to assess Rama's physical prowess. Now that Rama was expected to carry the burden of the world, would his chest and shoulders have enough power in them? As Dasaratha crushed the delicate body of Rama, he could sense the resilience and power beneath the soft exterior. Even a quarter of the power he had used in that embrace would have crushed an ordinary human, but Rama was oblivious of everything. All He felt was His father's loving embrace. *Bravo my son!* Dasaratha thought.

Dasaratha released his bear hug and gently ushered Rama to the gilded throne in his palace and sat beside Him, pouring out his

---

[28] In a fountain, water that gushes upward with zeal comes down with grace. Similarly, respect, when sent forth with genuineness, returns with elegance. Rama was respected because he was respectful.

heart. The delight on Dasaratha's face upon seeing Rama was the same as seeing one's happy reflection in the mirror.

Dasaratha lifted his index finger and said: "Deep gratitude. That's what I feel toward the gods for having allowed me to live and rule this long. In all these years, I have carefully struck off all the five debts a human being incurs. By performing sacrifices, I am no more indebted to the celestials. By studying the scriptures, I have fulfilled my debt to those sages who wrote them and taught them. By donating wealth and food, I repaid my debt to the *brahmanas*. By relishing in the comforts of desire, I have fulfilled my debt to myself. And of course, by begetting a wonderful son like you, the debt to my ancestors, too, has been realized. I seem to have only one duty left to complete – place the imperial crown on your head. Everyone in Ayodhya wants to witness it, and this will be the fulfillment of my life's greatest dream, too.[29]

"I consider you a good friend, so I wish to say a few things although I am aware you already know of it. Yet, as your friend,[30] it is my job to help you understand your responsibilities. A just ruler happily sacrifices the self at the pyre of world peace. The two swords that dangle above a leader's head are desire and anger. A good leader

[29] Clouds receive salty water from the ocean and return sweet water as rain. A cow eats grass and returns sweet milk. A coconut tree drinks water and returns nectar. What one receives is a debt that can be absolved by paying through selfless service. But being grateful vindicates one of the additional interest accrued.

[30] Only the inexperienced say that a father is only a father. He is in fact a protective father only initially, then a disciplining commander, then an encouraging teacher, then a transparent friend, then a respectable mentor and then a dependent elder. Holding on to a past role is like holding on to a moving car.

keeps these swords from felling him with the help of the cross-shields of satisfaction and patience.[31] The secret of a leader's success lies in his able ministry and not his personal talent. Keep the ministers satisfied in every possible way – directly or indirectly. A leader without followers is no leader at all. A leader's ability is always weighed against the satisfaction of his followers – keep the people happy through well-thought administrative schemes, ever-brimming coffers and easy accessibility."

Saying so, Dasaratha rose and began walking restlessly across the room. He was not sure about how to convey the message he actually wanted to. Rama understood that there was more to this conversation. If it was such a happy occasion afterall, why was His father upset and worried? A happy man does not behave this way. What was behind this mask of happiness?

Dasaratha opened up. He told Rama that at this point in time, his life was like a mother's, who, though happy at the thought of giving birth, was still writhing in labor, unsure whether to smile or cry. As he paced the room, Dasaratha clenched his fists, as if to stop the flow of time, and mentioned that bad signs were haunting him. He described all his horrifying nightmares, the ill omens he had spotted over the last few days, the falling meteors and even the royal astrologer's predictions that the planets Rahu and Mangal were stealthily approaching his birth star. These omens implied that the king would either die or meet with a fatal accident.

Dasaratha told Rama that he could no longer trust in his own mind these days as it seemed to have a life of its own. He wanted

---

[31] For a good leader, anger and desire are his loyal servants; he displays them when required. The day these servants peep out without instruction from the master, that day marks the beginning of the end of leadership.

to crown Rama king before his mind forced him to change his decision. His mind right now was as restless as a monkey, as strong as an elephant, as turbulent as an ocean and as stubborn as the bull. How could any sane human rely on something so unpredictable? He wanted to expedite things while he still had some control over his unstable mind.[32] "It has to happen tomorrow," Dasaratha concluded.

Shifting his tone from that of concern to jubilation, Dasaratha requested Rama to remain celibate for the rest of the night and observe a fast with His wife, Sita, and sleep on a couch made of *kusa* grass. As an afterthought, he also told Rama to ask His best friends to guard His palace all night. Sabotage was a weapon such ill omens often brought in their wake. What was Dasaratha expecting? He was not so sure if he was anticipating an attack from his disturbed mind or from somewhere outside!

Rama stood up to leave, sensing that His father had conveyed everything and given him enough instructions. As he was about to leave, Dasaratha muttered under his breath that the coronation should take place while Bharata was still away. Rama perked a brow, expecting a justification for that statement, but there was none. Instead, Dasaratha made two diametrically opposite statements: "Bharata is a righteous and compassionate brother and he will follow you. But men are inconsistent because of which sometimes impulse may throw up unexpected results." He then abruptly walked away.

---

[32] An unprotected and unpredictable mind is like an open pot of nectar. One blob of poison dropped into it will ruin all the nectar.

one king two bodies

Erect back, lotus posture, folded hands, a serene face, closed eyes, prayerful murmur – this was Rama's vision of His mother, Kaushalya. She was always the same every single time he visited her. Yet again, she stood there greeting Him as she always did. Rama admired her. She was the epitome of devotion and dedication.

What was surprising, however, was the presence of Sita, Lakshmana and Lakshmana's mother Sumitra in his mother's room. Their smiling faces at once implied that they already knew. Some guard or attendant desirous of earning either the favor of the Queen Mother or some extra wealth had perhaps informed her of her son's coronation the next day. His mother's prayer now was surely her way of offering gratitude to the Lord for showering such kindness upon her. Rama waited patiently, using this time to meditate on and appreciate his mother's divine qualities.[33]

Kaushalya gracefully got up to see her son. She walked up to Him with a knowing smile. Yet Rama formally informed her of His coronation the next morning. The happy mother poured out a river of blessings from her heart with joy and gratitude.

Rama then turned toward Lakshmana and Sita and told His brother: "Ayodhya will be ruled by one king in two bodies. Together We will rule the kingdom bestowed upon Us by Our father. I desire to rule the kingdom only for your sake." Conveying this, Rama departed

---

[33] Muscles develop and strengthen when one pushes a heavy object away from oneself. Similarly, our capacity to show appreciation grows by pushing away the craving for self-appreciation.

to His palace along with Sita to prepare for the fast and the other pre-coronation rituals.

darkness returns

Night fell on Ayodhya and a blanket of darkness enveloped the city. It slowly crept into Dasaratha, too. Dasaratha dreaded sunsets for it heralded the dark nights he did not want to face. He sat in front of his mirror, and once again, a strand of gray caught his attention. The gray glistened against the dark backdrop of the night, almost as if trying to say something to him. What is it? Why was he focusing on that one gray strand? Did the gray of the hair and the black of the night allude to something? What horrors lay ahead?

Chapter 2

The Ego Maniac

One swift swish, and the courtroom was blinded by the splattering of blood. The courtiers wiped away the scarlet splashes from their eyes to see the severed head roll out of the courtroom. Fountains of blood gushed out of the lifeless trunk that had instantly slumped to the floor. Everything had happened in the blink of an eye – the fierce lunge from the throne, the rash drawing of the sword, the sharp striking off of the loyal messenger's head. Throbbing silence stifled the bloodied room for there was no knowing the repercussions of this chilling act.

The mighty king stood hyperventilating over his victim, the diamond-studded golden hilt held in an unyielding grip, with the sword tip thrust into the still body of the unfortunate messenger. His big, strong hand swiveled vigorously in accordance with his heaving and puffing, his labored breathing controlled by sheer rage and unhinged anger![1]

---

[1] The danger of anger is that it suddenly makes one a stranger to others. Anger makes people behave differently from the way they usually are, which makes others around them wonder if it is the same person they know. An angry person is like the flower vase that falls on someone's foot; there's no doubt that it hurts the foot, but it also breaks in the process. The damage

The wheezing from his heavy breathing was the only thing audible in the room. Hundred pairs of eyes were glued to the intimidating king.

"Attack my stupid brother," hollered the king of Lanka, Dasagriva. The order was complete in itself. The chiefs of all armies scurried out to prepare for the siege, while some of the servants dragged the decapitated body to be dumped into the ocean. A hint of a grin crept up to the corner of Dasagriva's lips as he walked back to his throne. He hated losing control even momentarily. How dare that audacious messenger make him feel insecure?[2]

sibling rivalry

"Did I hear it right? Is our king Dasagriva planning to attack his own brother?" Kumyo, a low-ranking foot soldier, spoke to his colleague as he was sharpening his battle spear. While carefully dipping the tip of his arrow into a poison-filled pot, his elderly colleague nodded in affirmation. "Someone wanting take his own brother's life is unheard of, *even* among *rakshasas*. I thought Dasagriva had only two brothers and a sister. Where did this other brother come from? Did I hear his name as Kubera?" Kumyo wondered.

---

to the foot is reversible, but the vase can't be unbroken. Anger is seldom expressed without someone being hurt. It acts not like an antiseptic but as an inflammatory agent for the hurt heart, almost like sprinkling chili powder on an already septic wound.

[2] An insecure person constantly needs validation and wants to be worshipped every second to feel secure. Real security comes not from objects of luxury but from an upright character.

Expecting exhilarating gossip[3] that could possibly reveal their king's deep, dark secrets, a group of soldiers gathered around the two. With an eager audience now amassed in front, the elderly soldier instantly assumed the role of a wise old man and began bragging about his knowledge of old histories his young listeners had no access to.

He began to relate the story of two *rakshasa* brothers Heti and Praheti. Praheti was disinclined to be a ruler and instead chose to be a renunciant, so Heti became the king, who was eventually succeeded by his son Vidyut Kesh. Vidyut Kesh and his wife Sal Kankata, who were used to a life of luxury and sensuality, were averse to responsibility.[4] During one of their pleasure trips to Mandrachal hills, Sal gave birth to a boy. Not wanting to take the onus of raising a child, the debauched couple abandoned the baby there to return to the comforts of their kingdom.

Shiva and Parvati, who were in the vicinity, heard the baby wailing in the wilderness. They bestowed the baby with instant youth and arranged for aerial travel back to his parents' house. Because their child was now all grown up, Heti and Sal accepted him and named him Sukesh.[5]

---

[3] Gossip is like a cacophony of crows, where every crow seems to be saying the most important thing, but has neither the time nor the inclination to hear an equally important message from any of the other crows. For those who consider themselves unimportant, indulging in gossip gives them a fleeting sense of importance.

[4] Enjoyment is the free trailer to the movie called "Life", which comes for the price of responsibility. Responsibility is the fire that burns the weeds of indolence. Attachment to comforts is like rain that extinguishes the fire of responsibility and allows the weeds of indolence to malnourish the tree of sacrifice.

[5] The role of a wise person is to make a seemingly burdensome thing

Sukesh married a *gandharva* girl named Devavati and had three sons: Malyavan, Sumali and Mali. These three boys grew up to perform austerities to please Lord Brahma and received benedictions from him, which made them as good as invincible.

Bloated by arrogance, the brothers oppressed innocent people and conquered many kingdoms. After he had grabbed sufficient power and wrested enough control, Malyavan decided to build a magnificent abode for himself and his family. He approached Vishwakarma, the architect of the demigods, who gave him this island of Lanka. Malyavan and his family began living here. Eventually his other brothers, too, married and fathered many children. Their brutalities continued through it all, though.

No longer able to bear the atrocities of the trio, the saints and hapless inhabitants of the surrounding kingdoms begged Lord Vishnu for protection. Lord Vishnu then fought against the three brothers. The hair-raising battle culminated in the death of Mali, and as a result Sumali and Malyavan had to vacate Lanka and take shelter in *Patalaloka*, the underworld. Vishravas, the son of Paulastya and the grandson of the Brahma, then sent his son Kubera, the loyal treasurer of the demigods, to Lanka to rule as the king.

Meanwhile, the homeless Sumali's mind kept returning to Lanka, and all he desperately wanted was an opportunity to reclaim his homeland and regain his family's lost glory. It wasn't long before the opportunity presented itself, when one day, he fortuitously spotted

---

useful. Sukesh, who was considered to be a burden by his parents, was made useful by Shiva. Here Heti and Sal represent the "What is in it for me?" mindset. They were unable to see Sukesh as anything but a burden. Rejection and acceptance depend not on the value of the object but on the value our mind assigns to it.

Kubera's air chariot hovering over a forest hermitage. Sumali's cunning mind instantly deduced that Kubera was on his way to sage Vishravas' hermitage to pay his father a visit. The deceitful diplomat that Sumali was took this seed of a chance to craft a devious plan. Sumali had always wanted his daughter to marry a powerful *Brahmana* so that their offspring could have the best of both races – they would be *rakshasas* but possess the powers of great *brahmanas*. This would ensure that *rakshasas*' permanent rule over the demigods. He managed to convince his reluctant daughter Kaikashi to marry Vishravas, telling her that she would bear sons as mighty and bright as Kubera.[6] Sumali then devised Kaikashi's chance encounter with Vishravas, who fell in love with her and married her.

The elderly soldier paused after this enthralling description and stood up to stretch his stiff limbs and build up anticipation. He knew that his audience was hooked.

The rest, according to him, was folklore. Kaikashi gave birth to Dasagriva, Kumbakarna, Vibhishan and Surpanakha. Kubera's frequent visits to his father riled Kaikashi. She was always repelled by Kubera's landing at the entrance of their home in his highly adorned air chariot and his vulgar display of wealth. Meanwhile, instigated by their mother's envy and their desire to acquire invincible powers, the four siblings left home to perform intense austerities and gain the favor of Brahma. They finally returned to their proud mother and their even prouder grandfather; after all, Sumali had waited so long to see the fruition of his plans.

Inspired and goaded by Sumali, many loyal *rakshasas*, such as

---

[6] Diplomacy with selfless motives is necessary for love to develop between people. But when diplomacy is laced with selfishness, people use and manipulate other people and love material things.

Maricha, Prahasta, Nirupaksha and Mahodara, tried to persuade
Dasagriva to reclaim Lanka, their rightful land. Years and years
of intense austerities and an ascetic life had made Dasagriva soft-
hearted and sober; he was disinclined to fight, saying that Kubera
was his elder.[7]

Prahasta, a clever diplomat, convinced Dasagriva that fraternal
feelings were immaterial because the *brahmanas* and *rakshasas* were
both sage Kashyapa's offspring, but have been sworn enemies since
days of yore. The exhorted Dasagriva then agreed to send Prahasta
as an emissary to appeal to Kubera to hand over the kingdom to its
rightful owners. Prahasta soon presented himself in front of Kubera
and placed the request. Kubera then consulted with his father and
decided it was vain fighting with the near-invincible Dasagriva. He
vacated Lanka and, as per his father's advice, proceeded to settle
down in the foothills of Kailash to perform penances to please Shiva,
who asked Vishwakarma to create the city of Alaka for Kubera.

Dasagriva now became the unbridled king of Lanka.

No sooner than the elderly soldier ended his narration, Kumyo
became restless. He was convinced there was more because the
peaceful ending of the story defied logic. "If Dasagriva was such a
peace-loving man, how do we rationalize this new, gruesome side of
him? Surely, the man we saw in the courtroom today is far removed
from the one you are talking about."

"Blame it on the magic of the throne of Lanka! The day
Dasagriva sat on that throne, he morphed into a different man,"

---

[7] Desires are like waves in an ocean. If one hits the shores, rest assured,
another is on its way. Spiritual practice transfers one from the ceaseless
ocean of desires to the still lake of self-satisfaction.

the experienced soldier declared.[8]

Dasagriva always experienced unparalleled ecstasy every time he saw fear hovering in the eyes of the weak. That hounded look was like some supreme, matchless intoxicant he was so addicted to; so much so, that he was willing to go to any lengths just to catch a glimpse of that look. Vulnerable *rishis* and saints dwelling in hermitages in the forests became soft targets. He also distorted the justice system, turning it into a tool for torturing enough souls on a daily basis, so that he could keep experiencing that high.[9]

Dasagriva's atrocities had penetrated deeper into the kingdom and often beyond it. Clearly, he was fast turning into an interplanetary terrorist. Concerned that Dasagriva's evil deeds were tarnishing the reputation of his prosperous city, Kubera made an attempt to help his half-brother out of his gory reverie by sending him some friendly advice through a trusted messenger – a man the god of wealth considered intelligent, virtuous and sensitive.

A few sentences, a warning, yet another sincere attempt later, the messenger was history![10] Unknown to Kubera, that single swift swish had killed his noble intentions.

---

[8] An ordinary wire does not burn because it transfers power without holding on to it; however, an unqualified circuit blows up because it tries to hold power. A good leader, like the ordinary wire, is a good conductor of power, whereas a bad leader is a resistor who tries to hold on to power.

[9] The words "intoxication" and "controllership" are synonymous. In the beginning, you believe that you can regulate both, but soon you realize that these control you. What you try to control, controls you; therefore, control is like the genie that initially seems to be in your power, but has you in its clutches.

[10] Trying to enlighten fools is like trying to soften a bamboo by pouring milk over it.

winged wonder

A poisoned spear sliced the air to pierce precisely into the chest of the *yaksha* guarding Kubera's abode in Kailash. The *yaksha* had presumed wrong and paid with his life. This was no brotherly visit; it was a bloody war. Soon hordes of Dasagriva's soldiers were swarming around the Kailash mountains pummeling Kubera's army. The *yakshas* fought valiantly, but the *rakshasas*' destructive illusory tricks led them right into the hands of defeat. Rattled, battered and gripped by mortal terror, they surrendered meekly to death. With the *yaksha* army obliterated, Dasagriva entered Kubera's palace and forced him out.

Kubera stepped out armed for a bloodthirsty battle, but he appeared calm and poised. He made a final effort to drive some sense into Dasagriva. He invoked memories of his glorious father and questioned if Dasagriva's actions would make his father proud of his son today. Kubera advised Dasagriva that as a leader, he should lead a life of *dharma* and propagate love and peace rather than hate and violence.[11]

Dasagriva let loose an evil guffaw. He thundered, "You talk about love and peace when you are all set for war. How contradictory! Instead of a begging bowl and a loincloth, what you have is a mighty bow and a strong armor. If you are in the mood for renunciation,

---

[11] Kubera acted like Dasagriva's intelligence and tried to teach him self-criticism. Self-criticism is the microscopic analysis of one's own shortcomings. Most people are like monkeys who are so busy picking lice off their friends' bodies that they fail to realize the extent to which they themselves are infested. *Dharma* is a protective shield, whereas *adharma* is a bare chest.

step aside and let me take over your kingdom, else fight and die!"

Soon, a mace came hurtling at Dasagriva with sinister words closely following it, "You are cursed to ruin yourself!"

The blood brothers were now baying for each other's blood. What Dasagriva had thought would be mere child's play was in fact a serious threat to his near-indomitable strength. When matching his brother's might became tough, Dasagriva turned to trickery, changing shape in succession – from a tiger to a pig to a rumbling cloud to thunderbolts flashing here and there.

Kubera's bloodied head was reeling and soon he was in excruciating pain. He realized he was sinking, and the last thing he remembered was bolting pain in the nape. Dasagriva had suddenly appeared right behind the collapsing Kubera to deal the final blow with his mace.

As Kubera lay unconscious, every inch of his palace was ransacked, every treasure packed away and every piece of junk and untakable reduced to ashes.[12]

The pillaging had finally given what Dasagriva had always wanted, the real reason behind this war. He actually harbored no ill feelings against Kubera. If anything, he had profound respect for his elder brother. But Dasagriva had always coveted his brother's quaint possession from the moment he first laid eyes on it in his father's courtyard as a little boy – the Pushpak Vimana, the flying machine.

[12] The dark mood of selfishness unmasks the child in a person. Such a debunked person cannot tolerate anyone possessing something that he himself has lost.

Dasagriva had grown up listening to fascinating stories about this wonder chariot and everything it could do. He had heard that this fully automated machine with no mechanical parts could be remote-controlled by the will of its rider. It had inbuilt luxurious palaces and other comforts, and it was fully air-conditioned too! Not just that, it could expand or contract in accordance with the number of travelers, and with expansion, more features automatically got added in.

Vishravas had gifted this dream machine to Kubera, but had not left him even a dime. Dasagriva was a self-made man, but there was always something amiss – something that made him feel incomplete. The moment he touched the air chariot, he felt whole.[13]

the big toe

Thus far, watching the world from afar and from way high up in the air had only been a dream. Now, it was about to come true. Dasagriva stepped into the Pushpak Vimana with his uncle Maricha and an aide Prahasta to make an aerial tour of the Kailash mountain, his dream became a reality. But could this beautiful dream turn into a horrible nightmare?

Dasagriva found it difficult to control his mind. Should he admire the beauty of the mountains and vast landscape? Or should he marvel at his majestic plane? Just as the Pushpak Vimana was

---

[13] Success has to be built from a deep foundation of uncompromising character, strong bricks of nonmanipulated principles and steel frames of unbending determination. If instead, the foundation is shallow because of malleable character, the bricks hollow because of lack of principles and the frames paperlike because of unwarranted desires, the tower of success will collapse in the first storm of difficulties.

traversing the thick interiors of Kailash, known as the Sharvan forest, the air chariot began to slow down and deviate from its path. Panic gripped Dasagriva's heart and body. All he knew about this chariot's function was that it worked at the rider's will. Technically, *he* was in possession of the chariot and *he* was the rider, which meant that *he* was the owner; but practically, the chariot belonged to Kubera, which made the god of wealth the real owner. Did the Pushpak Vimana know this? How could a material object be aware of its real owner? Then again, if it was merely a material object, how could it move to the rider's mental vibrations? Dasagriva's head was reeling, his thoughts spinning like a tornado.[14]

Dasagriva talked himself into calming down, "Shhh... you are the king of Lanka and the undisputable Lord of all the worlds." Despite his efforts, he could not fathom the deceleration and deviation of the air chariot. "Why has this machine slowed down? It cannot happen without interference. How dare anyone override my desire!"

His uncle Maricha said, "You are right Dasagriva, this air chariot cannot make a mistake. This is not an ordinary contraption invented by mortals prone to breakdown. This automatic change of course baffles me. Perhaps this machine is programmed to slow down and deviate if stolen or wrested from the owner."[15]

---

[14] Metal detectors detect dangerous material on one's person. What if there were mental detectors that could scan dangerous thoughts? Whereas metal detectors are programmed for superficial external checks, mental detectors can look deep within the recesses of the mind. The appearance of the most well-dressed person may conceal an obnoxious mind filled with envious agendas, big-headedness, deceit and disrespect.

[15] The burning desire to have something is called ambition. A healthy ambition turns into a disease of greed when innocent desires turn into conscience-depleting obsessions.

As the uncle–nephew team was trying to make sense of it all, a unique creature with a robust torso and pillar-like arms emerged from behind the peaks of Kailash. One hand wielding a spear and the other placed on the hip, the creature's posture was certainly aggressive. His daunting personality seemed menacing and his booming voice sounded authoritative, just as loud as the rumbling clouds atop the mountains. "This is a restricted area. Ordinary mortals, *rakshasas*, *gandharvas* and even *devas* are not permitted here without the sanction of Shiva, the lord of this area."

Dasagriva was irked for being stopped, much like a child prevented from entering the kitchen to steal sweets. But something about the creature's demeanor tickled Dasagriva's funny bone. Although right in the middle of a warlike situation, Dasagriva began giggling impetuously, much to the surprise of his ministers. He tried to muffle his giggles with his hand, but this impudence did not go unnoticed by the daunting warrior from Kailash.

"You mock me because my face resembles that of a monkey's? Your pride will soon be vanquished in the most humiliating way, you haughty fool!" scowled Nandishwar, the loyal bull mount of Lord Shiva. "Very soon monkey-like men will destroy you. They will come in hordes and annihilate your entire race. When you are on your deathbed, you will remember this costly snigger. Then *you* will cry, and the monkeys will laugh. I could kill you this instant, but then it will not be a shameful-enough death. I want you to die feeling helpless, watching everything you value demolished right before your eyes."[16]

---

[16] Having fun at the expense of another is like buying misery with your post-dated check that is cashed at some unpredictable point in time, when your balance is zero.

This was indigestible! A tiny giggle had caused so much of turmoil in this monkey-faced creature.[17] All his arrogance was from the courage he borrowed from his hiding master, Shiva. It was time to give haughty challengers a tutorial on strength. Jumping off the almost stationary Pushpak Vimana, Dasagriva landed on the mountain with a thud and immediately disappeared from sight.

Almost simultaneously, Nandi found himself trembling and losing balance. The entire mountain was quaking. Scores of Shiva's followers ran helter-skelter scurrying out of the multiple caves and dwellings in Kailash's bosom. Horrendous laughter reverberated through the air. Dasagriva's ministers were awestruck by their master's terrific feat, and their admiration for him increased manifold. They gaped and gasped as he effortlessly performed a herculean task – Dasagriva had uprooted the entire Kailash mountain and was holding it aloft! Incredible! Superhuman!

As they chattered excitedly about their master's strength and considered themselves lucky to be led by such a mighty leader, Dasagriva's facial expression began to change – the sardonic smile gave way to a painful grimace and, eventually, a universe-rattling howl. Obviously, he was in pain, but what caused it all of a sudden? Did he lose his confidence or his strength? The telling smiles on the faces of Shiva's followers were proof enough.

Disturbed by the mayhem caused by Dasagriva's act, Shiva dug his big right toe into the Kailash mountain. The pressure was so intense

---

[17] A vulture never makes fun of the ugliness of another vulture. As humans, instead of investing energy in poking fun at others, we could explore humor in our own failures and use it as a tool to cope with our setbacks rather than use someone else's defects to laugh at.

that Dasagriva's fingers were crushed beneath the mountain, and the pain radiated all the way up his boulder-like arms. Neither he nor all his ministers together could move the mountain even by a millimeter. Dasagriva looked like a puny rat cornered by a big cat. The hapless Dasagriva saw no hope.[18]

"The one who can destroy you can also save you, if appeased. Shiva is *Ashutosh*, the one easily pleased. Pray to him Dasagriva, he will surely forgive you and relieve you of your pain," Maricha, his uncle, minister and well-wisher, and all his councilors implored him.

Writhing in pain and realizing that there was no way out, Dasagriva relented and began offering eloquent prayers from the Vedas to glorify Lord Shiva. After all he was the son of Vishravas, a saint who did teach him all the Vedas. The prayers were so replete with meaning and devotion that Shiva's followers were astounded. If this man was so well-versed in the glories of Lord Shiva, why was he challenging him with such arrogance?[19]

---

[18] The distance between two personalities drowning in a quicksand does not matter as much as the distance between a drowning man and a man on land. In fact, the more two people in a quicksand try to help one another, the faster they sink. Only a person on stable land can expedite the rescue process. The ministers were as helpless as Ravana here; someone else's intervention was needed to rescue him.

[19] The essence of any learning lies in its comprehension and the application of that lesson. The difference between realization and rote memory is the difference between the words converse and rehearse. To converse one needs application of learning and to rehearse one needs retention of learning.

Retention of learning is mechanical and monotonous, much like a garden filled with single-hued and single-species flowers. Comprehension and application of learning are as practical and vivacious as a garden filled with multicolored and multifarious flowers.

Eventually, pleased by Dasagriva's lament, Shiva soon gently lifted his toe and the weight of the mountain was lifted off Dasagriva's throbbing fingers. "How did it feel to experience pain, for a change? Despite your cruel nature, your courage and sincerity has pleased me. And, because you cause so much pain and make people cry, from hereon you will be known as Ravana. Ravana, nonetheless, you have pleased me enough to want to reward you with a boon. Ask Ravana!"

From Brahma, Ravana had received the twin boons of a really long life and immunity from death at the hands of demigods, sages, *gandharvas*, *kinnaras*, *rakshasas* and *nagas*. So Ravana told Shiva, "Considering I already have some invaluable boons, I only ask you to add the same number of years I have lived to my quota of life and a special weapon of your choice." Shiva then gave him an effulgent and divine sword named Chandrahasa. But with a rider: "Do not disregard this sword, for if you do, it will certainly come back to me."[20,21]

a n a r r o w e s c a p e

"Run! The flying tyrant has come." In a moment, the powerful controllers of the universe began squirming like worms at the

---

[20] In the past, objects were respected and named. These days, even people are disrespected and assigned numbers. When people are treated as things, they react like rigid stones. When people are treated with respect, they act like soft butter.

[21] The condition applied to an undeserved benediction, acts like a masquerade that disguises the problem, changes the perspective of seeing it, and obscures the result to be achieved.

sight of a savage bird. The sages were bewildered: where had the demigods disappeared? This jester had swooped down from nowhere and thwarted their universal *yajna*, which had attracted the most powerful of celestial leaders. The sages were visibly upset and unable to focus. Even the powerful King Marut was disturbed. A lot had gone into this *yajna*. It had taken prolonged periods of fasting, long hours of chanting *mantras*, relentless pouring of butter into the fire, tolerating days and days of blinding and choking smoke, offering unlimited charity and performing endless micro-monitored rituals to build up the intensity of the sacrifice. Now as the sacrifice was very near culmination, the last thing anyone wanted was an interruption. But this was no normal intrusion; a ten-headed man was looming over them roaring with laughter. The horrendous ear-splitting sound that boomed ten-fold louder was agonizing![22]

Ravana disembarked from his unusual flying machine as it landed in the arena, while Marut rose from his seat at the sacrifice. Marut did not want to predict the intentions of this impressive *rakshasa*. His mind was serene and calm from the constant incantation of *mantras* over the past several days.[23]

"Welcome, O great one! Thank you for joining us at this most auspicious time of the sacrifice. Do grace this occasion by accepting a seat of honor." Marut's gesture was kind, welcoming and genuine.

---

[22] The pain is supremely acute when an unavoidable and uncontrollable obstacle abruptly terminates an expectation that was very close to being met.

[23] The word *mantra* is a combination of two words – *man* meaning mind and *tra* (from *trayate*) meaning control. *Mantra* literally means that which controls the mind. *Mantras* are subtle sound waves that soothe the subtle mind.

"I am not here to listen to your mumbo-jumbo or run around this fire. Ravana is my name, and to make others cry is my fame. After having defeated my brother, Kubera, and usurped his kingdom and snatched his Pushpak Vimana, I am on a world tour of subjugating all the powerful warriors of the universe. My fame has spread far and wide, and universal controllers tremble when they hear my name, or so I am told. It is surprising that you don't recognize me. Surrender or perish! This is my command."

Nearby, a peacock stealthily peeked in from behind a tree, trying hard to hide its long, dull blue train and to control its quivering legs; a chameleon tried to camouflage itself the best way it could, lest the 20 gruesome eyes of the mighty demon detect it; a crow suppressed its caw even though its throat itched to make a noise; a swan buried its slender neck beneath its own black, fluffy body, realizing that it was better for its neck to bear the weight of its body than the brunt of a sword. Some sages from the *yajna* noticed the peculiar behavior of these animals. Why this deviant behavior? No, this was no time for contemplation. Despite fear gnawing at their hearts, the sages still wanted to find out what was forcing the birds and the reptile to behave this way.

A relaxed smile on Marut's lips raised a questioning arch on Ravana's brow. Such audacity to smile when in such trouble! Ravana invoked the Chandrahasa, the ferocious sword gifted to him by Shiva, to rattle Marut. But the smile was *still* on. That Marut was unfazed thoroughly infuriated Ravana.[24]

---

[24] A hollow puppet, though irritated, tolerates the hand stuffed into it. A hollow bell is shaken vigorously from the outside and beaten intensely from the inside. A hollow bubble is fearful of the weakest hand that touches it.

When a hollow person experiences the confidence of another, he feels like a stuffed puppet, the shaken bell and a vulnerable bubble.

As Ravana's exasperation escalated, a still-smiling Marut said, "Yes, I don't know or recognize you, and I am happy not knowing a shameless man who plundered his own brother. At this moment, when you leave here with nothing but your life at your disposal, you will cringe with humiliation and be stripped of all pride." Invoking his bow and arrow, Marut readied himself for a gruesome fight.

An elderly palm grabbed his taut biceps as his fingers curled around the base of the arrow held ready on the bowstring. It was chief priest Samvartan's effort to change the course of this heated discussion. If something wasn't done soon, putrefied blood instead of clarified butter would find its way into the sacrificial fire. "No, your Highness, you have vowed nonviolence and abstinence from anger till the end of *yajna*. Do not succumb to such provocation. Remember the higher purpose behind the *yajna*. In your haste to prove your supremacy, please do not lose sight of your goal."[25]

Appreciative of the timely wisdom from Samvartan, Marut swallowed his anger and detached himself from the desire to prove his supremacy. Returning to the somber mood of the sacrifice, he resumed the sacrificial worship.

Ravana mocked him and jeered at him, calling him a coward and a puppet in the hands of the priest. Boasting about having subjugated yet another king, he haughtily hopped into the Pushpak Vimana and whizzed off in search of more royal victims, more lands to conquer and more victories to claim.

---

[25] The route to the goal is lined with many bypasses, each of which misleads one to pits of gratification. Through intense introspection on the purpose of the journey and importance of the goal, one has to curb the tendency to be lured away from the objective.

While in flight, an agitated Ravana pondered, "Untrustworthy fools, each one of them! Even the spies are stupid these days! 'Prominent demigods will attend the sacrifice.' Bah! What were those imbeciles thinking? Where do they get such information? Had their tipoff been true, it would have saved me a trip to the heavens; I could have captured all those delicate demigods right here, right now. But only this joker was here. Ha, the pleasure of defeating yet another king is worth it, after all."

As soon as Ravana left, the timid peacock ventured out from behind the tree and took its seat on the mat meant for Indra, the king of demigods. The sages were aghast at its impudence. Whoosh! In place of the peacock was Indra!

He called out to all the peacocks in the forest and said: "A bird of your species saved me from the embarrassment of being captured by Ravana, and I want to show my gratitude in the form of a special gift that will be eternally remembered as my contribution to your species. Henceforth, the monotonous blue of your plumage will become iridescent and have a multitude of colors. Each of your feathers will also have an imprint of my eye. Furthermore, I make you immune to all diseases, and those who dare to kill you will meet their death. You will never fear snakes; in fact, snakes will dread coming close to you. My dear peacocks, I grant you that special ecstasy when your feet will automatically break into a dance of joy every time I shower rain on Earth. Your colorful feathers will add extraordinary effect to your dance. And thus my relationship with you will be eternally sealed."[26]

---

[26] The gift of health, fearlessness, talent, beauty and experience of joy is the result of grace. But real grace lies not just in possessing these qualities but also in being grateful for these qualities. The highest manifestation of gracefulness is gratefulness.

As the crow swooped down, it took the shape of Yama, the god of death. Yama blessed the crow with fearlessness of death. He granted the crow life till someone else kills it. Food offered to a crow would reach the donor's ancestors, who are residents of *Yamaloka*.

The black swan glided in and was suddenly transformed into Varuna, the god of water. Varuna blessed that the swan would be so spotlessly white that it would even put the moon to shame.

The chameleon perched on a small stone near the sacrificial arena was in fact Kubera, the treasurer of the celestials. He not only blessed the chameleon with the ability to change colors to suit the environment and camouflage to save itself when in danger, he also gave the reptile a golden hue. Kubera was, of course, the most grateful of all, especially since he had had a recent encounter with his cruel half-brother Ravana and wanted no more embarrassment.[27]

All the universal controllers returned to their seats and signaled the continuation of the sacrifice, much to the relief of the sages and King Marut. The demigods accepted their offerings, showered their blessings upon the king and returned to their abodes.

"Phew! Saved yet again from this decahedral demon! But how long luck will be on our side, hard to say." With this worry, they went back to their insecure kingdoms.

---

[27] A well can give only when it receives and what it receives. Just like the well receiving rainwater cannot be expected to give out nectar, similarly the universal controllers cannot be expected to share what they do not possess.

the invincible duo

"Of the seven *yajnas*, six are now complete. One more, and this boy will become invincible." Sukracharya, the *guru* of the *asuras* spoke animatedly to Ravana, pointing out to the effulgent, shaven-headed boy dressed in deerskin sitting in front of the sacrificial fire with his eyes closed and his lips chanting *mantras* with the ferocity and focus of a lion on a hunt.[28]

His first cry was a harbinger of his exceptional strength. Unlike the vulnerable yelp of a newborn, his roar shook the entire city of Lanka; cracks appeared on Earth, buildings collapsed, pregnant women had miscarriages and trembling elephants defecated and urinated with fear. The baby was named as Meghanada, the one with the voice of a rumbling cloud.

Now no longer a baby, Meghanada was a youth of sparkling majesty. The proud father Ravana looked at his powerful son, basking in the golden hue of the sacrificial fire housed in an ornately designed mega altar. He could not help but smile in anticipation of the immense good fortune his son would bring him.[29]

---

[28] Sunrays provide warmth, but when intensified by a lens, these cause fire. Shrubs that are otherwise useless, become medicines when scrutinized by expert eyes.

Stale food when experienced by a hungry belly becomes tasty. An inadequate penny in the hands of a miserable beggar is equivalent to gold.

Any aspect of life when focused upon becomes a source of inspiration and success. And the most important aspects of life when neglected become a burden.

[29] What you desire is what you see:

When you look through the pink lens of love, you feel kindness all around you.

As Meghanada sat deeply absorbed through the proceedings of the seventh *yajna*, Ravana walked around the exceedingly beautiful Nikumbhila gardens, the site of the *yajna*. Here, his advisors updated him about his son's achievements across the first six *yajnas*. Apparently, Lord Shiva was extremely pleased with Meghanada's stellar performance through these extremely difficult sacrifices. As a gesture of his appreciation, he awarded Meghanada a special auto-chariot that needed no driver to maneuver; it was a wish-driven chariot. He also bestowed the boy with expertise in the science of illusion, the crowning glory being the invisible smoke screen that would make him imperceptible to the enemy even if he were as close as their breath. Lord Shiva did not stop at this. He also gifted Meghanada an unbreakable bow and a multitude of deadly arrows. Just as Ravana was savoring this good news, Meghanada let out of his trademark shriek, which indicated the end of the seventh *yajna*. This boy had now become invincible!

As the beaming Ravana embraced his glorious son, his only words were, "Wrest the heavens!"

News of the invincible father-son duo spread far and wide, forcing the demigods to scurry for safety. Indra tried his best for protection from Lord Vishnu, but strangely, this time the lord had other priorities, which left Indra broken-hearted. After all, wasn't Indra

---

When you look through the yellow lens of optimism, you count the blessings that you should be grateful for.

When you look through the gold lens of giving, you look for opportunities for sharing.

When you look through the white lens of simplicity, you look for peace and a meaningful life all around you.

Ravana was looking through the red lens of power and he saw the supremacy of his son.

supervising the universal management on His behalf? Indra fought with the *rakshasas*, low on morale and even lower on desire.

The war had begun at a frenetic pace. Indra took on Ravana headlong as Jayanta, Indra's son, attacked Meghanada. During this point in the war, it seemed as if Indra would be the victor, especially when he strategically engaged his army to surround Ravana and capture him alive. But right then, Meghanada resorted to the art of *samadhi*, Lord Shiva's gift to him. Soon Jayanta swooned against his chariot and was carried off the battlefield by his men, to be safely hidden in the ocean bed. Assuming his son dead, Indra went ballistic with rage and launched a full-throttle attack on Ravana with his explosive thunderbolt. Ravana fell unconscious, unable to withstand the power of the bolt.

Everything seemed perfectly aligned for Indra's victory. And then, *everything* froze! A cold eeriness enveloped the atmosphere. Indra could move only his eyes. What just happened? Why did his body freeze? The army looked at him for orders as he helplessly looked back at them. Indra hoped that they would understand and forgive him, while they hoped he would speak and save them. Without his directions, his army was mercilessly chopped to death right in front of him, as helpless tears rolled down his cheeks.[30]

Soon a pair of muscular hands seized his shoulders in a crocodile grip and his body's was back in motion. But he was now tied up with ropes. Meghanada's magic had worked yet again. Hanging

---

[30] The mightiest roar of a lion is a tiny squeak in the midst of a thunderstorm. Recognizing its helplessness, the lion king withdraws into the cave of humility. Every king goes through such moments of helplessness, which teach him humility. Every negative situation in life has a seed of positivity. Here Indra learns a lesson in humility.

his head in defeat, Indra was hauled into the Pushpak Vimana and disgracefully tied to the flag post. With their leader captured alive, the demigods who saw no more sense in continuing the fight, dropped their weapons. They, too, were rounded up and pushed into the magical air chariot. At last, all the universal directors were under his control! What interesting plans Ravana had for them!

the cursed stare

As they sat huddled on the cold floor of Ravana's hot kitchen chopping vegetables, the demigods exchanged occasional glances of disgrace and disdain. The controllers under control! What happened to their all-pervasive power? Where did all the respect they commanded disappear? Where was their pride, their wealth? This low point in their life had turned them all philosophical! [31]

The demigods lay resting on their stomachs and spoke only in hushed whispers. Mangal was sniffling, "Shani, just look at what has happened to us! Is this really true? I can't believe such fate could befall the nine of us, the illustrious *navagrahas*, who were together unconquerable; we controlled the destinies of all humans. Our pride is being crushed under the weight of this bully."[32]

---

[31] Life is like a mega game of chess. Anyone who desires kingship should also familiarize himself with its pitfalls. The real control lies with everyone else except the king! While on the chessboard, the king lives a short life of self-pity and while inside the box, the king lives a long life of self-awareness (realizing that in actuality there is no difference between a king and a pawn – all are equally helpless).

[32] When glass shatters, it explodes; when pride shatters, it implodes.

Shukra agreed, "There can be no proof of Ravana's supremacy more explicit than this – the *navagrahas* lying helplessly on their bellies on the nine steps leading to his throne and him stepping onto each one of them to reach there. This is so mortifying! If this news reaches Earth, then humans will stop respecting us or consulting astrologers on how we influence their lives."[33]

"Today I will do something different. Let me set the dice rolling for Ravana's end." Shani decided, as an answer to end their misery.

Ravana stomped in amid much pomp and music. This was Golden Lanka's golden era. Ravana's oppressive, indomitable power left everyone shaking like a leaf. What a sight to behold: The king had demigods for slaves! But Ravana's favorite bit was haughtily walking up those nine steps to his throne, crushing each until-now-invincible planet under his feet. What sadistic pleasure he derived from digging his heels into their spines at every step. With every step, he guaranteed the supremacy of his fate.[34]

As he stepped on the ninth one, his eyes met with another pair of glowering eyes. "Huh!" He tripped for a moment. Was it a threat, a curse or something worse? Shani was lain on his back and was staring at Ravana. That was the infamous stare of Shani, the planet capable of causing the downfall with a mere stare. Now ploughing his heels deeper into the planet's stomach, Ravana caused those glaring eyes to wince in pain. The arrogant king stepped toward

---

[33] The fear of what's coming ahead comes from a lack of control over past events. Actions of the past shape the future, like an unshapely stone transforms into a beautiful figurine with fine chiseling.

[34] Personal joy derived by gifting pain to others is charity that creates a wooden heart.

his throne with a wicked grin. He was beyond the laws of this world, wasn't he?[35]

what goes around comes around

Brahma had been watching this grim drama play itself out. Realizing that everything was about to wheel out of control, he decided to resolve it by mediating with Ravana. Although he detested the very thought of asking Ravana for a favor, he had no option but to restore orderliness and universal peace.

Switching from grim to pleasant, Brahma stood before Ravana and his son Meghanada. "Indeed Ravana, you are glorious! Your fame has spread across the universe. Wherever I go, the only topics of discussion are your might and greatness. Your son Meghanada has taken your eminence to another level by capturing Indra, the king of the demigods. He will undoubtedly become an unparalleled conqueror in the history of this world. It is my honor to bestow upon him the title, 'Indrajit', the one who has conquered Indra."

"Everything you have stated about me actually goes to glorify your divine self. Had it not been for your benevolence, I would not have achieved a fraction of this. I owe everything to you!" Ravana

---

[35] Expressions of freedom are within the continuously monitored boundaries of law. As long as expressions are confined to the boundaries, the boundaries seem virtual to the naïve. As soon as an attempt is made to cross it, the same boundaries become vicious. Ravana tried to control the demigods, but when he overstepped his boundaries, Shani's stare ensured the beginning of his downfall.

beamed, unable to hide his pleasure at the generous comments made by Brahma.[36]

"The title Indrajit itself brings you unparalleled honor and fame. What would you achieve by still holding Indra and the demigods captive? If you release him now, I will reward you aptly." Brahma shuddered even as he offered bait to the father-son duo, not knowing what these demons would solicit.

"Immortality is the only thing I seek in return," said Indrajit instantly.[37]

"It is not in my hands to change the rules I haven't made. Inevitability of death is a rule that even I am subjugated to. In this universe, there are lawmakers and law keepers; I belong to the second category. Ask anything else within my reach." Brahma admitted frankly.[38]

Indrajit tried to checkmate Brahma by disguising his request and getting the Supreme Creator to gift him what he had originally asked for. He requested Brahma to ensure that every time a fire sacrifice was performed by him anywhere, his celestial chariot would fully load with weapons, and as long as he was seated on the chariot, death would not be able to touch him.

---

[36] Praise is the temperature at which any human melts. It is the garment that warms a cold body. It is a password to log into the software of any heart.

[37] This statement reveals a deep fear – a fear that plagues and engulfs all other pleasures.

[38] Every leader has a leadership threshold that is defined by his capacity, ability and role. A wise leader has to be aware of the tendency of his followers to push him beyond this ceiling. The push initially seems like an encouragement, but it could quickly become a stranglehold noose. True wisdom lies in accepting one's threshold and being honest about it.

Spotting the loopholes he was desperately seeking, Brahma quickly granted the benediction. Noncompletion of the sacrifice and descent from the chariot would mean annulment of the boon.

The contract was sealed with two smiling faces. Indrajit grinned with total conviction that he had successfully fooled Brahma, the most intelligent being of the universe. And Brahma beamed knowing that intelligent fools are the easiest to fool.[39]

His head hung in shame and grief, a battered Indra walked out of Ravana's palace following Brahma. The bemused and mocking smiles of the *rakshasas* scalding his skin like hot, dripping candle wax. Oh, why was he subjected to such traumatic humiliation despite selflessly serving the universe?

Reading the turmoil in his mind, Brahma philosophized, "Do you remember that day in your life when you tortured a helpless person? Tears flowing out of that pair of eyes have been the cause of your humiliation today; Meghanada and Ravana are merely two instruments."[40,41]

Indra's mind flashed back to that fateful wee hour when he was trying to satiate his basest instincts. His stubborn, sinful mind had sealed not only his fate but hers too. Poor Ahalya had borne the brunt of his failure to subdue his obstinate mind. That failure had directly resulted in this failure, according to Brahma. He could now fathom the meaning of that disgusted look on the face of Lord Vishnu

---

[39] God's intelligence is to make a fool feel that he is intelligent.

[40] Helplessness caused becomes a helplessness causer.

[41] When your actions boomerang as reactions, rather than wondering who threw it at you, you should wonder when you threw it.

(which he had misread as the Supreme Protector being preoccupied) when he had approached Him for help in staving off Ravana. Everything made sense now. Guilt crept into his mind, replacing the shame he had felt earlier. He wanted to fall at the feet of that virtuous lady whose honor he had violated through trickery. His present suffering was probably not even an iota of what Ahalya had gone through then. Ravana no longer seemed to be as big an enemy as his own mind.[42]

a tide reverses

The day's events raced past his mind as he sat all knotted up inside the dark prison cell covered in cobwebs. Ravana could hear his own voice.

"I don't believe that a mere human being can reverse the flow of a river and that too with just his hands. Impossible! Get your eyes tested," Ravana barked at his ministers and walked away. Ravana did not believe in miracles. If there was a feat he could not perform, none else could. And he surely could not reverse the flow of a river like Narmada.[43]

Yet, one corner of Ravana's mind kept drumming about the realities he was possibly fleeing from. The easiest way to evade truths was

---

[42] Past mistakes are like a man dressed in black running after you with a knife. No matter how fast you run away from your past, it catches up with you. And when it does, it plunges that knife right into you, causing suffering. When you know that your present suffering is related to a past mistake, shame is replaced with guilt.

[43] Doubting one's own ability makes one modest, whereas doubting others' ability makes one haughty.

to shrug them off as fantasies spun by fertile minds, rather fearful minds.[44] But just too many people had warned him with sagas of the thousand-handed Kartivirya Arjuna.

Hearsay is one thing, experience is quite another. Ravana gaped in disbelief when he saw river Narmada flowing in the opposite direction. Although for a short time, it did flow in the opposite direction and that too with a strong current. In fact, all his *pooja* paraphernalia, for the worship of the *Shivalinga* (idol representing Lord Shiva) had been washed away because of the reverse flow. He had not felt anger, instead felt total powerlessness. He had meekly watched everything flow away. He had then ordered his ministers to investigate the reason for this phenomenon, and they had brought news of a reality check he wasn't ready to take.[45]

In prison now, Ravana bit his lips as he remembered ordering his army to attack earlier that noon, more out of frustration than because of anger. He had foolishly wished to conquer the city of Mahismati when the king was making merry with his queens in the river. Was it Ravana's war strategy or was it the deep-rooted fear of not wanting to face Kartivirya Arjuna?

The vicious joy he felt when butchering Kartivirya Arjuna's

---

[44] The most convenient way to handle a problem is to assume that the problem does not exist. Just like an ostrich buries its head in the sand in the face of a calamity it cannot handle, a man turns his face away from a calamity when unable to deal with it.

 Neither the ostrich nor the man need ever face such a calamity again, since both of them will not survive to encounter another calamity, anyway.

[45] Realities of life and our expectations from life are like adjoining sliding cliffs. To the degree we further our expectations from the realities of life, the gap between the two increases. The wider the gap, the greater is the frustration.

helpless ministers and unprepared soldiers was soon drowned by the agonizing pain Kartivirya's mighty blows were causing him. This legend had appeared within minutes of Ravana's attack and taken full control of the situation. Not that Ravana failed to put up a tough fight. He fought hard, but how long can a butterfly fight an eagle? Each of Kartivirya Arjuna's blows smashed the very core of Ravana's bravado, crushing him to a pulp.[46]

Staring at the cold stone floor of the prison cell kept reminding the helpless Ravana of how his strength had betrayed him. He was not expecting to be released any time soon, so he was surprised when the iron door opened and he was ushered respectfully to the palace.

It all dawned on him when he saw Sage Paulatsya, his grandfather. Oh no! The old man had taken a favor. How he hated this! He did not need an old man taking care of him! Whatever the old man had told Kartivirya was working. Kartivirya was so impressed that he began interacting with Ravana like a friend. He even declared aloud his friendship with Ravana. Ravana was relieved, if not happy, at the turn of events. He returned to Lanka on his Pushpak Vimana with a friend gained and a lesson learned – overconfidence will drown you in the river of reality.[47]

a revenge foretold

Crushing smaller rulers had become Ravana's free play. He traveled extensively just to challenge as many independent kings as he could.

---

[46] Nature's way of humbling one is known as ego therapy. It is not a soft massage, but a strong message.

[47] Confidence is a key to all locks, but overconfidence is the lock to all doors. Confidence leads to inspiration, but overconfidence leads to perspiration.

Most never even put up a decent fight and surrendered to Ravana's supremacy. Ravana's kingdom thus spread far and wide.

He met a match in Anaranya, the king of Ayodhya, who seemed weak but was not willing to throw away his kingdom. A terrible fight ensued, tragically ending with Anaranya on the floor, a spear pierced through his chest. As he took his last breath, Anaranya cursed Ravana that his death would be avenged by a descendent.

Ravana had a good laugh, as he did not believe in tales of the future. He lived in the moment, and here and now, he was the winner![48]

covert lessons

Ravana blissfully soared across the sky in his precious Pushpak Vimana, totally oblivious that someone from above was observing him. Not that he cared, but this meeting would change the course of his life, at least his image as the king of the universe.

High above, Narada *muni*, the divine spaceman, was waiting for the Pushpak to attain enough elevation. His discussion with Ravana had to be private and confidential. What better place than space?

Narada decided to craft his words carefully to open a conversation with Ravana. This man was always suspicious and quick to anger. He would not take Narada's words seriously if he became even

---

[48] The entrance to the present is flanked by two doors – the past that opens inward and the future that opens outward. If we focus on the present, the future goes into the auto-care mode. The enemy of the present is disregard of the future.

remotely suspicious. Narada knew this from his experience with him.

Not too long ago, when flying over Ravana's mansion in Lanka, the king spotted the *muni* and beckoned him. Reluctantly, he went and met the mighty king. Ravana expressed his desire to learn the *Om mantra*. Despite Narada's polite refusal, Ravana remained persuasive. Narada patiently explained that Vedic *mantras* were taught not on the basis of competence, but on the basis of the student's character and that a teacher reserved the right to impart knowledge according to his assessment of the student. Ravana drew out his Chandrahasa sword and threatened Narada with an icy tone, "When a student wants to learn something, the teacher must comply."[49]

Narada, shocked at this *rakshasa*'s audacity, decided to teach him a lesson on humility, somewhat different from the lesson he actually wanted to learn. He laughed at Ravana, inciting him even more. "Not everything in this world can be bought with money or controlled with power, Ravana. Your experiences have taught you that your wealth and power bring everything to your feet; however, you are wide off the mark. There are many more things that humility can bring. Your reckless arrogance will one day be the cause of your destruction."[50]

Unaccustomed to hearing words of disrespect, Ravana erupted

---

[49] Eagerness expressed without the right attitude should be spelled as arrogance. A teacher is like a tap, and a student is an empty pot. For the pot to fill up, it has to sit below the tap. If the pot sits above the tap, it will remain dry even if the tap is running.

[50] When money travels from your pocket to your head, it triggers the secretion of a liquid known as hauteur. This liquid gives rise to a disease known as disrespectfulness.

with anger. In a fit of rage, he slashed Narada with his sword in an attempt to make a clean sweep across the audacious *muni*'s torso. Ravana had invested all his energy into the act, but the sword passed through Narada's body as if cutting through air. Ravana tripped; Narada was unharmed! How was this possible?

Narada guffawed at Ravana's ignorance. How could his sword cut a spiritual body? Awestruck by Narada's supernatural powers, Ravana fell at his feet pleading for a body like that. Narada smiled at Ravana's change in attitude. Here was a shrewd man; willing to go to any lengths to gather anything that would establish and reaffirm his supremacy. A moment ago, he was wielding a sword, and now, all of a sudden, he was down on his knees, pleading. Chameleons could learn a lesson or two from Ravana on changing colors![51]

Narada chastised Ravana, "If you chant the name of Vishnu, you could also gain a spiritual body." That was it! The name of Vishnu had such an unexpected effect on Ravana that he stormed right back into his palace with, "I don't need a spiritual body. You wait and watch, I will make this body eternal." Narada was left stunned by his conceit.

Even as Ravana was in the Pushpak Vimana that was flying toward him, Narada's position was still that of a teacher, and Ravana's still that of a student, although an unwilling one. Narada wanted to teach Ravana another lesson and reveal to him another aspect he had yet to learn.[52]

---

[51] Diplomacy is an art that changes your body language drastically with no change in the language of the heart. In a moment, Ravana's body language changed from wielding a sword to holding the feet of Narada, but the language of his heart remained unchanged.

[52] A good teacher is like a fisherman, always looking for a good catch, to share his wisdom and give life lessons to all who need it.

"Congratulations! From the time I met you last, you have become a powerful universal monarch. I am so pleased to have known someone of your stature and valor. In my travels across the universe, I am yet to meet a warrior stronger than you. Your recent conquest over the universal controllers is testimony to that; however, I wonder how great people like you occasionally show lapses in common sense." Having said this, Narada stopped in his tracks.

Ravana was intently listening to the sweet music of praise, so when it stopped abruptly, he felt like a child whose favorite toy had been snatched. "Lapse?! What do you mean by lapse? As far as I am concerned, there is no lapse in my rule. Come clear with what you mean."

"Yes, Ravana, let me explain. You are painstakingly conquering so many kings and rulers and celestial beings. But all these beings are all already conquered by death. Can't you see these tiny human beings are always suffering from disease, old age and other frailties? Each will perish and be taken by death. More than you, people fear death. Instead of wasting your time with these insignificant people, it would be wiser to first conquer the god of death, Yama. If you do that, naturally everyone will submit to you." Narada could not help suppress a smile when Ravana immediately got up for mission impossible.[53]

---

[53] Death is a universal virus installed in every individual, programmed to terminate and dissolve the machine itself. Narada was encouraging Ravana to find the anti-virus software for the virus named death. A mission impossible!

a close brush with death

The first glimpse of hell sent a chill down Ravana's spine. Torture wasn't new to his dictionary; in fact, it was one of his favorite words. But what he saw here was beyond horrendous, even by his standards.

The most ferocious of *rakshasas* in Ravana's kingdom would probably look like *apsaras* (beautiful heavenly damsels) in front of the vicious looking *yamadutas* (assistants to Yama). Each *yamaduta* was in charge of a department that dealt with a specific punishment for each sin. Although there was variety in the punishment, the effect was the same – intense pain.

A man was being flogged with a whip, and he was howling in agony. Another was being chased by a ferocious dog biting into his legs and tearing away chunks of his flesh repeatedly. Men were thrown into a deep pit filled with poisonous worms and creepy insects that were gnawing away their bodies inch by inch. In the middle of the torture city was a vast river of blood, and men were being tossed into it with stones tied to their necks. On the banks, men were walking on hot, burning sand; their blistered feet bleeding, but they had no recourse of any kind except to continue walking and crying.

The worst sight was the plight of those in the forest. They were tied up with ropes and forced to climb tall trees with thorny trunks and razor sharp leaves. Once they reached the top, they were mercilessly pulled down, their already-bruised bodies scraping over the thorny trunks and leaves. This was repeated endlessly. Some were dunked in salty water tanks, others were made to walk on sharp swords, yet others were buried neck deep in mud with no food or water for weeks and weeks. Hunger and thirst were constant companions for all. If anyone were to express a wish, the answer would be death. But alas, this was the death kingdom where no one could die. Hadn't all of them already died to come here?

All people could ever do was suffer for their sins. Ravana was no saint, but it did not take long to recognize that he, too, would be here soon. He visualized himself being flogged as he ran on the hot sand, jumping into the bloody water and being subjected to all forms of punishment.[54]

"Stop all this nonsense! Attack the bullies! Stop this persecution, release the victims." Suddenly Ravana was overcome with a bout of compassion in his heart, an event that probably occurs not even once in a demon's lifetime. Ravana wheeled around in his plane and rallied his soldiers against the confused *yamadutas*. Never before had the hells been attacked like this! The *yamadutas* were trained to persecute, not fight. Ravana's soldiers began creating havoc. This activated the security system, and all hell broke loose on the Pushpak Vimana. The air chariot was damaged badly, but within moments, the damage was undone! Nevertheless, Ravana was so incensed that someone dared damage his favorite vehicle. He lunged off the Pushpak Vimana and charged at them with his *Pasupatastra* (the weapon given by Lord Shiva). The *Pasupatastra* could release hundreds of flame-tipped arrows simultaneously. Wherever these arrows found target, destruction was certain.[55]

---

[54] Like Ravana, everyone wants a life where fun is welcome, but punishment is not; enjoyment is welcome, but responsibility is not.

[55] Fake compassion and cruelty exhibited simultaneously reveal hypocrisy. On the one hand, Ravana showed compassion to the suffering victims in hell and on the other hand, he exhibited cruelty by killing the *yamadutas*.

As the victory shouts of Ravana and his army reached Yama's ears, he began to worry. Such cries were unusual in hell. This implied that an intruder had attacked hell. In the past, many fools had wanted to change the system of punishment and reward, but in vain.[56]

The situation turned grave; Yama quickly mounted his chariot to set things right. As he assumed the role of the punisher, his eyes became red with anger and hot fumes billowed out of the pores of his body. Two imposing personalities mounted his chariot and stood on either side. Death and Time were Yama's assistants. Glancing at the two invincible aspects of his own realm, he grinned.

All of Ravana's army, including his prominent ministers, suddenly had the look of ashen horror. Ravana was so engrossed in revelry that he did not even hear Yama's chariot drawing closer. Fear gripped him when he turned to see three dreadful beings atop a chariot staring down indignantly at him. He recognized the one ahead as Yama, the god of death. But who were the other two? Did inquisitiveness make any difference at a moment like this? If they were on the same chariot as Yama's, they surely hadn't come to congratulate him or dance with him in celebration!

Swallowing his fears and staring straight into the eyes of Yama, Ravana tightened his waist belt. A volley of arrows emerged from Yama's bow. The force and relentlessness of the arrows took Ravana completely by surprise. This game wasn't going to be easy. But he wasn't ever the one to give up!

---

[56] Aspiring to change the unchangeable without ability reveals an entertainer. Humbly accepting the unchangeable despite ability reveals a discriminator.

He sent a spinning arrow at Yama's chariot driver and seriously wounded him. He followed it up with another powerful missile at Death who stood just behind Yama. As the missile whizzed past Yama, Death slightly adjusted and averted the weapon. Yama was shaking in frenzied rage. Never before had anyone dared challenge Death so brazenly. If this man was allowed to get away, the masses would lose respect for Death and it would lead to proliferation of more Ravana-like men wanting to challenge Death and even obliterate it.

Yama's rage erupted as a fiery river flowing out from his mouth. The temperature shot up creating an appalling atmosphere. *Rakshasas* began perspiring profusely; some even fainted, unable to tolerate the intensity of the battle. At this juncture, Death decided to speak in its ear-splitting, heart-shattering and fear-evoking voice. "Never have I let you down my master! Give me the opportunity to serve you yet again by finishing off this puny insect that was foolhardy enough to attack an elephant. Many such fools in the past have rushed into my vicious fold and ceased to exist – Hiranyakashipu, Namuchi, Nisandi, Dhumketu, Virochan, to name a few. Ravana has still not come within my range, but now I feel his time has come. Can I do the honors?"

"Indeed you are capable of doing all that you said and more. But this fool is my prey. Rare is an opportunity to vanquish fools such as him. Let me have the pleasure." Yama held out his hand to attract an effulgent golden staff, the Yama *danda* (the staff of death), which appeared with a flash of lightning and a deafening sound. *Rakshasas* began scurrying like ants. Ravana was perspiring, but he pretended to be composed. Just as Yama was about to put an end to Ravana with the staff, Lord Brahma appeared.

"Spare Ravana, O merciful Yama. I have unfortunately given him a boon that he cannot be killed by a demigod; so please do not make my promise go in vain. If you kill him, I will be always blamed for making false promises and you will be accused of going against a senior. The Yama *danda* is the ultimate weapon in this universe. Undoubtedly, it will destroy Ravana, but if by any chance it does not, then that will be the ultimate tragedy for this world. This man will become invincible and will fear no one and nothing. Considering all this, please desist from using your weapon and cease this war."

Yama saw merit in Brahma's words, withdrew his attack and returned to his palace.

Ravana of course had not heard the conversation between Brahma and Yama, but he assumed that Yama had accepted defeat and withdrawn. He declared himself the winner and returned to Lanka. He coined himself another name, Trilokeshwar, the lord of the three worlds.[57]

waiting for hope

Darkness enveloped the city of Lanka. The evening of partying and revelry ended. Laughter and voices slowly died down and all that was heard were the loud snores of intoxicated *rakshasas*. It had clearly been an evening of triumph, with Ravana returning after

---

[57] Withdrawing requires maturity and following the directions of superiors requires humility. The combination of maturity and humility is called leadership. The attack of Yama was not to prove his superiority but an act to defend the superiority of the laws of god. Ravana on the other hand conveniently forgot how he was to die. But rather felt that the interference of Brahma was also his own greatness.

subduing none less than the god of death, Yama. Ravana had been godlike to them, but post this victory, he *was* god.

High above, another group was not as ecstatic as the ones below. The defeated demigods rued every moment, upset with the way Ravana was treating them and disturbing the natural balance of the universe by inflicting unlimited atrocities. Would Ravana's sins ever fructify and cause his destruction?[58]

Their gaze turned from Lanka to a distant land up north, a land of hope, Ayodhya!

Ravana's black sins had taken shape as white hair on Dasaratha's head, which urged him to act for the benefit of the world. He had done it; at least, that's what declaring Rama's coronation seemed to do, until yet another plan began to unfold. A plan that would yield results much faster! After all, the world couldn't wait for too long...

---

[58] Just as some spiders eat their mothers, the sins of Ravana born from Ravana were soon going to eat him up.

CHAPTER 3

BOONS BECOME CURSES

The two eyes carefully inspected the entire city; initially just scanning, but eventually zooming into details. Something was different today! How could such an important event escape the microscopic scrutiny of the two ever-watchful eyes?

The rooftop of the palace of her mistress was ideal for a bird's eye view of the entire city. The last massive celebration had taken place two-and-a-half decades ago when Dasaratha was blessed with four sons. What could it possibly be this time?

All that the beady, darting eyes could see across every corner of Ayodhya was excitement. Tree-shaped lanterns lined every lane and by-lane of Ayodhya. Such brightness! Were one to walk down these lanes ignoring the lanterns, one would mistake night for day!

Ayodhya's citizens were exulting, invigorated by the triple joys of the gentle drizzle. The scented showers caressed, colored and calmed the people. Water droplets, color sprays and flower showers rained from the mellowing skies on the mirthful citizens clambered over rooftops and trees. Rainbow colors floated in the air as the joyous people of

Ayodhya soaked in the soothing atmosphere. As the indolent sun slowly set in the distant west, an effulgent one seemed to rise over Ayodhya's horizon. Yet all this revelry stung so much that the two wicked eyes just rained loathsome anger![1]

As the wrathful eyes scanned Rama's cheerful abode, they crinkled. The palace that was once her mistress's (and, as a consequence, hers, too) was swamped by people. The spiteful eyes glanced at the slender-waisted maidens in twirling skirts and ornate blouses swaying to the festive tunes. As they pirouetted and pranced, the darting pair of eyes froze.

The dark eyes turned darker with fury with each passing hour. It was well past bedtime, but the night was still young for Ayodhya. Won't these people fall asleep at all tonight? Why was everyone so restless? What exactly was going on?

The now-confused eyes turned toward the gateway of the glorious city, swallowing in every flower, every flag, every festoon adorning the houses, street corners and temple domes all the way up to the palace entrance. Besides the luxuriant dazzle of the diamond-studded gateway decorated with flowing shimmering silk, plantain stems and betel nuts tree barks, what struck the eyes was the sheer number of people streaming into Ayodhya even at dusk.

---

[1] Beauty resides not in the eyes but in the vision of the beholder. Just as a person who has fallen into a mucky valley constantly finds fault with the filth he is lying in and cannot appreciate the scenic beauty of the mountains, one cannot appreciate the beauty of things around when lower nature prevails.

Strange! Why would so many people want to enter a city at such an hour?[2,3,4]

When her eyes alone could not decode the festive puzzle, she opened her mouth to ask a happy maid, who was gawking at the festivities below, "What's happening in our city? What's this occasion that I am unaware of? Why is there so much fanfare? My mind is unable to comprehend. Are you aware of what's happening?"[5,6]

"What are you saying? Don't you know? It's the most auspicious news Ayodhya could ever have heard! The king of Ayodhya, Dasaratha, has decided to coronate his first son, our dear Rama, as the king of Ayodhya tomorrow morning. People from across the world are longing to witness this event. I have never seen so many people from so many distant lands thronging our city. Aren't we

---

[2] Real vision is not so much the property of the eyes as much as it is of the heart. What the society needs today is not an eye transplant but a vision transplant. An eye transplant grants the gift of sight and a vision transplant grants the gift of direction.

[3] Confused eyes, sad eyes, smiling eyes, confident eyes, microscopic eyes, blank eyes, joyful eyes, graceful eyes – our eyes expose our emotional state and are the windows to our mind, which is hidden from the world.

[4] Weak eyes feel blinded by bright light; here, weak eyes and a defective vision were analyzing the bright light of Rama's coronation. Weak eyes need the protective goggles of humility and acceptance to withstand bedazzling light.

[5] Knowledge gained through the sense of hearing–, especially from the right source with the right intention and of the right purpose, – is more reliable than the self-guided sense of seeing.

[6] When analysis with one's abilities fails to give answers, questioning the right source certainly works. Such questioning, when progressive, helps one align with the deeper truths of life, but when regressive, it merely aligns truths forcefully to one's personal paradigms.

fortunate to have such a virtuous king? Surely, our pious deeds have taken birth in the form of Rama." That said, the maid cavorted away from the spellbound questioner.

The thick eyebrows knotted to resemble a stretched bow; her breathing became heavier, her teeth gritted, her fists clenched and her ears fumed. This was a live ball of fire!

Manthara, Keikeyi's hunchbacked maid and haughty associate, became livid and decided to take matters in her own hands.[7]

For one last time, she scoured the city below with the same pair of eyes, but these were now enlightened with the knowledge of truth. The view made perfect sense now. Suddenly, she spotted something that hadn't caught her attention earlier. Kaushalya, Rama's mother, was making generous donations with a confident smile on her face. This was a rare sight for Manthara. Her queen, Keikeyi, was always the one making these distributions on behalf of the king, because she was his favorite. She was the one with access to all the king's resources, not Kaushalya, who was always the neglected wife with nothing much to offer. Her world would change overnight if she did not act soon. This night was crucial for the future of her mistress and, more importantly, her own.

Plotting and planning in her frenzied head, Manthara lumbered down the terrace stairs into her mistress's inner chambers. Climbing down the stairs had always been tough because of the huge effort

---

[7] Valmiki describes that Manthara's visit to the terrace that night was *yaddrcchaya* or accidental. An accident may get you somewhere, but what you do upon getting there is no accident. Manthara may have gone to the terrace by chance, but her actions from that point on were no accident, they were intentional.

that went into trying to keep her leaning body from toppling over. But today, her fast-ticking mind was miraculously pushing her through the entire ordeal.[8]

revelry and reverence

Winding his way through the bubbling crowd of onlookers and dancers, Vasistha's assistant reached Rama's palace. The joyous enthusiasm of the citizens resembled the excited sea on a full-moon night. As he gazed away from the crowd, the white marble structure atop Lord Rama's palace reflected the moon beams and seemed to outshine the moon itself. The lower half of the palace building shimmered, because of the brilliance of the golden flames from lanterns all around it.

The assistant found the noise deafening, yet inspiring. Ayodhya's citizens were in the throes of uninhibited celebration and seemed determined to sing and dance the night away. They wanted to be the first ones to greet Rama at sunrise.

As Vasistha's assistant passed by the first doorway of Rama's palace and then through a series of gateways and arched doors into the

---

[8] The success of a leopard lies in the failure of the deer; this is the rule of the jungle not a human tenet. Even in a jungle, between similar species, there is love, not war.

When humans learn to celebrate each other's success rather than plan one another's failures, they develop concrete relationships rather than concrete jungles.

Manthara had concretely decided to turn Ayodhya into a jungle and the jungle into Ayodhya.

inner most chamber of Rama's palace, the tumultuous noise faded into a serene silence and then slowly gave way to a soft murmur of Vedic chants.

The calm inside was in complete contrast to chaos outside. As he soaked in this scene, he was certain Rama was the ideal person to rule Ayodhya!

Seated on simple *kusa* mats (grass mats) around a sacrificial fire was the divine couple, Rama and Sita. Maids and servants stood around, waiting for orders to be of assistance in the religious ceremony. The couple was absorbed in prayer, Their eyes closed through the chanting of the *mantras*. Occasionally, Rama opened His eyes to guide His soft hands to offer clarified butter into the sacred fire as Sita opened Hers to speckle the flames with pounded rice and other holy ingredients. With folded palms, Rama then gently reminded Sita about the enormity of the responsibility They were about to take on and that They ought to sacrifice all Their personal needs and expectations in this fire. Whatever time, intelligence, energy and resources They possessed had to be henceforth poured into the fire of sacrifice for the welfare of Ayodhya's citizens. Sita nodded knowingly.[9]

Vasistha's assistant soon began drawing comparisons in his mind between the celebrations outside and inside. Outside, the citizens were reveling in the fortune of being blessed with a king such as Rama, and inside, Rama was rejoicing in the opportunity He had

---

[9] Why were fire and sacrifice interconnected in Vedic times? Because both burn! Fire burns lumber and sacrifice burns slumber. One cannot sleep when one is on fire. A person who chooses to sacrifice for the sake of the world cannot expect a life of ease when burning with the desire to serve.

been given to serve His people. The outside was pompous, the inside sober; the outside danced to festive songs and the celebration inside bowed to prayers of devotion.[10]

What touched him most was that Rama was unfazed by the high position and role to be bestowed on Him the next morning; He was not arrogant and proud, rather he was contemplative and focused. Rama had decided to devote all His energies into serving Ayodhya. Rather than dwelling upon the immense power awaiting Him, Rama took refuge in the higher powers to empower Himself to dispense His responsibilities better.[11,12,13]

a m i n d g a m e

With every descending step, the plan became clearer and clearer,

---

[10] Rama and Sita burned Their desires for personal comforts in the fire of sacrifice. Sound sacrifice is a silent affair.

[11] In a fountain, water lying at a low level touches great heights only when propelled by the power of a motor. Similarly, elevation from one's current level of responsibility occurs only when thrust by the power of commitment.

[12] Just like a motor can function only as long as there is electricity, commitment sustains for as long as integrity motivates it. For electricity, one needs a powerhouse; to live a life of integrity, one needs the power of prayer.

[13] Despite being God, through His own example, Rama teaches how to prepare one's consciousness before accepting a higher responsibility. Whether it is the responsibility of a king, a teacher, a mother, a father or any other position that arouses expectations from followers, the same preparation must be invested. We equip ourselves with skills for an exulted position, but do we prepare our consciousness to qualify for it?

as if some unknown force[14] was guiding Manthara to stoop lower and lower.[15]

Annoyance took over the respect that Manthara had for Keikeyi when she saw her nonchalant demeanor. Keikeyi's delicate and almost fragile body rested on the soft bed much like watercress floating on the milky ocean.

"How can she sleep so peacefully amid such calamity? Her father has rightly sent me along to protect his innocent and docile daughter. But to safeguard her, I need to wake her up from her deep slumber of ignorance," Manthara mumbled and went charging to her mistress as if an evil planet were out to destroy some unsuspecting person.

Clasping Keikeyi's petal soft feet, Manthara tried to wake her up. Keikeyi stirred but did not really get up.[16] "Get up you fool!" Manthara screamed, still holding her feet. The shrill voice broke Keikeyi's slumber. "Just like the moon that keeps sharing its cooling beams unabated, oblivious of the poison-filled planet Rahu's

---

[14] It is believed in some circles that when Dasaratha decided to crown Rama king, the demigods and Mother Earth became worried that if Rama were to become entwined in ruling, there would be no one to slay the horrible Ravana and his demonic army. So they went to Saraswati, the goddess of intelligence, (or Vani, the goddess of speech) to change the minds of Dasaratha and his queens. They were asked to first go and corrupt Manthara's mind and then Keikeyi's. Saraswati then went to Ayodhya and found the hunchbacked Manthara and messed with her mind enough to get Keiekyi to send Rama to exile and thereby fulfill His mission on earth.

[15] Ravana's sins and the demigods' prayers were the forces guiding Manthara to act for the welfare of the world.

[16] On the one hand Manthara was at Keikeyi's feet, on the other hand, she was screaming at her. Being at someone's feet denotes humility, whereas screaming at someone shows haughtiness.

approach, you lie there blissfully unaware of calamity that is at your doorstep."[17]

Keikeyi leaped up to sit on her bed and replied, "A woman who has four powerful virtuous sons need not fear any bad situation or any ill person in this world. With my sons Rama, Bharata, Lakshmana and Shatrughna around me, why should I worry about minor calamities?"

Manthara likened Keikeyi to the thoughtless person sleeping despite his house being swept away by a flash flood. Manthara was certain the flood of troubles the next morning would carry Keikeyi away if she did not get up and act immediately.

Exasperated that Keikeyi was too naïve to interpret her analogies, Manthara took on a more direct approach. She told Keikeyi, "Dasaratha flaunts you as his favorite queen, but in reality he favors Kaushalya more. His action today is proof enough, and your fortunes will now dissipate like a stream under the summer sun."[18,19]

Keikeyi could sense some disturbing insecurity in Manthara's words and assured her of her protection, but Manthara became more and more frustrated with Keikeyi's inability to grasp the gravity of the situation.

---

[17] Conflicting actions are permissible when the intention is clean. But when the intention itself is conflicted, then actions lead to confusion, not clarity. The confusion in the mind manifests as a confusion in one's actions.

[18] Reciprocation of love when demanded is obsession, and when commanded natural.

[19] Manthara was trying to convince Keikeyi that Dasratha's favoring Kaushalya symbolized the non-reciprocation of love. Favoritism displayed by children is innocence, but by adults it is guile.

"You have been carrying a poisonous snake in your bosom and showering it with love. Nourished and strengthened by your love, it has now driven its poisonous fangs into your flesh. Its name is Dasaratha!" Manthara spat out, flashing an intense, angry look at the meek Keikeyi.

"You were always conceited about the complete control you had over your husband and his other wives. You were wrong, my dear! Kaushalya has monopolized Dasaratha now. He showers you with sweet words, but it comes to action, Kaushalya is his biggest beneficiary. The king is outwardly truthful, but inwardly cunning. Despite being born a royal, how can you be so gullible and not know of the cruelty in kingly diplomacy? Kaushalya, through Dasaratha, has cleverly set your future on fire."[20]

Keikeyi was disturbed by Manthara's constant babbling. She said, "Don't go in circles or mince any words; just speak clearly, without fear. What's on your mind?"

Manthara rambled on, "Dasaratha has decided to appoint the useless Rama as the king of Ayodhya, that incompetent son of Kaushalya who killed an innocent woman named Tataka with his arrow.[21] The entire solar dynasty is embarrassed about this fellow's

---

[20] When magnitude of love is equated with quantity of facility given, relationships become transactions, mutual understanding becomes contracts, serving becomes an investment and denial becomes breach of agreement.

[21] A shrub may have flowers and thorns. Thorns play as important a role as the flowers; in fact, sometimes more. If it weren't for the thorns, the flowers would not survive to serve their purpose.

A ruler has dual roles – to be like the flower, showering love and affection on his people, and to be like the thorn, staving off people with

shameful deed, but can you imagine how foolish it is of your beloved husband to appoint him as the heir apparent?[22] This news has left me drowning in fear. To me, this marks the beginning of torture for you and your son, Bharata. It feels as if I have been hurled into the bottomless pit of anxiety."[23]

Unable to contain her joy, Keikeyi lunged out of her bed and rushed toward Manthara, "O Manthara, thank you! This is the best news I have received in my entire life! Rama is going to become the king of Ayodhya! This is nectar to my ears! Thank you, Manthara, once again. You have filled my life with immense pleasure. Surely, you want a good reward for bringing this news, which is why you express so much fear. Here, take this gem-studded necklace, it will fetch you a fortune.

Why do you contradict yourself by saying that Rama is going to become king and not my son. Rama *is* my son. I do not see any difference between Rama and Bharata. My affection for Rama and Bharata are the same. Right now, my mind is like a golden pot filled

---

ill-will toward his kingdom. It is important to appreciate a ruler for his gentleness as well as his harshness.

[22] Manthara bemoaned Rama's killing of the woman Tataka without mentioning anything about the atrocities for which He was duty-bound to kill her.

Finding good in a bad person is good as long as the effect is good. But here, Manthara was intent on finding good in Tataka at the cost of finding bad in Rama. Presenting the wicked as innocent and the innocent as wicked with a vicious agenda is itself a heinous act.

[23] When in fact the whole of Ayodhya considered the killing of Tataka a reason to glorify Rama, Manthara saw this as His fault. She is free to have an individual perception. But here, she is projecting her views as that of the entire kingdom. Such extrapolation can only be the result of a deep-seated grudge.

to the brim with honey. In fact, I am so convinced that you can give me no better news than this for the rest of your life. Keeping that in mind and knowing my state of bliss, ask me a boon; ask anything you want, Manthara, and it will be yours."[24]

Manthara became near hysterical when Keikeyi handed over the jewelry. All of sudden, Manthara's mind raced back to that moment when a fleeting arrow had swished and landed with a thud on her young back.[25] The arrow tip, loaded with a mud ball, had burst open sparking squeals of laughter. Rama had shot the arrow, and the four boys were laughing their guts away as the hissing Manthara had walked away, brushing the mud off her back but gathering lifelong vengeance in her heart. That incident had dug deep into Manthara's mind and sown the seed of everlasting hatred for Rama. Today, that seed had borne the fruit of vengeance.[26]

---

[24] Just like a river does not differentiate between two banks, a pure mind does not differentiate between what is the self's and what is not; like the river, it is so absorbed in others' welfare that it finds no time for self-absorption.

Keikeyi had such a pure mind at this point that she saw no difference between Rama and Bharata.

[25] When one makes an event the epicenter of one's entire life, one pauses it at that small event and magnifies it to such gigantic proportions that it engulfs one's whole existence. The world moves on, but one remains stuck there.

Even 25 years later, Manthara was still stuck on that event of perceived insult, and she made it the center of her life. Revenge became the goal of her life.

[26] The tool of forgiveness helps one release the anchor of frustration from the mud of revenge and allows the boat of life to go forth into the ocean of joys. If this tool is not used soon enough, then the whole life is wasted on the frustrating banks of hatred.

When seen from Rama's perspective, we can understand that jokes

Manthara looked at the jewelry in her hands and let out a sigh of deep frustration.[27] She began shedding profuse tears; she slapped her own head hard, pulled at her hair and tore her own clothes. She then flung the necklace on the floor with all her might; it created a dent in the hard marble floor, and thousands of pieces of precious stones scattered all over the room.[28] In the process, she managed to grab Keikeyi's attention and shake her out of her joyful trance.

At the end of all her theatrics, Manthara succeeded in getting her queen to hear her out. Keikeyi got carried away by Manthara's conduct, and she felt that it was her jealousy that was guised as concern.

Manthara uttered words as violent as her actions, "O foolishness embodied, you are writing your own story of doom. Imagine a person in the middle of the ocean drilling a hole in his own boat. O fish-eyed one, you are like that person – you are in an ocean of troubles, your position as queen is like that of the boat and your laughter (taking the situation lightly) like the drill about to drown you.

Which intelligent woman would be happy with the fortune of her stepson? A stepson and a co-wife are a woman's primary enemies. Wise people say that one should deal with fire and enemies right

---

can be costly. Although meant to lighten life, when shared with the wrong people, jokes could end up burdening our lives.

[27] Manthara had always believed that Keikeyi trusted her and she could control her queen very easily. But here she was, devastated and frustrated as she could no longer control her queen.

[28] Anger is an outcome of the frustration of unmet desires. To fulfill their desires, people sometimes destroy themselves. It is actually easier to destroy oneself than to destroy one's desires.

away. Your timely action will not only save you and your son but also me from reaching a state of poverty.[29] If not, very soon you will become Kaushalya's maid along with us, and your son will become Rama's servant.

Rama's wives will be happy to see Him in this position of respect and power, and your daughter-in-law will become sad to see Bharata wane like the moon and slowly fade away into oblivion." Manthara chose her words wisely, ensuring that she drove home her point. [30]

Keikeyi mustered all her kindness and composure to convince Manthara about her understanding of Rama. "Manthara, stop spurting all this twaddle, I know Rama more than I know myself. He has a mountain of gemlike qualities. He is trained by His elders to act righteously. He only speaks the truth, and His conduct is stainless and clean. He will not abuse His brothers with His position; in fact, He will serve and protect them like a kind father.

Not only that, O Hunchbacked One, Rama is Dasaratha's eldest son. The Suryavanshi or solar race is like a peacock, and it follows the laws laid down by Manu closely. In the solar lineage, the eldest

---

[29] Insecurity about the future creates a kingdom of fear in everyone's heart. Just like the a herd of elephants running to save themselves from some disaster cause insecurity among the hundreds of smaller animals who face the risk of being trampled to death, our attempts to make ourselves secure may become the cause of insecurity for many others.

Manthara was trying to secure her personal life and, in the process, was ready to disrupt the entire kingdom.

[30] Assumption is the mother of many deceptions.

Manthara mentions Rama as having many wives, assuming that as any other king, Rama would also marry more than once. As is evident, she is assuming too many things at this point.

son of the king inherits the throne. In a pride of peacocks, though the hens lay many eggs simultaneously, only the eldest one grows wings the earliest. No one can change nature. You cannot prevent Rama from ascending to the throne as much as you cannot prevent the eldest peacock from spreading its wings first.[31]

Manthara, if anyone else had spoken these words instead of you, I would have slit the tongue of that person. You are actually our enemy, my son's and mine.[32] The reality is that Rama serves me more than my own son does. I would even go to the extent of saying that He actually serves me more than He serves His own mother, Kaushalya. Why should I be envious of such an adorable boy?"

Manthara argued, "O slender-waisted Keikeyi, if everything is as innocent as you say, then tell me why did Dasaratha send Bharata away and why is he crowning Rama in his absence? Did you even think about that? You can't, Keikeyi, because you are innocent. The only explanation is 'fear'.

---

[31] An oyster automatically opens when the pearl inside is completely formed. If opened forcibly before maturity, dirt, not the pearl, will be visible inside.

The laws of nature cannot be changed to accommodate our whims. One who tries to change the laws is at a loss.

[32] A kind heart is a grateful heart. Keikeyi's kindness and pure heartedness is visible in her expression of gratitude to Rama.

But kindness can sometimes become an impediment against a strict action. Instead of merely saying so, had Keikeyi actually punished Manthara, the situation would not have reached this stage.

The fine balance between kindness and strictness is called justice or *dharma*.

Bharata is the only competition for Rama.[33] In fact, he has equal rights to the throne. Lakshmana and Shatrughna are both too young to compete for the throne; only Bharata is closer to Rama by age. Besides, the crafty Rama has wisely won over Lakshmana, and the young boy will not utter a word in opposition. Shatrughna is a non-entity anyway, so no one will bother about his opinion.[34] Bharata is equipped with finer qualities than Rama to rule the kingdom, and Dasaratha and Rama both know it all too well. No wonder then that they are rushing to finish the coronation tomorrow itself without Bharata getting a hint of it."[35]

Keikeyi was now convinced that Manthara was unnecessarily worked up about Rama's coronation. She was hopeful Rama would hand over the reign of his kingdom to Bharata after countless years of ruling. And since that joyful moment was sure to come in her lifetime, why should she look at Rama's coronation in a negative way now?

Manthara could not believe her ears! How daft can this woman be? Her mistress was not as blessed with intelligence as she was with beauty. Thus far, it was Keikeyi's beauty that had got her success. But now, if any success were to be achieved, it would need more

---

[33] When the conclusion is drawn and an opinion formed, data can be manipulated to achieve the desired results. Valmiki calls Manthara *vakya visharaddha*, which means word wise. Manthara was clever with words.

[34] She deftly analyzed the love between Rama and Lakshmana as part of Rama's diplomacy and Shatrughna's loyalty as lack of opinion.

[35] In any given situation, different people can have different opinions. If someone else's opinion becomes the basis of our decision, then whose opinion to take seriously and whose not to becomes crucial.

If extreme selfishness, and not the greater good, is the basis of opinions, then those opinions must be reconsidered.

than just beauty. Now, more than ever in the past, Manthara felt that she had to be Keikeyi's intellect. Now was the time for this intellect to act sternly and decisively.[36] The decision had been made. Now no matter what it takes to enthrone Bharata, it will be done.

Taking a long and deep sigh of despair, Manthara spoke to the naïve Keikeyi, "My dear innocent queen, kingship is always offered for a lifetime. With the coronation of Rama, your son's claim to the throne will be wiped out forever. After Rama, His descendants will occupy the throne. What Bharata will give his progenies is eternal servitude to the descendants of Rama. Yours will be a servant chain tied mercilessly to the legs of the throne of Ayodhya.

If, as you say, the senior-most person should be king, then why is Dasaratha making Rama king when he is still alive. Generally, kings do not choose the right candidate to rule the kingdom carefully, they merely mechanically pick their eldest son. If this system were allowed to prevail in your son's case, then Bharata will surely become an orphan in his own kingdom, or be sent to some other kingdom, or worse, die a miserable death."[37]

Manthara was like poison without an antidote, untreatable with medicine or magic. She was determined to destroy Keikeyi's consciousness with the poison in her mind. She said, "Hear me, Keikeyi, there are three reasons why you should follow my advice.

---

[36] The only success-achieving technique that does not change with the ever-changing world is 'flexibility'. A flexible person gives up rigidity and focuses on the goal. Innovation is another name for flexibility.

[37] Just as a blind person sees darkness all around and fails to identify the darkness within, an obsessed person looks for faults all around rather than look within. Manthara was an expert at finding fault with every system in Ayodhya, but she found no fault in herself.

The first will save you, the second will save your son and the third will save your father.

O Keikeyi, hear my first reason carefully, it will save you. Follow my advice if you do not want to live a life of insult and poverty. All your life, you have been proud and vain, knowing that your beauty has controlled the king. This arrogance has often led you to hurl unlimited insults at Kaushalya, some knowingly and many unwittingly. You have always considered Dasaratha a plaything. All these years, Kaushalya has been at the receiving end and had withdrawn to a state of self-pity, neglected by the king and with minimal facility. But don't think she is a fool; she has been sharpening the sword named Rama by making Him Dasaratha's favorite. Now that the sword is sharp and drawn, it will plunge into your back tomorrow morning. Once Rama is installed as the king, Kaushalya will avenge every insult and disrespect you had shown her in the past. Can you withstand your co-wife's domination and can you bear to be her maid? The egoistic person that you are makes me think that you'd rather embrace death than play second fiddle."[38]

Try to understand your pitiable future, Keikeyi. If the poor come to you for a favor, what will you give them? Will you beg of Kaushalya to appease them?[39] Or would you rather die of shame? Just imagine, when your father or relatives come to ask you for a favor, what will they think when they see that all the wealth belongs to your co-wife and that you need to beg from her to help them?

---

[38] Assuming one will always be in control is like assuming that ice will never melt. The power of time is the heat that melts the coldness of vanity.

[39] Manthara is using the good quality of being charitable in the future as a reason to be cruel and selfish in the present. But how can the selfishness of the present turn to selflessness in the future? She is assuming that sowing bitter seeds of a *neem* tree will blossom into sweet mangoes in the future.

The second reason why you should take my advice is because it will save your son from disaster. Although you are Bharata's mother, you have been so busy enjoying the palatial luxuries and comforts all your life that you never took time out to pay any attention to your son. You allowed Bharata to spend more time at his uncle's place than in Ayodhya because of which Dasaratha has no love lost for him. Kaushalya never allowed Rama to be out of His father's sight and hence the king has such deep affection for Him.

If a tree marked to be felled is covered by the prickly *ishhika* grass,[40] there is a chance it will be saved from being cut. Likewise, had Bharata stayed in Ayodhya more often, Dasaratha may have supported him.

Your foolishness will result in Ayodhya's history ignoring your son and all his descendants.[41] But that's not the only concern. When Rama becomes the king, He and Lakshmana will protect each other because they are inseparable, like the *Ashvini Kumaras* (the celestial demigod twins). That will not be the case with Bharata; Rama will hunt him down like a lion hunts down an elephant. I would advise you to rather send Bharata directly from his uncle's kingdom to the forest because that would be a much safer place for him than Ayodhya. The animals in the jungle would definitely be kinder to him than Rama.

"O Bharata, how unfortunate you are my dear! Your father is cruel and partial. Your mother is also cruel and unmindful of your

---

[40] True culture is to respect all. Manthara's culture is to respect only those that are useful to her. She is comparing Dasaratha to a prickly grass because right now he is the thorny impediment to her happiness.

[41] The active mood of Ayodhya was cooperation. The spirit of active cooperation means everyone enjoys together and everyone suffers together.

impending troubles. O prince, your unparalleled beauty, valor, charming youthfulness, boundless energy, rare skills in archery and impeccable virtues are as useless today as spilt nectar. Bereft of these comforts and luxuries, how will you be able to live a life of poverty?[42]

Keikeyi, at least now understand that Rama is your enemy, send Him to exile and secure all the comforts for your son.[43]

The third reason that I am about to mention would never have crossed your mind. But it will save your father from calamity.

The decision to make Rama king bodes nothing but death for your father. Your father, Ashwapati, has always lived in fear of Janak, the king of Mithila and your father's sworn enemy. But so far, Janak had not attacked your father's kingdom, Kekaya, only because of his obligation toward Dasaratha. But when Rama becomes king, Janak will become all the more powerful by virtue of being His father-in-law and will definitely take over your father's kingdom at the first opportunity. You surely cannot expect Rama to do anything because he has no real relation or love for your father. So, is your father protected then? What will you do to protect him? Will you keep quiet?

Did you know that Dasaratha has called the whole world for Rama's coronation tomorrow morning except your father and Sita's? He

---

[42] Assigning a quota of suffering to others and only enjoyment to oneself changes the mood from active cooperation to destructive competition.

[43] Manthara always talks about one group enjoying and the other suffering. How about the possibility of all enjoying together, which was always the mood of Ayodhya?

knows of their enmity and, as of now, he does not want that to come to the fore till after the coronation. Once that is over, he will hardly be bothered. Keikeyi, you are surrounded by schemers, wake up!"

p o i s o n t a k e s r o o t

"Savior! Savior! Bravo! Bravo! O beautiful one, indeed you have saved me from falling headlong off a cliff. It seems that the safe rug named Dasaratha has been pulled from under my feet and I am falling into a bottomless pit named Kaushalya. Just as I was about to meet death, O Manthara, you have come as an angel to my rescue. I do not see a better well-wisher than you for me and my son in all the three worlds. I have treated you as a maid so far, when I should in fact have been treating you as a confidante.[44]

My illusion is now shattered; I am ready to follow your advice. Guide me, O Noble One! Be my guiding stick as that for the blind; guide me with your wisdom. Gift me potent magic to make my son the king of Ayodhya and spell doom to the shameless Kaushalya and her son."[45]

---

[44] Keikeyi's heart is compared to a shallow pond during summer. Fish that exist in deep waters cannot reside in a shallow pond; similarly, deep feelings of love cannot exist in a shallow heart. Though she had love for Rama, it wasn't really deep.

   If an indolent buffalo enters this shallow pond, the dirt lying at the bottom will surface and pollute it; similarly, Manthara, like the buffalo, entered Keikeyi's shallow heart to stir up the dirt and pollute her heart.

[45] Keikeyi is compared to Chandrakanta, a precious stone. When moon beams fall on this stone, it helplessly melts. But when weeds and creepers cover this stone, the moon beams can no longer melt it. Keikeyi was

Finally Manthara had succeeded in her attempts.[46] She spoke with a knowing smile, "The gift that you are looking for lies in your past, Keikeyi. Good deeds done in the past come handy during calamities. In this most tragic moment of your life, your past good deeds will become the saving grace.[47]

Many years ago when you had married Dasaratha, you had told me a story about your heroism. You may have forgotten it, but I remember every tiny detail, almost as if it all happened just yesterday. I have kept this in mind because of my love for you, and I knew that this information would be crucial one day.[48] Remember the battle between Dasaratha and the lord of magic, Sambarasura, also known as Timidhvaja. You had valiantly assisted Dasaratha by being his charioteer. On two occasions during that battle you had saved Dasaratha's life, once when you drove him away from the battle scene after he became unconscious, wounded by enemy arrows and next when you daringly and painstakingly braced his loose chariot

---

covered over by a creeper named Manthara because of which her heart did not melt despite hearing the glories of Lord Rama, who was like the soothing moon beams.

[46] Keikeyi is also compared to an ocean of good qualities, and Manthara to the Mandara mountain that was used to churn the milk ocean. To disturb such an oceanic heart required someone as powerful as her. Manthara was successful in churning this ocean and extracting the poison that would destroy Ayodhya.

[47] If past good deeds lead to present good events, then won't present bad deeds lead to future bad events? Just as a cataract blurs vision, selfishness leads to blurred conclusions.

[48] Complicated people like Manthara extract small things for a lifetime from some corner of their memory and expertly lay it out at the opportune time. If so much of human energy goes into such remembrance, naturally, there will be no energy left to love people and life.

wheel just as it was about to come off. Out of genuine gratitude that stemmed from intense appreciation for your sacrifice, Dasaratha had offered you two boons. At that time, O Queen, you had no unfulfilled desires; therefore, you chose to claim these boons at a later date. The time to claim what is rightfully yours has come – the boons and the kingdom!"[49]

Mesmerized, Keikeyi said "Manthara, how do you remember something that happened so many years ago? I had forgotten about it.[50] Tell me now; I am excited to hear what more goodies are stored in your hunchback? It definitely is a storehouse of thousands of astounding tricks that can challenge Sambarasura's supernatural illusions! O blessed Manthara, your hunch is actually like the magic box full of super-excellent thoughts and solutions. I am sure you have a solution to all of Ayodhya's problems."

Manthara excitedly began sharing more of her ideas with her mistress, "Keikeyi, these two boons will destroy Kaushalya and build your fortunes. For the first boon, ask Dasaratha to make Bharata the king of Ayodhya instead of Rama and for the second, ask him to send Rama to exile to the forest for 14 years.[51] These 14

---

[49] Manthara was encouraging Keikeyi to change her relationship with Dasaratha from that of her life partner to a business partner. Rather than a love transaction, Manthara was encouraging the transaction of Ayodhya.

[50] Unflawed use of memory space is in remembering others' acts of nobleness toward us. The flaw in recollecting the good that one has done for others is that it is invariably linked with the expectation that those favors will be returned.

Where there is flawed use of memory, especially between a husband and wife, what develops is a business deal rather than selfless love.

[51] Manthara chose 14 years for Lord Rama's exile because the legal system of claiming proprietorship in the *Tretayuga* (the time when Ramayana is

long years of Rama's absence from Ayodhya will help Bharata win the confidence of the citizens through his intimate interactions.[52] Rama will slowly lose His position in the hearts of the people, just as new leaves replace old ones after winter. Once replaced, no one remembers the old leaves.

To convince Dasaratha to agree to grant you these boons, you have to first weaken his heart.[53] A weak heart cannot analyze; he will then be compelled to give in to your desires. To weaken his heart, I suggest that you enter the sulking chamber (*krodhagraha* or room of anger) and lie down on the empty floor in a disheveled condition. As soon as Dasaratha enters the dark room in search of you, begin to sob and wail unceasingly. Do not even look toward Dasaratha. Do not care for the petty facilities and riches of diamonds, gold and other valuables that Dasaratha may offer you with the desire to pacify you.

---

supposed to have occurred) decreed that if the legal owner does not claim proprietorship for 14 years, then the resident of that place can proclaim it as his own. Manthara calculated that if Rama were to be away for 14 years, Bharata could legally claim ownership of Ayodhya.

In the *Dwaparyuga*, the duration for claiming proprietorship was 13 years, which is why the Pandavas were exiled for 13 years. And in *Kaliyuga* (the present age) the same is 12 years.

[52] From the spiritual perspective, acharyas have an interesting justification for the choice of 14 years. Sita is compared to a struggling spiritual aspirant who desires to reach the spiritual abode to eternally reside with the Lord. The 14 years represent the struggle of the aspirant to overcome the 14 planetary systems to reach the spiritual world; thus, Sita's journey – from the time she enters the forest to the time she returns to Ayodhya and is coronated along with Rama – is compared to the journey of an aspirant who achieves perfection after enduring unlimited struggles.

[53] The decision to make decisions has to be made in moments of strength, not in moments of weakness.

The moment you see that he is completely helpless and is agitated enough to do your bidding, remind him of his two boons and narrate your desire to claim them now.[54]

Relieved that you have finally expressed your need, he will rush into promising you anything you want. That's when you should plunge the two daggers into his heart – throne for Bharata and 14 years of exile for Rama.

Make sure you ask Dasaratha to send Rama to the forest. If He is exiled, only then will happiness will come your way. For as long He stays in Ayodhya, your happiness will remain exiled."

Keikeyi' eyes sparkled with joy. She was certain this idea would yield the desired result. Her innocent smile took the shape of a sinister smirk. Manthara's poisoning was complete. Keikeyi's consciousness was dead!

Keikeyi began showering Manthara with effusive praise, thanking her profusely for saving her from calamity. She crooned, "The hunchbacked are generally sad to look at, their bodies warped and unpleasant. O Manthara, but you are an exception. You, unlike other hunchbacks, seem like beautiful lotus bent by the breeze. The beauty of your navel is shyly hidden from the world. Your thin waist, encircled with a golden belt, swings with your graceful movements creating a euphonious music. Like the royal swan, you glide gracefully on your long legs, hidden within the folds of a beautiful silk *sari*.[55] As soon as my Bharata is on the throne and

---

[54] Drinking while running cannot bring satisfaction; similarly, a disturbed mind cannot make satisfactory decisions.

[55] Perceptions change with changing ideals. When the windows of

Rama walks off toward the forest, a golden garland will adorn your hunchback and golden dots will ornament your forehead. Your already beautiful looks will be embellished even more by the myriad garments that I will bestow on you.

Soon all of Ayodhya's hunchbacked women will become your maids, and you will rule over them.[56] You are indeed the best hunchbacked when it comes to making intellectual decisions, so you definitely deserve this honor."[57]

Manthara began to pirouette like a little girl when praised for her beauty. As she was twirling, the huge bun of hair mounted on her head and adorned with flowers began to shake rhythmically with her movements. Keikeyi laughed hysterically seeing Manthara so happy.[58]

Suddenly Manthara stopped and stared menacingly at Keikeyi, completely changing the mood of the room. Words sprang from her mouth like froth from a vessel containing poison. "The dam has to be constructed before all the water flows away; there is no point in

---

perception are tainted, one can see beauty in ugliness. Keikeyi was able to see beauty where there was none.

[56] Crookedness of the body is not as bad as the crookedness of the mind. When a crooked mind comes between two people, love become hatred and simplicity become duplicity. Keikeyi allowed Manthara, whose mind was more crooked than her body, to come between her husband and herself and thus permanently twist their relationship.

[57] Seeing good in whatever is bad or bad in whatever is good is the role of the coached mind. Choosing the right coach is more important than blaming the helpless mind.

[58] One ounce of immaturity coupled with ten ounces of ill advice is the perfect recipe for a life of disaster.

doing it later. Stop all this imagination! Enter the sulking chamber and coerce Dasaratha to accept your desire."[59]

payback time

Dasaratha had been staring too intently into the mirror for a while now. Was he becoming so self-absorbed at this age? This is when he should slowly have started becoming detached. At least that's what he had declared today earlier at the assembly in front of all his citizens and followers. But within the privacy of his chambers, another disturbing aspect of his life tortured him – a reality he seemed to be struggling to come to terms with.

From the time Rama left his palace for His own abode, Dasaratha had been contemplating and unwittingly staring at himself in the mirror. He closed his eyes, hoping to bolt the doors to worries. But what was he so worried about? Sabotage of the coronation? Something worse? Harm to Rama? No sooner than he shut his eyes, he saw a beautiful pair of lotus-shaped kohl-lined eyes with thick, long lashes open up. The eyebrows were arched like bows releasing arrows through a deadly pair of amber-colored eyeballs.

The mere vision of these mesmerizing eyes made Dasaratha jump up with joy. These were the eyes he had drowned in probably millions of times in the past – the eyes he loved more than anything else in

---

[59] When rainwater enters into a snake hole, snakes rush out and strike at the closest person. Manthara's words were like rain waters that entered into Keikeyi's ears, which were compared to snake holes. Naturally two snakes in the form of two boons will come out of her mouth and strike Dasaratha to death.

the world. Of course, except Rama! Every time there was a crisis in his life that could not be solved, every time there was a feeling of emptiness in his heart and every time he needed to experience love and peace, he would endlessly stare into those eyes. The oceanic peace he found within those eyes was something that he could never explain to anyone. Tonight he just wanted to immerse himself into the beauty of those eyes and calm his agitated, overworked mind.[60]

Dasaratha rushed out of his palace like a very thirsty man at the sight of a well. He felt that he was running toward an ocean, not a well.[61] Queen Keikeyi was his oceanic source of relief in frustrating times such as this.[62]

Dasaratha gazed longingly at the steps leading to Keikeyi's palace. He realized that he had climbed these steps hundreds of times, and every time he walked down these steps after spending time with Keikeyi, he had always found himself much more stable and composed. Indeed, she was the one person he had allowed to influence him more than anyone else in his life.

The love between them was definitely not onesided. Keikeyi always took extreme care and did all she possibly could to receive and

---

[60] Man tries to forget his worries by focusing on something else; sometimes, the very thing he focuses on to forget his worries becomes the cause of greater worries to him.

[61] The ocean may be deeper and wider than a well and contain more water. But the ocean with its unlimited salt water only increases thirst, and the well with its limited water instantly satisfies it.

[62] Need and personal capacity are two points to be considered before deciding whether you need a well or an ocean. When the need is to quench thirst and one has a personal capacity of being able to handle only a few glasses full of water, the wise would choose a well.

serve Dasaratha. Every time Dasaratha walked into her palace, an amazing feeling of comfort, care and peace oozed from every corner of the building. Keikeyi had turned her palace into heaven on earth to please Dasaratha. Sweet, soothing music reverberated through every nook of the palace. Peacocks, parrots and swans graciously hovered around, adding their melodies to the divine music. Beautiful paintings, ornate furnishings of ivory, silver and gold were strategically placed to rouse a range of emotions among onlookers. Varieties of foods and drinks were made available at all times of the day. All of these sensory inducements combined evoked lusty desires even in a dead man, and here was Dasaratha, alive with many expectations.

Today, however, was different! Why was Keikeyi's palace so dark? Why did she not arrange for any special reception today? Why are all the guards and maids avoiding the gaze of Dasaratha? Why was the feeling of comfort he associated with Keikeyi's palace replaced by an eerie feeling of insecurity?[63] Where was Keikeyi?

After several enquiries, a nervous maid, trembling like a leaf, explained to Dasaratha that Keikeyi had entered the sulking chamber a couple of hours ago and had refused to eat or drink or even meet anyone. Dasaratha's heart sank. On this auspicious day when he had come to share the most joyous news with her, what had made her so angry?

As Dasaratha descended into the sulking room at the basement of Keikeyi's palace, he was engulfed by this sinking feeling, as if inching closer to some unknown fear with each step. It is funny how life takes such rapid turns! Only moments ago while alighting the stairs

---

[63] Uncertainty becomes a joy when you welcome flexibility instead of set expectations.

to meet Keikeyi, he was so full of hope and security,[64] and now as he climbed down the stairs of the same building to meet the same person, he was gripped by despair and fear.

Suppressing a shriek, Dasaratha was aghast at the sight in the dark, sulking chamber. This couldn't be happening, his mind screamed. He quickly scanned the room to absorb as much information as he could to logicize whatever he saw. Strewn carelessly across the floor were Keikeyi's ornaments – amulets and anklets everywhere. Her tiara was flung across the room so hard that it had lost its shape. The delicately framed golden waist belt was now only pieces of gold dangling together after being mercilessly thrashed on the floor. Infinite small particles of gold that had once formed part of the belt were scattered everywhere.

What disturbed him most was his dear wife Keikeyi's condition! How can a queen lie so disheveled? Even an ordinary citizen of Ayodhya could not be in this state. She was sprawled across the cold floor like a distorted gold wire. Like a creeper separated from the tree, her usually beautifully cascading soft hair was so tousled that she almost appeared like a ghost. The usually meticulously dressed Keikeyi was today draped in untidy clothes. The flowers from her hair were ripped apart and thrown down in anger. What devastated Dasaratha was the sight of her beautiful face; the red vermillion on the parting of her hair to signify her marital status was violently rubbed off and that on her forehead was smeared across her brow.[65]

---

[64] Claiming to predict life accurately is like bragging about being able to predict the next move of a restless monkey – in other words, it is impossible.

[65] Before one externally rubs off any symbol of relationships, one rubs it off millions of times internally. By rubbing off her red kumkum (vermillion), Keikeyi indicated that her priority was now personal comfort and that it had overridden this sacred relationship.

Lying in distress, Keikeyi resembled a fallen angel, or perhaps a tied up deer, or a jasmine branch devoid of flowers. Her face was covered with the negative emotion of anger and her mind resembled a starless sky on a gloomy night. Slowly and delicately, Dasaratha inched toward her, his heart in pain.

The couple had actually nothing in common at this point. He was very old and she was quite young. He was stainless and she was tainted with wickedness. He was like an elephant and she was delicate like a doe. With extreme care, he tried to lift her up knowing how fragile she was. A tight slap across his arm made him stagger two steps back. Did his wife hit him? How can his ever-loving wife hit him so hard?

Why Do People Who Love Each Other Suddenly Realize That They Have Nothing In Common?

Changes in the externals of relationships occur when there is change in the motto or loyalty on the internal level. Dasaratha was in his usual mood, but something had changed in Keikeyi's life that made her different.

Keikeyi was like a female elephant wounded by the poisonous arrow of a hunter named Manthara, and the poison had not only wounded her but also driven her mad. The poison of distrust had been injected, which changed Keikeyi's loyalty toward Dasaratha.

Dasaratha had come to Keikeyi seeking happiness and peace. But Keikeyi could only think about her own happiness as the result of her discussions with Manthara. Each became self-centric and so had nothing in common.

> Between two people, the common center has to be selfless love.
> When this common center is displaced by individual selfish centers,
> mutual love turns into self-love and lovers into strangers.

"O most beautiful enchantress! O Queen of Ayodhya! I cannot fathom the reason behind your anger. I am extremely hurt to see you in this state, lying there on the cold, barren floor. Why are you hurting your body and my mind by sulking like this?

Has anyone disrespected you causing you misery?

Or are you ill? If so, just tell me the symptoms, and I will order the best of royal physicians to start treating you immediately.

O Keikeyi, I am the monarch of the entire earth; I own every corner a chariot wheel can go. Countries I own like Sindu, Sauvira, Saurashtra, Vangam Anga, Magadha, Matsya, Kasi and Kausala are filled to the brim with unlimited opulence. All my people and I are subservient to you. You have more authority over my authority over these kingdoms. Your wish is my command. Demand what you want, and I shall deposit it at your feet. Even the smallest desire you hold is like a precious unpolished diamond. Allow me the opportunity to make these diamonds sparkle in the sun light.[66]

---

[66] These words are not really spoken by Dasaratha, it is lust speaking through him. Valmiki *muni*, at this juncture, uses two words to describe Dasaratha. He calls him *jagatpati* or Lord of the world and *mahaayasaah*, a person of great fame. Using these words, Valmiki teaches the world that even the most powerful monarchs become weak and pitiable when under the influence of *kaama* or lust.

Do you want me to do anyone a favor? Do you want me to pick a fight with someone? I can render mercy even to the most undeserving soul just for you. I can come down heavily on someone honest and genuine just at your bidding.

Keikeyi, for you, I am willing to kill an innocent person and release a prisoner on death row. I could make a poor person rich and a rich person poor, if you so decide.[67]

You are precious to me, Keikeyi. Trust me. Just like the sun rises to melt away all the mist, I will chase away all your fears. You just need to name them. Just utter your desire once and see your husband fulfill it in a jiffy."

Keikeyi broke into a subtle smile. Seeing that, Dasaratha felt relieved that at least there was some reaction.

"O Lord, a desire has arisen in my heart like the moon on a dark night. If I am assured of your promise to get me this moon, I will speak up." With this statement, Keikeyi instantly filled Dasaratha with hope, and he lovingly caressed her silky hair.

"O Keikeyi, I may be the Lord of *the* world,[68] but you are the mistress of *my* world.[69] Don't you know that I gave myself to you long ago,

---

[67] To please his beloved and end her miseries, Dasaratha was ready to make anyone's life miserable. This is called wicked love.

[68] Life of a leader is centered around accountability and not on privacy. Accepting the position of leadership means embracing accountability persistently and forsaking privacy endlessly. In fact, a leader is more accountable for his privacy.

[69] By separating *his* world from *the* world, Dasaratha is separating his privacy from his accountability.

why do you need such a promise? There is nothing dearer to me than you except Rama. If this is what will make you peaceful and reassured to speak your heart out, I swear on Rama that I will fulfill any desire of yours. Ask, Keikeyi, ask!"

As if jolted by a surge of electric current, Keikeyi sprang up and dramatically raised both her hands toward the ceiling and facing it, she spoke rapidly with her voice gradually reaching a crescendo. "Today, the Lord of Ayodhya, King Dasaratha, has made a promise. I invoke all the celestials to come and bear witness to this oath. O *agni* (the god of fire) come along with 33 celestials, O sun god, O moon god, O god of the skies and O god of houses, I invoke your presence here. I call the planets, the day and night, the eight directions, the universe, the earth personified, the *gandharvas* (celestial musicians), the demons, the spirits wandering in the nights and all other spirits, come one, come all to bear witness to this matchless vow my husband has made."

Dasaratha was bewildered by Keikeyi's drama. But his wife was totally involved and was very serious. In fact, he had never seen her as serious as this ever before.

She continued in the same tone, "Maharaj, do you remember once long ago during your war with Sambarasura, I had assisted you and saved your life twice?"

Dasaratha instantly responded, "Of course I do, Keikeyi, and that's precisely why my love for you has grown so much, having seen your desire to serve me without caring for your own life. I still remember the agony on your face while supporting the wheel of my chariot with your delicate fingers. Why do you recall that incident now?"

"There is a connection – a deep connection. As a mark of gratitude, you had promised me two boons, which I had kept safe with you to claim another day. The time is now, Maharaj." Keikeyi's eyes squinted menacingly, reflecting new determination, one that had not even surfaced while driving Dasaratha's chariot to fight Sambarasura. What could be driving such a mood in her, Dasaratha wondered?

"Of course Keikeyi, don't hesitate, just ask." Dasaratha was like a deer that entered a hunter's trap, allured by the hunter's sweet flute.

"With the first boon, I claim the throne of Ayodhya for my son Bharata and with the second, I want Rama to be exiled to the forest of Dandakaranya for 14 years, where He will live like an ascetic wearing tree barks, deerskin and have matted hair. That's all I want, O king!"

The two vows struck him like daggers on his back!

As if not satisfied with striking her husband twice, she continued speaking about how truthfulness is important for a king and how Dasaratha should not abandon it under any condition. Keikeyi was digging the daggers deeper into the already wounded Dasaratha, taking away his very life.

Dasaratha's legs felt weak; he could no longer stand. Dasaratha lay sprawled on the floor of the sulking chamber, and Keikeyi stood over him staring at him, without compassion and full of anger.

How life changes within moments! He had come to pacify her, but who will pacify him now?

PAUSE TO THINK

Let us ponder over a few minutes about what transpired as Dasaratha lay unconscious.

Have you ever wondered why pubs are dark and classrooms bright? Why are pictures of people with mighty muscles put up in gyms and pictures of beautiful people put up in beauty parlors? Why are pictures of people with good smiles hung in dentists' chambers?

The environment thus created influences the mindset and decisions of people.

Obviously one enters a gambling den with the desire to win wealth. An environment of ignorance (darkness) is created to facilitate wrong decision-making. If this is coupled with overconfidence and lack of proper guidance, then one loses everything.

The two biggest epics of India have a common theme. In both the Ramayana and Mahabharata, the stories revolve around decisions made in wrong environments, influenced by misplaced priorities and with extreme overconfidence.

Here in the Ramayana, Keikeyi created an environment of ignorance and darkness into which Dasaratha entered with lust and desire in his heart. He was over overconfident about his abilities to satisfy any of her desires. He made her a promise without considering the consequences. He did not consider consulting with any one before making the vow either. In his craving to experience momentary pleasure, he accepted the gift of lifetime misery.

In Mahabharata, Satyavati created an environment of ignorance and darkness into which Bhishma entered wanting to satisfy the lust and desire of his father, King Shantanu. Again, Bhishma was overconfident about his abilities to satisfy her desires. He took a vow of lifelong celibacy, not getting married all his life. He took this vow without considering the consequences. Nor did he think of consulting anyone before making the promise. Wanting to give his father experiences of momentary pleasure, he awarded the gift of a lifetime of misery to the entire kingdom including himself.

(Satyavati wanted to secure the kingdom for her to-be-born sons. The only obstacle was Bhisma, the elder son of king Shantanu. By taking a lifelong vow of celibacy, he assured Satyavati that only her sons would rule. But later that very vow became the cause of anxiety for Satyavati and Bhisma when Satyavati's sons died, leaving no heir.)

CHAPTER 4

ACCEPTING DIFFICULTY WITH DIGNITY

Such stifling darkness; it was almost as if the lights had gone out inside his head.

The mighty Dasaratha lay there on the marble floor – weak and unconscious. Like the feisty deer frazzled and stunned by the ferocious lion, or the colossal elephant stung and brought down to its knees by the venomous serpent, Dasaratha was writhing on the cold floor, his energy, his strength and his power completely drained out of him.[1]

He was screaming in agony; such pain was alien to him. Never before had anyone managed to strike at his very being, his heart, with such precision. He let out a long, excruciating wail – a cornered prey's final cry of help before being devoured by the predator. His breath was hot like a brick-kiln, his tongue dry like parched land and his eyes crimson like the setting sun.

---

[1] Disease-causing germs not only destroy immunity internally, they then declare external victory by manifesting as symptoms of various diseases. Similarly, when there's turbulence in the mind, the disease takes root, and it's only a matter of time before the body shows symptoms by succumbing to the rulings of the sick mind.

Drawing together the last ounce of his strength, Dasaratha spoke feebly, "O cruel woman, do you wish to annihilate the Ikshvaku race? Why could I not see that I was marrying a lethal female serpent? O Keikeyi, you have never behaved this way before. I am shocked that such a sinister person existed under that honey-coated skin. Perhaps, this isn't you talking; perhaps, you are mouthing someone else's words; perhaps, someone else is controlling you; or perhaps, you are possessed by some evil spirit![2] I can't think of anything else that justifies such petty and condemnable behavior by a queen of the Ikshvaku race."

Keikeyi snarled back, "I am not controlled by anyone, nor am I haunted by some evil spirit. The only thing haunting me right now is a question: Is my husband, the king of Ayodhya and the protector of *dharma*, a liar?"

Dasaratha heaved himself up, his legs still trembling. He looked down at Keikeyi and tried to persuade her to rethink: "At least retract one of the two wishes. I have no problem with Bharata becoming the king, but why are you adamant about sending Rama to the forest? I thought you claimed not once but multiple times that Rama is better than Bharata! How can you ignore the fact that Rama always treats you as His mother and serves you more than he does Kaushalya? In fact, He takes care of you much more than your own son Bharata does. Rama is a gem who has won the heart of each citizen of Ayodhya. Even innocent children in Ayodhya

---

[2] When someone's spirit influences your actions, you are said to be possessed by a ghost; when someone's thoughts influence your actions, it is called possessed by a concept.

When a spirit possesses you, your behavior changes, and when malicious thoughts possess you, your intentions change along with your behavior.

will mock your wicked shenanigans. Give up this desire unless you want to embrace a lifetime of infamy."[3]

"For once the world can do without the sun and crops can survive without water, but Dasaratha cannot exist without Rama. Rama's beauty is the tonic that has rejuvenated my fading youth. No good wife schemes the death of her husband. That's what you will be known for if Rama were to leave for the forest.[4] If I ask Rama to give the kingdom to Bharata, He will happily part with it. Please abandon this idea of banishing Rama. I am an old man now; I am tired and need comfort, not anxiety. I, Dasaratha, the king of Ayodhya, humbly beg you to relent. As I implore you, I touch your feet with my head. O lady, be gracious to me and the entire kingdom."

Saying so, Dasaratha lay prostrate on the floor. Only this time, he had his helpless head placed at the feet of a woman he had mistaken for strength.[5] The cold and haughty tight-faced Keikeyi stood unmoved!

---

[3] Famine leads to a lifetime of hunger; infamy leads to a lifetime of disrespect.
Insufficient rain or a long drought leads to famine; insufficient control over our actions or a single misstep leads to infamy.

[4] In the process of fulfilling the boon of one person, we may be cursing many others, including ourselves. A boon should be spelled as a bane if it creates more sadness than joy
For Dasaratha, fulfilling Keikeyi's boon meant pushing himself toward death. Granting her fulfillment of her desire meant granting himself the misery of death.

[5] Helplessness is a result of the inability to summon strength around you. Ice melts helplessly when exposed to heat, but remains firm when safeguarded by cold.
Raising an army and then facing calamity alone is like cooking food and then going out to beg. Dasaratha had his counsel and the big M, which were equipped to handle any calamity, but the cloud of Keikeyi had hidden the moon of clear thinking.

Unaffected, Keikeyi shook Dasaratha off her feet and walked away from him. She began sermonizing with words that pierced Dasaratha like dart pins: "The ocean never crosses its limits once it makes a promise. It is more important for the person to keep his end of the unconditional promise he made rather than question the ethics behind the conditions put forth by the receiver of that promise. A person who says something and does something else lacks integrity. How will you face the virtuous sages? What will they think of you? Will you tell them that your wife saved your life and despite vowing to recompense her for it someday, you are yet to repay that debt and are living off her mercy merely because of your weakness for your son?"

"O King, you belong to the dynasty of King Shibi, who ascribed more value truth than anything else. I am sure you remember that once a pigeon had sought his protection as his subject, and he had promised to keep her safe. A little later, an eagle had attacked the pigeon claiming her to be his natural food. But the king shielded the pigeon and saved her life. The eagle questioned this bias, reminding the king of another responsibility – that of providing food for the eagle, too. There was logic in the eagle's argument, yet nothing could convince the king to break his promise and let the pigeon free for the eagle to feed upon. To be fair to both, he traded a portion of his own flesh equaling the weight of the pigeon and offered it as food to the eagle. Don't you feel inspired by such a powerful promise-maker in your ancestry?"

"The great king Alarka attained fame by keeping his promise. He had granted a boon to a blind *brahmana*, who wanted his eyes. The king sacrificed his own eyes to fulfill his promise and thus, restored the eyes of the *brahmana*. I am neither asking you for your flesh, nor your eyes, Dasaratha, I am only asking you to send Rama away.[6] The Vedas glorify truth as the highest goal to be pursued. In fact, the Vedas declare truth to be *Omkara* or *Pranava* or God Himself. One should adhere to truths without thinking of the consequences. Truth itself becomes a shield that protects one from all calamities and difficulties.[7] Now I make a promise, if Rama is coronated and not exiled, I will consume deadly poison and embrace death. Better death than a life forced to witness my rival Kaushalya being honored."

Dasaratha's head was throbbing and pounding, and he was convulsing on the cold floor. Despite all the pain he was going through as a father, Dasaratha was still king of Ayodhya and he was conscious of his responsibility toward his people. He forced himself up on his feet yet again; this time to save Ayodhya from disaster and, more importantly, to save himself from inglorious death.

"People will label me a fool if I pander to your every whim. What will I tell all the kings and well-wishers with whom I had consultations this morning? What will I tell Kaushalya, Sumitra and the innocent Sita? People will say that I have sold my son. How can you be happy seeing Rama wearing garments made of coarse tree barks?"

---

[6] By asking for Rama to be sent away, Keikeyi was in fact asking for both Dasaratha's flesh and his eyes. Dasaratha loved Rama dearly. If Rama were to go away to the forest, it would be akin to having his flesh torn off him. And he only wanted to use his eyes to see Rama. So what good are eyes if they cannot see what they long to see?

[7] Scriptures are like gold, which can be molded to any shape, size or form. Similarly, knowledge from the scriptures can be molded to justify any cause. The intentions and the character of one who uses the scriptures determine the effective use of it.

Keikeyi's diatribe was no less outrageous than the devil citing scriptures. So when an insensitive person such as Keikeyi tried to mold the scriptures, she was doing so in accordance with her malintentions.

As he spoke, his grief took the shape of anger and he burst out: "A hunter plays soft melodies to entice the innocent deer, and when the poor animal approaches him, he slits its throat. All these years you have been enticing me with your kind words and now that I am innocently close to you, you are cutting off my sustenance. Just as a man naïvely keeps a rope, unaware that it could be used to strangulate him, I have nurtured you, never once knowing that you could become the cause of my death. Bharata is as virtuous as Rama; he would never accept the kingdom this way. And, if he does, I will disown him and bar him from performing my last rites. If Rama leaves Ayodhya, this city will become haunted and your son will rule a barren kingdom. What kind of a wife are you? You have desires that are so harmful for your husband."[8]

Just as suddenly as Dasaratha had erupted with rage, he became vulnerable again; yet again, he fell at her feet: "I beg you Keikeyi, don't ruin everything I have so painstakingly created. I am your husband, an old man and a king, but I still fall at your feet and humbly beg you to change your mind."[9]

Dasaratha seemed like a demigod flung down from the heavens upon completion of a deserved duration of stay in the heavens. His waxen eyes stared at the bright moon, but they reflected deep darkness. It

[8] An ideal marriage is when a wife and husband reside not just in the same house, but when they house the same desires. More important than physically clasping hands is to clasp each other's desires. Marriage is a ceremony that aligns desires.

[9] Anger is a result of unmet needs. Dasaratha came in with a need for love and comfort, but Keikeyi gifted him envy and discomfort. Keikeyi was so busy taking care of her needs that his needs were not met.

Whenever there is a clash of needs, there is an eruption of volcanic anger.

seemed almost as if he was stopping the moon from disappearing and the sun from appearing. Although he wanted Keikeyi's torture to stop, he certainly did not want a new day to unfold and bring with it the horror he was so trying to avoid, and a change he was so desperately trying to stave off.[10]

Dasaratha contemplated how a frightening dream had woken him up from his sleep the previous night and how tonight life itself had become a nightmare. The previous night, he had ached for the horror to end, but today he seemed not to want the torturous night to end, for the end of the night would bring with it a lifetime of destruction. He wanted to hold on to night that was fast slipping away.

As the eager sun rose over the horizon, its tender rays spreading cheer among the hopeful citizens, Dasaratha covered his face, not wanting to face the sun; sunbeams had never seemed harsher than at this moment. It was about time, the sun bowed to her wishes, thought Keikeyi.

Royal musicians and bards entered the room to wake up the king and queen according to stately traditions. Dasaratha waved them off. What meaning did royal traditions have, now that loyal traditions had been abandoned?[11]

---

[10] Permanence of change in this temporary world acts as a reminder of its transient nature.

Expecting permanent enjoyment in the temporary world is like committing suicide to find a permanent solution to a temporary problem.

[11] One can enjoy luxuries when one is in a peaceful state of mind, but where the mind is restless, the first luxury it desires is peace itself.

External rituals of show are like royal traditions that impress others' minds. Internal rituals of substance are loyal traditions that inspire one's own mind.

Dasaratha felt like a horse flogged with the morning star (a mace with spikes) a hundred times over. Through the night, Keikeyi's words had felt like lashings that had drained the life out of him; feebly, he requested her to summon Rama, before passing out yet again.[12]

hope rises...to fall

As Dasaratha shut his eyes to hope in a morose corner of his once-favorite palace, Vasistha, the royal priest and spiritual preceptor of Ayodhya, stood on the banks of the Sarayu river and closed his eyes in a silent prayer to the rising sun. With cupped palms full of water and a heaving heart full of hope, Vasistha looked toward the sun god, the originator of solar dynasty: from this day forth, a new sun would rise over the solar dynasty – the sun prince Rama. Vasistha asked the sun god to shine on this son of Dasaratha and make Him resplendent.[13]

Money, fame, glorification, grandeur add to external rituals of show. Kindness, accommodation, appreciation, integrity add to internal rituals of substance.

[12] When a bent mind controls weak intelligence, the innocent soul becomes vulnerable.

Manthara's hunch was a manifestation of her crooked mind. Dasaratha represents weak intelligence that is not strong enough to assert itself in front of a robust mind. Keikeyi represents a person caught up in the tug of war between the mind and intelligence. Being weak, Dasaratha is unable to pull her away from the clutches of the strong and controlling Manthara. This is the mind game of life.

[13] At two different ends of the same city, the same sun held different meanings to two different people. Dasaratha perceived the rising sun as the foreboder of approaching woe, whereas Vasistha saw it as the harbinger of hope.

Fresh after the morning spiritual practices, Vasistha stepped into the city with cartloads of auspicious ingredients for the coronation ceremony. As this grand procession entered the city, hundreds of beaming citizens, guests and onlookers, who had lined the street to watch the biggest spectacle of their lives, hooted and cheered. Each of them had spent hours the previous day cleansing their homes, their courtyards and the streets of Ayodhya.

In the hundreds of cartloads were pots containing various essential items; there were pots full of holy waters from every river in the world, honey, milk, yogurt, clarified butter, pounded rice, innumerable fruits, flowers, color powders, blades of *darbha* grass, a special sword called *Nistimsa*, a golden jug, tiger skin and various types of fragrances. An elephant walked right behind, preceded by a golden chariot drawn by four royal horses. And just ahead of it four bearers carried an ornamental palanquin and right in front was Vasistha. As the carts passed by, citizens lost count. They were astounded by the preparation and the detail that went into it; there was promise of never-before-witnessed grandeur.

Vasistha entered the royal courtroom of Ayodhya and soon began making arrangements for the coronation. His expert management ensured that everything was meticulous down to the last detail and all was set for Rama's coronation. A quick consultation with the royal astrologer, and Vasistha knew it was time to call the king for the initial proceedings before the actual ceremony. He instructed Sumantra to invite the king.

Vasistha had spent his night in prayer, thus, invoking positive vibes, whereas Dasaratha had spent his tortured by lower powers, thus, invoking negative vibes. The environment you surround yourself with either raises your hopes or dashes them.

Dasaratha was not in his palace, so Sumantra went to the next obvious place – Keikeyi's palace. He knew Dasaratha all too well and was certain that whenever he needed solace and comfort, Keikeyi's was the palace he chose to spend his night. Sumantra had noticed traces of nervousness in the old king as everyone left the courtroom the previous day after the announcement of the coronation. He did not know why the king was ruffled, but he was wise and experienced enough to sense it. And having observed that the king was out of sorts, Sumantra guessed that he most likely spent the night with Keikeyi.

This old minister, advisor, charioteer and confidant of Dasaratha was loyalty personified. Although a *suta* or a charioteer by birth, Sumantra's wisdom, accurate foresight and immense loyalty had seen him being installed as the senior most minister in Dasaratha's Big M.[14] He had free access anywhere in the kingdom of Ayodhya; be it to the innermost precincts of the palaces or the private chamber of the king,[15] Sumantra could slip in and out of all the corners of the kingdom as and when he felt like it. But Sumantra made sure that he did not misuse this freedom and honor; he always remembered his humble beginnings and was grateful for the opportunity to serve.[16]

---

[14] Birth only provides the facility and not the ability to become qualified. Keeping a sword close to a grinding stone will not make it sharp. Real qualification comes when one polishes oneself on the grinding stone of hard work.

[15] The pass code to enter private chamber of another's hearts is consistent loyalty.

[16] Remembrance of one's humble beginnings even after achieving great heights is the pill that prevents the acidity of arrogance.

Sumantra walked into Keikeyi's palace and announced his presence in front of the king by singing his praises: "Just like the sun awakens the earth that sustains all beings, I awaken our glorious king, who is like the earth that ensures the welfare of his subjects. With the passage of the night, the most awaited day has arrived. With each new day, the sun renews hope in everyone; similarly, a new king renews hope in the kingdom. Get up, O King and instruct the waiting sage Vasistha, so that the coronation proceedings may commence. A kingdom without a king is no better than an army without a commander or the night without the moon."

Ignorant of the nightlong drama, Sumantra innocently continued with his eulogy until he thought he heard the deep sigh of a wounded lion. "Why do you flog a dead horse? Your words, which would calm my frayed nerves on other days, are today provoking me."

Immediately sensing that he had inadvertently overstepped some boundaries, Sumantra retreated and stood reverentially in a corner waiting for some direction from the royal couple. The queen reacted first. With an air of authority, Keikeyi walked up to the rattled minister and told him, "The king is brimming with joy about Rama's coronation, and all this excitement had kept him awake through the night. That lack of sleep is taking its toll on his aging body. There's only one solution to the king's fatigue – Rama's presence." Sumantra understood what was expected of him and left the palace to do his bidding.

Outside, many of Ayodhya's prominent citizens and experienced *brahmanas*, who had performed an all-night vigil chanting holy *mantras* to invoke auspiciousness, were waiting for the king to step out, when instead they saw the lone minister. They were perturbed. They hurled a barrage of questions and doubts at the minister. Why don't you have the king with you? What's wrong? Didn't you tell him that the *Pushya* star had already set off on its arc and the auspicious time for the coronation is fast ticking away? With so many heads talking and pushing him back, Sumantra realized that precious time was being lost and that he had to retrace his steps to the king. Keikeyi had no doubt implied that he should fetch Rama, but Sumantra decided on a reconsultation with the king on his priorities at the moment.

No sooner than Sumantra opened his mouth to convey the *brahmanas'* anxiety to the king, Dasaratha, on seeing his minister walk in without Rama, cut him short and snapped: "What's wrong with you? Why did you not follow her advice? Get Rama here this instant."

The king's irritation unsettled Sumantra. For a moment, he felt like a ball tossed around in different directions.[17] If he had to be a ball anyway, he'd rather be hurled toward Rama's magical palace, where hope and confidence resided in abundance. Assured he would be better off fetching Rama and being near Him, Sumantra walked toward the gates of Rama's palace.[18]

---

[17] The feeling that one is a mere ball at the hands of others creeps in when one is tossed around aimlessly. One then only finds comfort when one is with a safe pair of hands that treat one with respect and grace and not as a plaything but as an upright acquaintance.

[18] Balls are meant for using and if balls were to feel, they would definitely hate being abused. Abuse may not always necessarily be physical, but may also be emotional and verbal.

    When handled with care, a ball bounces back even when dropped. But when abused, it punctures and drops flat. People when treated well stay hopeful, when treated badly they become disillusioned.

soothing smiles

As Sumantra inched closer to the palace, he could see large gem-studded doors and coral-embroidered festoons. No matter how many times, he walked through these corridors, the art along the walls always fascinated and enthralled him. There were intricately carved exquisite ivory, metal and wood sculptures placed at regular intervals, enhancing the beauty of the grand furnishing. Sumantra shook the daze off his indulgent mind. He was here for a very important job and hurriedly walked past the seven enclosures that led to Lord Rama's private chamber. The surrounding beauty magnified with each step he took toward the chamber, but he refused to allow himself to be swayed away from his purpose of visit.[19]

When he finally reached the door, he sent a guard clad in orange uniform to inform Lord Rama that His servant was at His doorstep with palms folded in *anjali mudra*.[20]

The guard returned and ushered him into Rama's chamber. Sumantra carved this moment into his memory for recollection at a later date. Rama was all dressed for the coronation – yellowish robes, a diamond pendant on His broad chest, earrings dangling from His ears and amulets stretching across His powerful biceps, sandalwood perfumeon the body. He was seated on a golden swing

---

[19] The mind has the unique ability to churn out the weirdest of thoughts in the most urgent of situations. To maintain a pure mind constant filtration of thoughts is necessary. When a filter does not function, impurities seep into water, leading to sickness; similarly, when the mind filter is faulty, impure thoughts make sick decisions.

[20] The *anjali mudra* indicates veneration and respect to another.

draped with bright red silk laced with gold. He swung gently as Sita stood beside Him, endearingly waving a peacock feather fan. The pair was immersed in a loving conversation and closely resembled the shining moon accompanied by the *Chitra* star.

Sumantra had come with a purpose so he couldn't afford to immerse himself in Rama's beauty. He moved closer to them. As soon as he stepped into their midst, Sita and Rama stood up and greeted the elderly minister. Sumantra blessed Rama with the *abhaya mudra*[21] and uttered, "*Ayushmaan.*"[22,23]

"My dear prince, King Dasaratha and Queen Keikeyi want to see you this instant. I have come to fetch you."

Rama instantly turned to Sita and said, "Surely father and mother Keikeyi have decided something wonderful for our well-being, benefit and prosperity."

Sita smiled, acknowledging His sentiment and understanding His mind. Her smile filled Rama with confidence. Rama followed Sumantra, and Sita followed Him till the doorway of the inner chamber. Just before leaving to meet His father, Rama stopped,

---

[21] The *abhaya mudra* allows greater energies to descend and protect the person in front.

[22] *Ayushmaan* is a profuse outpouring of blessings of a happy heart.

[23] Being related to a person at multiple levels is always a challenge. Sumantra was Rama's father's minister, he was His natural subordinate and a respectable elder. As a subordinate, Sumantra followed etiquette as a minister and sought permission before entering Rama's palace, as a subordinate he offered his respects and as an elder, blessed Him. Through his various gestures, Sumantra conveyed not only his genuine love for Rama, but also the different roles he played in His life.

exchanged glances with Sita, removed the fragrant garland from around His neck and gently placed it around Hers and smiled. Sita looked at the garland for a few moments and broke into a smile. She then wove an imaginary garland around Rama's neck by moving Her beautiful eyes and smiled again. Sumantra assumed this as some act of intimate love between the couple. Or, was it? Could this be some kind of deep, inaudible communication between the two?

What Is True Communication?

This brief episode between Rama and Sita teaches the essence of good communication.

They speak so little but understand so much. The answers to the four questions in this episode teach us how to maintain good relationships.

Communication is, therefore, not so much verbal as it is integral or heartfelt.

1. Why did Rama say that mother and father are surely planning something good for Them?

Seeing the positives in every situation is the nature of a pure mind. Preparing the mind not to see faults but rather the hidden good in everything is the first step to good relationships. A successful gold digger focuses on the gold in the dirt and an unsuccessful one is bothered by the dirt around.

Rama was trying to convey to Sita that no matter what instruction/s

Dasaratha and Keikeyi had for Him, it was for Their welfare even though it may not seem that way.

Good relationships begin by helping each other see good intentions in every act and keep away from criticism.

2. Why did Rama place the garland around Sita's neck?

Rama implied that the only gifts He would henceforth be able to give Her would be forest flowers because He was going to lose all His wealth. He merely wanted to ascertain if She was willing to accept Him despite the change in circumstances?

Sita did not speak, only smiled, indicating that she was happy to follow the mood and mission of Rama. Sita knew that the time had come for Them to leave Ayodhya to carry out the mission of His incarnation. She had come to assist Him in His mission.

For Sita, being with Rama at all times was more important than being with Him only during happy times.

Good relationships grow when both the happy and sad phases of life are shared and complaints are kept at bay.

3. Why did Sita weave a garland about Rama's neck with her eyes?

She wove a garland as token of recognition of His love for her.

When one is accustomed to tangible gifts, one tends to forget the value of intangible gifts. From the tangible perspective, the silent exchanges between Sita and Rama were value less, but from the intangible perspective, these were invaluable.

Good relationships survive when those involved realize that the greatest gift two people actually have is each other. Anything else added to this may enhance but should not replace it; thus, one should refrain from competing with each other.

4. What does Sita's invisible garland represent?

Sita is also called Sudikshana, which means one who has both skill and strength. She offered both these types of flowers to Rama interwoven as an invisible garland to Him.

She was conveying that through Her skill, She would deftly handle complicated issues that would raise their head from time to time and through Her strong will, She would face these difficulties with determination.

Good relationships thrive when people trust each other and use their strengths to serve each other selflessly, thus keeping away from cynicism.

For healthy relationships and good communications, it is recommended that one embrace four principles and refrain from four bad attitudes.

1. Embrace the habit of seeing the good in others, and refrain from criticism.
2. Embrace the habit of finding joy in all phases of life, and refrain from complaining.
3. Embrace the habit of valuing one another, and refrain from competing.
4. Embrace the habit of serving each other with selfless trust, and refrain from cynicism.

Sita then invoked the protection of all the gods on Rama. Rama stepped out of the threshold of His inner chamber like a lion coming out of his cave. Just outside the room stood a bowing Lakshmana with folded hands, ever eager to serve his elder brother. Ever since he was a baby, Lakshmana had always felt duty bound to protect and serve the body of Lord Rama. The feeling was instinctive; no one really taught him to do so, nor had he ever tried to fathom why he felt that way. But the feeling was so strong that he allowed it to dictate and direct his entire life.[24]

As the two brothers trailed Sumantra out of the palace, a sea of enthusiastic people rushed to greet them. The jostling onlookers were huddled together with not even an atom of space between them. Some voices kept urging for space for more people to cram in, but people could not move. There was no space! To make things worse, hundreds more continued to throng the courtyard to catch a glimpse of their darling prince, who was to become king. Rama surveyed His subjects as a cow would its calf before feeding it. Even though there was just one Rama before the multitude of people, each felt that He had exchanged glances solely with them and reciprocated their feelings.[25]

Sumantra knew time was running out, so he created a pathway to

---

[24] Monitor the trigger that sets off your feelings of love toward someone. If the trigger is ignited by the core values of selflessness, integrity and strength of character of the other person, feel free to be drawn to that person. If, on the other hand, the trigger is ignited by the external qualities of beauty, power and influence of the person, restrain and curb the urge to mingle with that person.

[25] A leader's toughest role is to satisfy scores of expectations. Only God can satisfy all expectations simultaneously, yet individually. God has the ability and the desire to respond to each.

allow Rama and Lakshmana to mount a silver chariot. As Rama continued reciprocating the love of His subjects, Lakshmana held an umbrella over His head with one hand and waved a *chamara* (fly whisk) with another. The crowd parted to allow the chariot to pass. As Rama's chariot came out of the precincts of His palace, it resembled the sun rising over the horizon.

Soon everyone began following the chariot, mounting on their horses, elephants or chariots, not wanting to miss a moment with Him. With the flower showers rained heaps of praise, blessing and prayers. Some prayed loudly, offering the merit of their entire *tapasya* to Rama, some prayed for years of their lives to be added to His, so He could live forever. Everyone seemed to have gained the world merely by looking at Him.

Once at Keikeyi's palace, Rama hopped off His chariot and walked toward the door. Upon entering the palace, He greeted thousands of eager citizens in accordance with their age, position and relationship with Him. As He slowly disappeared into the palace, the people stood outside with bated breath, eager for the coronation to begin. Just as the ocean waits for the rising moon, the tide of Rama lovers waited for Ramachandra to shine on them. Rama had long disappeared from their vision, but their eyes remained transfixed to the direction of His departure. Their life's hope had stepped into the palace.[26]

---

[26] As lifeless iron filings are drawn toward a magnet, the citizens of Ayodhya were charmed by Rama and felt drawn toward Him. Faithlessness is the rust that prevents humans from attracting God's grace.

promises to keep

After offering prostrated obeisance to His father and mother Keikeyi, Rama stood to one side of the room in *vinaya mudra*,[27] His body bent a little as a mark of respect, one hand covering His mouth and the other clasping His ornaments to prevent them from creating disturbance.[28]

Rama looked around. The stark difference between the ambience inside and outside did not go unnoticed. Rama was very disturbed by what He saw. He felt a pang.[29]

In each of Rama's memories of Dasaratha, the king was on a throne or some ornate seat, dressed in the most regal manner almost to perfection, grave and power-exuding. But here was His father lying on the bare floor, disheveled and dressed in the previous day's wrinkled robes, extremely weak and lifeless.

---

[27] *Vinaya mudra* symbolizes humility and a desire to hear and not speak, thus, enriching one's life with knowledge, which is a by-product of humility.

[28] Packed as He was with good qualities, Rama could see better qualities in His superiors. Like a full-fruited tree, Rama was bent in the humility of the recognition of His own shortcomings.

Just as one has to bend to draw water from a deep well, a heart has to be humble to draw the best out of everyone.

You speak when you have something of value and importance to utter. Rama felt it wiser to keep His mouth covered and ears open for instructions when in the presence of His superiors and those more qualified than Him.

[29] Outside were people who loved Him and accepted Him.
Inside were people He loved, but they were rejecting Him.
Outside were people who expected Him to lead.
Inside were people who expected Him to follow.

Some steps away stood Keikeyi, nonchalant and ignorant of the king's condition. Rama could sense a combination of anger, sternness and cruelty. She did not seem composed, but she looked firm.

Rama's eyes then turned to His beloved father, who was sobbing inconsolably with his eyes shut tight. His pallor made him seem like a rainbow shorn of its color, or a sage who has lost his luster by deviating from *dharma*. Glistening tears ran down his cheeks, baring his aching heart. Only one word escaped through the painfully parted lips, "Rama!" For a second, Dasaratha opened his eyes to see Him. The moment they locked their eyes, Dasaratha turned away, unable to hold His gaze. In that instant, Rama saw an ocean of suffering, almost as if Dasaratha was drowning in that sea of sorrow.[30]

Seeing His father suffer, Rama's heart became agitated like the ocean on a full moon night. Usually, the sight of Rama turned Dasaratha's anger to bliss. But today, the one who always brought him pleasure seemed to have become the cause of his misery. Rama realized that His presence had caused his father much distress. He began wondering if He had done something inadvertently to have disturbed His father so much. Rama turned to Keikeyi for answers to the questions in His mind.

"Is My father suffering from some sudden bodily affliction? Or, is something disturbing him mentally? Has some inauspiciousness affected Bharata or Shatrughna or My mother? Or, did your pride and anger make you say something harsh to him? It is not always

---

[30] Our eyes reveal to us what is outside, but a discerning person's eyes reveal what is on our minds. Eyes are the balconies that allow others to witness the drama unfolding in the theater of our minds.

possible to obtain happiness; however, it is My duty to try and rid My father of his misery."[31]

Keikeyi could sense Rama's apprehensions regarding His father's emotional well-being. She swooped down on the moment. She spoke, choosing her words carefully, ensuring that they made the biggest impact: "A son is born only to solve a father's dilemmas. It is time You prove Your worth Rama. Many moons ago, Your father had offered me two boons. Now that I have chosen to claim those boons, he is reluctant to grant them, because he is worried about Your reaction. Only if You promise to do whatever You are told, without considering personal loss or gain, will I reveal what is expected of You. The scriptures expect a king to uphold *dharma* or righteousness and to be a role model. Now Rama, it is up to You to ensure that the king keeps his promise."

Keikeyi's words shattered Rama, not because He was expecting bad news, but because she had doubted His obedience and loyalty to His father. He said: "At my father's command, entering fire is like walking into a cool pond, consuming poison like licking honey and drowning in the sea like liberation. Mother, I promise you that

---

[31] Surprisingly, Dasaratha was trying to relieve Keikeyi from her misery a little while ago. But the difference between Dasaratha and Rama lay in the attitude with which they approached the problem at hand.

- Dasaratha was arrogant that he had solutions to all of life's problems, whereas Rama was certain that even though one could not always rid others of their misery, one should try nonetheless.
- Dasaratha felt that he could beckon happiness as and when he wanted, but Rama knew that finding happiness was not always possible. He knew that what was possible, however, was to stabilize one's mind enough to be unaffected by the misery that could follow.

The right attitude, more than self-belief, is the key to shield one from misery and helps handle others' misery.

I will abide by My father's desires, even if it comes at the cost of self-destruction. The world knows Me as *eka-vachani, eka-patni and eka-bana*. I believe in one word, one wife and one arrow. Once given, I don't go back on My words; once married, My life is for My wife and once an arrow leaves my bow, it has to reach its mark. My name is equated with truth, so please don't doubt Me, mother. Just tell Me what am I expected to do?"[32]

Keikeyi should have been named Yama for her coldness was no less than that of the death god. She thundered: "Both You and Your father are bound by Your words now. Let the world see how You help Your father fulfill his vow. He has vowed to crown Bharata as the king of Ayodhya in Your place and banish You to the forest for 14 years."

With no trace of disappointment in His voice or change in His expressions, Rama said: "Mother, let father's wishes be fulfilled. This very moment ask Bharata to return from his uncle's palace. To see Bharata coronated in My place is of great joy to Me, because My mind does not distinguish his joys from Mine. And I will happily go to the forest to celebrate Bharata's coronation. The only thing that disturbs Me is why did My father not tell Me all this directly? Does he have no confidence in My loyalty? Does he think I am attached to wealth and kingdom? It bothers Me that My father has no confidence in My character."

Keikeyi was quick to answer: "Your father is extremely ashamed at this point in time, because of which he finds it difficult to speak

---

[32] The difference between Rama's confidence and Dasaratha's overconfidence lies in its application. *Svartha* or self-interest governed Dasaratha's overconfidence. And *seva* or service was the reason behind Rama's confidence.

to you directly. As soon as You leave Ayodhya, he will return to normalcy. As You have mentally decided to proceed to the forest and seem so enthusiastic about it, I suggest that You leave right away. There is no need to wait for Bharata's return. In fact, Your father won't bathe or touch a morsel of food until You leave Ayodhya. Rama, let Your father live, leave for the forest immediately."

When Dasaratha heard this, he could no longer bear the pain and began weeping profusely. "How much misery can a man suffer?" His attempts to rise up failed and he collapsed yet again. Rama rushed to hold His father. Gently caressing him, Rama fondled His father back to consciousness and then got up to leave.

He looked at Keikeyi with utmost respect and said: "In all the years that I have lived, I have not been able to win your confidence at all. And it seems that you have never understood Me. For Me, there is no greater pleasure than fulfilling the words of My father. If this was what you had always wanted, you needn't have involved him at all. You just had to instruct Me and I would have happily left for the forest. I am no seeker of fortune, neither is it in Me to seek the sympathy of the people of Ayodhya to gain a throne. I have always wished to be a hermit and sought to gain knowledge from the exalted sages residing in the forest. You have now become instrumental in making My wish come true. These 14 years will not be years of exile, but years of learning. Just give Me enough time to pacify My mother Kaushalya and wife Sita." With these words, Rama paid His final respect to Dasaratha and Keikeyi and walked out of the room.[33]

---

[33] When an eagle is attacked by a murder of crows, it chooses to fly higher and out of the crows' reach rather than fight back.

Rather than delve in negative situations, Rama chose to focus on the positives awaiting Him.

When one tries to sort out the negativities in life, one becomes

Not much had changed in the room from the time He had walked in – Dasaratha was still on the floor weeping and Keikeyi was still standing. But the emotions had undergone a sea change – Keikeyi's anger had transformed into immeasurable joy and Dasaratha's pain had transformed into a catastrophe.

As Rama walked out of the room, He passed by Sumantra, Ayodhya's loyal minister, who was in a state of shock. Sumantra knew that he had no right to comment on family affairs, but as a minister, he realized that what had just transpired bode disaster for the kingdom. Left with no choice at this point, and more importantly, unable to withstand the shock, Sumantra thought it best to follow Rama out.

The drama in Keikeyi's life had ended (or so she thought), but the drama in Rama's life had just begun.[34] Rama's world had changed drastically over the last few minutes – he had walked in as a king to be and walked out a pauper. Could the weight of one desire turn a king into a pauper?[35]

Rama felt relieved at the thought of being able to lift a big burden off his father's back. He felt light that He could help ease His father's

---

muddled. Instead, when one focuses on the positives, one is able to soar high.

[34] Life as a whole is a drama. One scene in that drama may have ended in your favor, but that does not mean that the entire drama will end in your favor. Shortsightedness makes one focus on scenes, whereas farsightedness makes one look at the entire drama. Keikeyi assumed that her role was over and that she had won accolades, little realizing that she had only changed roles.

[35] Keikeyi gave more weight to her desires than to the traditions of Ayodhya, the fame of the Ikshvaku race and the distress of her husband.

pain. Never one to shy away from responsibility, Rama seemed just as happy when asked to rule as when asked to renounce the crown and go away into the forest.[36]

No sooner than Rama stepped out of the threshold of Keikeyi's room, He saw a fireball making its way to burn everyone and everything on its path. Fists clenched, teeth gritting and eyes flashing intense hate, Lakshmana was pacing furiously neither able to enter the room because of respect toward the king, nor able to resist entering to express solidarity with his beloved and wronged brother. Understanding Lakshmana's predicament, Rama chose not to speak to him at all and just walked past him.[37]

Lakshmana felt as if a cool ocean had swept past him. When a burning log of wood falls into the cool ocean, it is swept away by the ocean currents without causing any harm.[38] Soon realizing

---

[36] What actually burdens one is self-imposed expectations.

When Rama was to be the king, He was ready to take up this burden happily as a burden of love. When He was told not to be the king, He was still happy to experience other joys of life without that burden of kingship.

Under both circumstances, He continued to remain happy, because in both cases He was doing what He was told to do and not what He wanted to do.

[37] The worst place to help angry people is in front of a public gathering, and the worst way to deal with them is to discuss the matter when they are most agitated.

By walking away from Lakshmana, Rama did not allow him to express his anger. And by exhibiting extreme calmness, He confused Lakshmana.

[38] Angry people love other angry people because their emotions match and their language of expression is the same. But anger can be converted to love only when one forgets the language of hate and learns the language of affection. A teacher who does not speak it cannot teach the language of affection.

that Rama was no longer around, Lakshmana rushed toward Him with the umbrella and whisk. Rama waved those away, signaling to Lakshmana that He no longer wanted luxuries fit for a king. Lowering the accessories, Lakshmana followed Rama helplessly, tears welling in his eyes. Sumantra followed the brothers in tears.

ayodhya weeps

There was a burst of joy the moment the waiting crowd spotted Rama on the first step outside Keikeyi's palace. One glance at Rama could evoke more emotions in people than what a mother experiences at the sight of her newborn. Everyone was mesmerized by Rama's beauty and they kept staring at Him, without a blink and began whispering endlessly.

Rama bowed with folded hands to the vast crowd waiting for Him. He gazed at the morning sun. The sun can have no attachment to a particular tract of land; it has to constantly travel to every inch of land on earth. As a representative of the solar dynasty, Rama realized that the time had come for Him to follow the nature of the sun and associate with remote lands and serve people who needed Him in faraway places. He shut his eyes for a moment and prepared Himself for the service and mission that lay ahead.[39]

The whispers continued unabated. One man said: "Rama looks more effulgent after coming out of the palace. I wonder what has happened inside that has made Him so bright and determined. I

---

[39] The reason for His incarnation was about to unfold to the world. As Rama prepared to move toward the fulfillment of His mission, the demigods in the heavens smiled. Finally, their troubles would end and the tyrant demons would meet their match.

am sure that Rama now wants to shine on the world like the sun."
Another said: "I could probably have described Rama's beauty before
He went into the palace, but now it is beyond words."

Yet another old man said, "When Rama went in, His face was like a
beautifully closed lotus and now it resembles a fully blossomed one."

"Look at His eyes! They are like oceans, and whenever I look into
them, I feel lost. If one loses something in an ocean, what is the
hope of ever recovering it?" said another enthusiastic citizen.

Just then Lakshmana appeared behind Rama, the umbrella and
whisk lowered, and his head stooped even lower. He stood silently
beside Rama, not for one moment lifting his head. Sumantra stood
on the other side, with tears streaming down his cheeks, his chest
heaving in sorrow and a look of helplessness on his face. Quite aware
of the confusion the two people beside him seemed to cause in the
minds of the people below, Rama stood still – calm, composed and
unaffected. He could see hope transform into fear in the eyes of
the thousands of people below.[40]

"Aaagh! What's happening? Why is Lakshmana not shielding Rama
with the royal umbrella? Why is Sumantra sobbing? Could someone
explain before our worst fears kill us?" The citizens wept, looking
at each other, trying to solve the puzzle – the sight of a sobbing
Sumantra, a despondent Lakshmana and a composed Rama was
confusing them.[41]

---

[40] Hope turns into fear when one cannot comprehend what one sees. On
either side of their hope were standing their worst fears.
   Life always cocoons our hopes in a sheath of fear.

[41] Puzzles are fun to solve on paper but when life itself becomes a puzzle,
then fun fizzles out.

Rama descended, one step at a time, carefully and lovingly looking at every citizen. Lakshmana and Sumantra followed quietly.[42]

As he passed by the scores of citizens, He glanced lovingly at each of them, inquiring about their well-being as He walked. Tears began to stream down the eyes of the people as Rama passed them, but they had no idea why they were crying. The atmosphere had equal measure of love and sorrow.[43]

Doubts that had begun clouding the minds of the citizens turned to conviction when they noticed Rama not climbing into His chariot. It was common knowledge that if a king rejected the royal umbrella and the royal chariot, it meant that he had forsaken the throne. But things became even more confusing when Rama began to walk toward the coronation arena. Why would a king walk toward the coronation venue if he had apparently rejected the throne? Thousands of people lined up after Rama, the long train appearing like a massive extension of His shadow.

On reaching the coronation venue, Rama offered His respects to the surprised Vasistha. Without speaking a word, with folded hands He began encircling the paraphernalia collected for the coronation ceremony. After circumambulating the venue thrice, Rama quietly walked away. All doubts were now laid to rest. Rama was not going to be their king. A wail broke out in Ayodhya – a wail so loud

---

[42] As the first stone of difficulties drops into the pond of our minds, it releases ripples of hopelessness; however, the minds of great people like Rama are not like water but like ice – firm. They continue to live and lead their lives gracefully, unaffected by the changes in their circumstances.

[43] Rama demonstrated that an ideal leader hides his sorrows and is concerned about the welfare of his followers.

that it could have silenced a thunderclap. Ayodhya began to cry profusely and unstoppably. As Rama walked out this time, no one dared follow Him. Only an unsteady and devastated Lakshmana tagged along with the serene Rama a little distance away, of course now empty-handed.

Rama's countenance bore no trace of disappointment or sorrow. His subtle smile still remained encouraging as it had when He had entered the palace as king-to-be. Just as the darkness of night cannot hide the glow of the moon, the darkness of disappointment and setback cannot hide a moon like Ramachandra. Only from Lakshmana's expressions could one ascertain that something very unpleasant had happened. Tears strolled down his beautiful face. Just as his clenched fists and heavy breathing gave away the anger he harbored, his limp body revealed a sense of helplessness. He wanted to burst out and express his angst, but something was stopping him.

The wails and cries of the onlookers only grew louder as the duo walked farther and farther away from them.

HOW DOES ONE HANDLE REVERSALS IN LIFE?

Most people feel that handling reversals is one of the most difficult things in life. The *Bhagavad Gita* clarifies that more difficult than handling difficulties is handling joys. The word reversal refers to both extremes of life. Sanity is lost in the presence of too much joy and too much sorrow. The *Bhagavad Gita* is a book of balance. It teaches one to remain unaffected by both joys and sorrows.

What Krishna spoke in the Gita, in His incarnation as Lord Rama, He had demonstrated it.

Four situations in Lord Rama's life teach us four aspects of handling reversals.

1. When Rama travelled with Vishwamitra muni, He slept on the rugged forest floor as soundly as He would have on a soft palace bed. The lack of comforts and austerities did not bother Him. Flexibility is the first key to handling negative reversals effectively.

2. When Rama broke Lord Shiva's bow, Sita came to garland Him. The presence of a beautiful girl eager to marry Him did not disturb His focus on principles. Focus amid beautiful temptations is the second key to handling positive reversals effectively.

3. When Rama was informed that He would be crowned King of Ayodhya the very next day, He spent the entire night preparing to focus on the responsibility placed on Him. Sudden access to wealth and power did not wean Him away from his focus of responsibilities, because He knew that these had been given to Him to facilitate rendering more service. Awareness about the power of responsibility is the third key to handling positive reversals effectively.

4. When Rama was told to go on exile a day after being offered the throne, He remained as unaffected as He was when awarded the kingdom. Sudden loss or failure did not make Him depressed and despondent. Steadfastness amid failures is the fourth key to handling negative reversals effectively.

Yet seeing Lakshmana cry, one may conclude that he was not as good at handling reversals as Rama. Crying is considered as a sign of weakness and an indication of failure to handle a personal loss. But if one cries for another's loss, it is actually another type of strength and is known as love. Lakshmana teaches the fifth key of selflessness to handle reversals effectively.

kaushalya's lament

Seated exactly in the same spot as He had found her the previous day, Rama's pious mother was worshipping her deity with deep attention and devotion. This time, there was no smiling Sita and Lakshmana beside her. Lakshmana was in fact behind Him and definitely not smiling. Rama had not dared to see his face, but knew exactly what the expression would be. Not wanting to allow Lakshmana to react, He had not spoken to him since walking out of Keikeyi's palace.

No guard or servant had informed her about the bad news as they had for good news the previous day. Who wants to be a harbinger of sorrow?

Kaushalya had elegantly draped a silken white saree. Constant austerities and fasts had made her emaciated and seem as serene as a wise sage, yet there was no mistaking the air of regality to indicate her glorious birth.

Neglected by a husband who favored Keikeyi more than any other queen, Kaushalya had accepted her fate and chosen to utilize her time serving the society and God. She thought this noble than trying to grab her husband's attention back to herself and causing a rift in the family. She had maintained a *gurukul* and sponsored hundreds of poor students. After having raised a son to perfection and getting Him married, Kaushalya decided to completely focus on developing her spirituality by choosing a path of devotion to God and incessantly serving her family deity.[44]

---

[44] Using neglect as an opportunity to serve society rather than brooding

"Countless blessings, son! I wonder if there is anyone in this world who has attracted more blessings than You. Through Your good qualities, You have won over the hearts of everyone in Ayodhya. Envy never existed in this city, but Your becoming king will drive the word itself away from the dictionaries of Ayodhya. Your father has given a word, which he is sure to fulfill even at the cost of his life. By his desire You will soon adorn the glorious throne of Ayodhya and will continue the *rajarishi parampara* (detached saintly kings) in the tradition of glorious ancestors like Raghu, Kakutsu and Muchukunda," Kaushalya spoke as she gently stroked His head with one hand and embraced Him tightly with the other.[45]

Realizing that her son had been fasting since the previous evening, she had arranged a special feast for Him before He proceeded to the coronation arena. This was the last feast she would be able to serve her son before He became king. Once a king, the codes would be different. Gently pulling Him to sit on a special seat that she had fashioned for a future king, Kaushalya urged Rama to dig into the dishes she had herself prepared.

Rama steadied Himself before speaking to His innocent mother. He took a deep breath. He had to become hard-hearted now. It was not

---

over her misfortune was Kaushalya's way of teaching the world a positive way of dealing with an extremely negative situation.

[45] The words of Kaushalya can be seen from two perspectives.

From one perspective, she is wrong because envy had already entered Ayodhya through the words of Manthara and her husband had not really kept his word of coronating Rama.

From another perspective, she is right because Rama does not allow envy to enter Ayodhya by Himself leaving it and He ensures that Dasaratha is able to keep the promise He had made to Keikeyi before making one to His mother.

natural for the ever-kind Rama to become stone-hearted. But, the fate of Ayodhya rested on how he behaved now. He had decided in Keikeyi's chamber that it was better to make personal sacrifices than to allow chaos and disharmony to prevail in the kingdom. He was certain that He would not utter a word that would be misconstrued as His dissatisfaction with Dasaratha's decision. This was His first step toward breaking hearts. Many hearts and many expectations had to be broken to become a selfless leader.[46]

Mustering enough strength, Rama poured out His heart, "This royal seat is not meant for Me anymore. My father has selected Me for a special mission. After seeking your blessings, I will immediately depart on a voyage to the Dandakaranya forest for just 14 years, dressed as a recluse. Bharata, My dear brother will rule the kingdom instead. My meal from this day will be roots and fruits, and my drink will be sweet river water and honey. Mother, I know this will shatter yours as well as Sita's hearts, but rest assured this is for the welfare of all."

Kaushalya froze. Rama's words pierced through her eardrums and benumbed her mind. She stopped breathing and like an axed branch, she began dropping to the floor, almost as if a neglected angel was falling from the heavens. Rama swiftly held her, breaking the fall. Ushering her to a nearby seat, Rama caressed her back to consciousness. "Rama" was all she could say.

All under an hour, Rama had to witness both his parents in the exact same state of despair and helplessness. The only words that would bring succor to His parents He could not utter – "I won't leave

---

[46] Gold is soft and diamond is hard, but both are valuable. Diamond-like sternness and gold-like sensitivity are valuables that only exceptional leaders possess.

Ayodhya." Yet he had to speak the very words that were killing them, "I must leave Ayodhya." Did He really want to kill His parents? The first scene of the drama had unfolded this morning at Keikeyi's palace, and because the first scene alone could not reveal the entire story, Rama chose to be a cooperative actor in this drama of life.

Rama began to stroke her cheeks and comfort His mother. But comfort, there was none. Kaushalya cried her heart out and years of hidden woes began pouring forth as tears and words. "Perhaps, I would not have felt as helpless as now had I remained childless. But ever since You were born, You are my life. All my hopes, desires, joys and sorrows all rest on You. How can I have You torn away from me? The word *happiness* does not seem to exist in the lexicon of my life. While my husband was king, I have never seen happiness. Being the neglected wife was not as painful as being treated by him as the servant of my co-wife. I have patiently waited for 25 years (*dasa sapta cha varsani*)[47] expecting to find some respect, dreaming about the day you would be king. But it appears that I am destined for insult. Respect may come to me but only in dreams. My dreams have been shattered by the hammer of reality, O Rama!"

---

[47] The words "*dasa sapta cha varsani*" are supposed to indicate the age of Rama. In Sanskrit, *dasa* means 10, *sapta* means 7 and *dasa sapta* means 17. Most people conclude based on this simple interpretation of Sanskrit numbers that Rama's age at this point of the Ramayana was 17, whereas actually His age was 25. What is the secret?

The secret lies in the word *cha*. In Sanskrit whenever the word *cha* is used after a number it means that the number prior to it has to be added again, which means it would become 10 + 7 + 7 = 24 which is actually the right age of Rama.

The use of even a small word like *cha* actually goes on to highlight the effort that has gone into preserving such ancient texts not only in their physical form as verses, but also in their spiritual form as wisdom from these verses.

"Keikeyi's plans will fructify as You depart. What hope will be there for me in this kingdom? I have lost count of all my fasts, the painful vows, the hours of meditation, all with only one result in mind – Your kingship. All those prayers for Your well-being seem to have gone to waste! Like seeds sown in saline soil are wasted, all my austerities are wasted. You will now face hardships that I have never wanted you to face. I can't imagine the trials and turmoil you will go through each moment in the wilderness. O Rama, even after hearing this news if I am still breathing, surely my heart must be made of iron, else it would have burst by now. The only option left for me now, if You do not disobey Your father, is to follow You to the forest like a weak cow follows her calf."

ARE PRAYERS, VOWS AND AUSTERITIES PERFORMED TO ATTAIN A PURPOSE?

Prayers, vows and austerities can be performed in two moods. The *niskama* mood and the *sakama* mood.

When there is expectation of physical gratification, such spiritual practices are called *sakama* practices, which means full of desires.

When there is no expectation of physical gratification, such spiritual practices are called *niskama* practices, which means no personal desires.

Praying is like exercising. Just like the tangible result of exercise is a shapely body, the tangible effect of prayer is fulfillment of desires. But just like the intangible result of exercise is increased immunity (which is far more important) and freedom from disease, the intangible result of prayer is freedom from misgivings.

"Did the king personally tell You to leave Ayodhya and go to the forest?" asked Kaushalya, well aware of the answer. "No," said Rama, realizing the direction this discussion was headed.

"If the king did not tell You directly, how is it the king's instruction?" Kaushalya wanted to know.

"I am not following any instruction; I am just doing My duty. To rescue a person from drowning, one does not wait for instructions; one's just helps." Rama's reply silenced Kaushalya.

Though these words silenced Kaushalya, these fell like heavy bricks into Lakshmana's shallow cup of tolerance, forcing angry words to spill out of his thus-far silent mouth. Kaushalya's tears merely added fuel to a raging fire.[48]

Lakshmana breathed fire and spewed: "How can a king surrender his mind to a vile woman? The command of an unsteady king whose sense of judgment is governed by lust for a beautiful woman should not be followed. Trust cannot be placed on innocent children and incapacitated oldies. The king has become senile. Finding fault in Rama is like trying to find a bitter *neem* twig on a sweet mango tree. Even Rama's enemies cannot find a fault in him. In 25 years, I have not heard a single person even indirectly speak ill of Rama. That being the situation, what treason or act of immorality did Rama commit to be evicted from the kingdom this way? Today, at the gates of Ayodhya will stand the mighty Lakshmana. Let me see who dares send Rama away from His rights. History has seen that injustice is never dealt appropriately through mere politeness.

---

[48] Suppressing emotions unnaturally and expressing emotions violently are both indicators of a lack of a balanced manifestation of emotions.

Rama, your politeness will not work here. Let me use my strength to fight this injustice."

Realizing that His brother's overprotectiveness had resulted in disrespect for his father and mother, Rama clarified His stance. He said: "My mind cannot deviate from the path of dharma or righteousness just like the honey bee cannot be deviated from its path to nectar. Lakshmana, you claim to be strong, but let Me tell you, I am not strong enough to go against the wishes of My father. For a son, going against his father does not depict strength but weakness of character. The highest dharma or duty of a son is to obediently follow his father's orders. There are several examples from the past.

Maharishi Kandu killed a cow on the instructions of his father even though a cow is the most revered animal. Similarly, Parashurama unhesitatingly sliced off His own mother's head following his father's orders. Our own ancestors, the Sagaras, set the right precedence by digging up the entire earth and eventually giving up their lives upon the instructions of their father. These exalted personalities have committed gruesome acts, but what am I doing? Merely going away to reside in the forest for 14 years. My father has been kind enough not to ask for more. If I cannot fulfill even this, how am I to be called a good son? Lakshmana, excitement obstructs clear vision of the truth."

Kaushalya interrupted: "You always talk about following Your father's instructions, but what of Your mother's instructions? Aren't You duty-bound to obey Your mother, too?"

"Definitely, it is My duty, too, dear mother, but the nature of obligation is such that one cannot cancel out another. I have already committed to My father that I will leave for the forest immediately. After I follow the instructions of My father, which in this case will last 14 years, I will surely obey every word of yours." Rama spoke with such ease and clarity that Kaushalya had nothing more to say.

He continued to counsel Lakshmana, "My dear brother, don't you realize that Our father needs Us now more than any other time in the past? Instead of increasing his burden, We should plan to release him from the miserable state he is in. I cannot even imagine acting in a way that would be disagreeable to My father or mother. Our behavior should not add to the anxiety of our already anxious parents. Birds are born totally dependent on their parents, but once they develop wings, they should relieve them of the burden of their maintenance by taking care of themselves. Are we worse than birds that we cannot relieve our parents' burden? Right now Our father's anxiety is that I may not obey his words. And mother Keikeyi's anxiety is how soon I will leave so that she can focus on Bharata's coronation. The expected action from you as an obedient son is to immediately get tree barks for Me to wear and once I am gone you should focus on Bharat's coronation and use all those things that you accumulated for My coronation."

Still seeing lack of conviction and pain in Lakshmana's eyes, Rama took the philosophical approach. "My angry brother! Don't you see the hands of destiny working out a divine plan? If not, how can one explain the fact that Keikeyi who loved Me more than she did Bharata till the day before, change so drastically? When something is beyond Our reasoning, it is called divine ordinance or destiny. The kingdom that has been offered to me by destiny has been reclaimed by it, why should I argue against it? The king has never committed a mistake thus far nor has he committed one now, it is my destiny that has spoken through him."[49]

---

[49] When destiny shapes us, we grudgingly hold on to the chips that fall rather than focus on the beauty being revealed.

"Sometimes the most meticulous of plans fail miserably, and at other times, things work out perfectly even though completely unplanned. How do We explain such occurrences unless destiny is at play?[50] One must learn to develop a deeper philosophical outlook to events that happen in life keeping personal agendas aside and allowing divine will to prevail unobstructed. This is the only way to change Our sorrows into joys."[51]

Lakshmana shrugged off Rama's hands and walked away from Him, seething. "To hell with destiny! I knew that You would sermonize this as the hand of fate. But not fighting fate is the philosophy of the weak. The mighty create their own destinies and carve their own futures. My arrows are not just ornaments to decorate my shoulders, they can sting my enemies to death."

"Just stand by my side Rama, and I will take care of everything with these mighty arms. Let us act before everyone in Ayodhya becomes aware of Keikeyi's evil strategy. Even if it means making Ayodhya desolate, I will place you on the throne. If Bharata comes my way, he will learn a cruel lesson in warfare. Instigated by the witch, if Our father becomes a hurdle on my path, I will imprison him and if necessary kill him. Hear O world, for the sake of serving Rama, Lakshmana is willing to enter the fire smilingly."

On either side of Lakshmana, stood two people Lakshmana loved more than his life. His bravado brought a smile to the lips of one and a frown to the other. A mother wallowing deep in the ocean of

---

[50] To bring a chicken out of an egg, one only needs to wait. Similarly, destiny unfolds itself of its own accord.

[51] Trying to make destiny respond to our urgency or shape it to our needs is like breaking an egg to hasten the hatching process.

sorrow smiled and a brother standing atop a mountain of principles frowned. He was simply attempting to bridge the distance between their expectations. Kaushalya smiled knowing that Rama was not alone in this struggle as long as Lakshmana stood by Him. Rama frowned failing to understand how so much hatred had seeped into Lakshmana. Yes, His brother loved Him, but that did require him to hate everyone else.

To set things right and to bring the pointless discussion to an end, Rama spoke. He voice reverberated through the room: "I, Rama, the descendent of the Raghu dynasty, will go to the forest instantly on the orders of My father."

These words broke the dam of anger inside Lakshmana and a floodgate of tears burst forth.

Learnings from the Volatile Behavior of Lakshmana and the Composed Behavior of Rama

1. Rama was willing to accept the situation His life had put Him in, but Lakshmana was trying not to deal with it. When you learn to live with what comes your way, you develop patience, and when you learn to deal with what comes your way, you develop confidence.

2. From Rama we learn that when we judge others, we should see their positive intentions and when we judge ourselves we should monitor our actions.

3. Rama concluded that His going to the forest was His karma or fate due to some past action of His, whereas Lakshmana concluded that Rama was being sent to the forest due to

Dasaratha's mistake and mistakes ought to be corrected. From Rama, we learn to take responsibility for events in our lives. And from Lakshmana we learn that love cannot see mistakes in the object of love.

Lakshmana was called Shesha, which means leftover. It also means that he is like an object, which is not meant for itself. It is only used to show the greatness of another object. He could never see an iota of fault in Rama because of the immense love he had for his brother.

4. Lakshmana was happier to be known as Ramanuja, which means the younger brother of Lord Rama, than Saumitri, which means the son of Sumitra. He was like a protective circle around the center called Rama. If any disturbance occurred to the center, the entire circumference of the circle would vibrate with anger. From Lakshmana's anger, we learn what it really means to love someone loyally.

Both knew Rama enough to understand that the discussion had ended. Acceptance was the only option left. Lakshmana sobbed bitterly. Gone was the angry young man that could take on the whole of Ayodhya and here was a helpless brother defeated by love for his brother.

A heart-broken mother mustered all her strength to graciously deal with the inevitable. She wiped away her tears, washed her hands and legs and sipped the holy waters before speaking. She began to invoke the presence of all the different gods and demigods to protect Rama while He lived in exile for the next 14 years.

"Let Your righteousness, which you so ardently respect, protect You; let Your service to Your mother and father protect You; let truthfulness shield You from dangers.

The blessings of the saintly people will protect You, the weapons of Vishwamitra will surely aid You and the sacrificial fires invoked by the saints will constantly guard You.

May all of nature's resources protect You. The mountains, oceans, rivers, the earth and even the heavens will protect You.

The six seasons, the fortnights, months, years, nights, days and hours will act for Your protection.

The scriptures will become Your protection.

I pray that let there be no demons in the forest and let no wild animal harm You.

Let all the demigods and the trinity of Lord Shiva, Lord Brahma and Lord Vishnu work to protect You."

Throwing auspicious grains over the head of Rama, Kaushalya tied an amulet on His delicate wrist. She told Him that it contained a herb called *vishalakarni*, which could painlessly extract an arrow stuck to a body. After tying the amulet, she whispered a silent prayer holding the amulet, empowering it with the power of her purity and motherly blessings.

Rama fell at the feet of Kaushalya and for the first time since morning, cried. He shed unlimited tears that completely wet her feet. Realizing that it was time for the final departure, Kaushalya picked up Rama and embraced Him, drenching His head with her tears.

Gathering composure again, Rama straightened up and wiped off His tears. Instantly, He became the same undisturbed, unemotional and equanimous person He had always been. It was these small instances of emotions that Rama expressed which won the hearts of everyone.

With "Mission Kaushalya" accomplished, Rama steadied Himself for the toughest one– "Mission Sita." Will He be able to hold His emotions there? Will He be able to logicize everything there? Will He be able to handle the conflict between the *dharma* of a truthful son and that of a faithful husband?

CHAPTER 5

AYODHYA PARTS WITH LIFE

The auspicious time for the coronation ceremony was slipping away and no invitation, no proclamation, no action seemed to occur! Sita paced back and forth in the inner precincts of Her palace. What could be the cause of such delay? Nothing inauspicious could happen as long as Her husband Rama was around – that was Her deep-seated belief ever since she witnessed her husband confront Parashuram without the slightest hint of fear in His eyes. Nothing could be fiercer than Parashuram's attack. Every time Sita walked to the door, She sensed disturbances, but seemed to regain Her composure just thinking of Her husband's abilities.

Once again, Sita turned toward the door, and the vision brought tears and fear to Her anxious eyes. The image of Her husband standing firmly in front of Parashuram flashed across Her mind followed by the image of Him holding the broken bow of Lord Shiva. Those distant flashes of power, however, vanished like the sporadic streaks of lightning in dark of night, but what remained etched were the dark, anxious eyes of Lord Rama. How would Sita handle the news? How could They stay apart? Downcast eyes, pursed lips and a dismal expression all compounded Sita's anxiety.

Her palace had fallen silent with Rama's entry – the victory music, the chanting of auspicious hymns and the swaying celebrations had all stopped. Why? Why had the king-to-be come to the palace alone? Why wasn't the ever-eager-to-serve Lakshmana holding the royal umbrella over Rama's head? Why was the servant not swinging the yak fan? Why were there no guards accompanying the future king? Shouldn't the entry of a king herald joy? Why was the air so heavy then? Why was the prospective king so pensive? Rama was synonymous with stability, and His apparent instability left Sita extremely baffled.

The woman in Sita understood the need of the hour. She closed Her eyes for a moment to gather all the compassion in Her heart. She had always depended on Him for protection; now, *He* needed *Her* compassion. As She invoked every ounce of compassion from every inch of Her body to gather in Her eyes, tears of uncertainty rushed out of them.

Although She wept, Sita spoke to reassure Rama of Her love and support through whatever turmoil had crept into Their lives. "What's wrong My Lord? Today is the day of Your coronation. I know that You do not get affected by position or power. Tell me, what's on Your mind? Why is there no royal umbrella over Your head? Why is no one fanning You? Where are the singers who relentlessly sing Your glories? Where are the *brahmanas* who should have been reciting auspicious Vedic *mantras*? Where is the royal chariot? Why hasn't the royal elephant come? Is this one of Your tests to see if I am prepared to be queen?"

For a few moments, Rama dropped His guard. In front of the whole world, He had always projected Himself as being unaffected by reversals. The common citizen finds it hard to look up to a leader who shows signs of weakness; however, every leader needs room to express his feelings. For Rama, Sita was not merely that space, but a deep lake He could pour His emotions into and experience splashes of calm and elation.[1] The anxiety and worry in Sita's eyes, however, forced Rama to gain composure enough to show a negative situation in positive light.[2]

Rama spoke, "A negative situation cannot always be changed to be a positive one, but surely one can perceive the negative situation in a positive spirit.

Ruling the kingdom from a throne is like ruling the sea from a small boat. The rough sea of politics can toss off even a seasoned and confident sailor. By virtue of belonging to a royal family, Sita, You surely understand the volatility of kingship. Despite such unpredictability, the sharks of *adharma* cannot swallow one who does not judge intentions on the basis of solo events and one who does not abandon *dharmic* principles because of self-perceived injustice.[3]

Mother Keikeyi has redeemed two boons she acquired from Our father long before Our birth. She has desired kingship for Bharata in Ayodhya and hardship for Me in the forest."

---

[1] Everyone needs someone in his or her life with whom he or she can remain unjudged. The fear of being judged transforms a strong human into a weak tortoise with strength only in its shell – the shell of distrust.

[2] The costliest currency in the market is trust. With it, one can buy the share of confidence, which, in turn, can buy everything else. The real exchange rate of the currency of trust can be determined only during troubled markets.

[3] Testing a single grain of rice from a cooker is enough to judge if all the others are cooked.

But the same principle cannot be applied to judge people. The behavior during a single event can never be enough to judge a person's character.

Although sad, it was apparent that Rama had not abandoned His righteousness even in the face of difficulties.

Rama continued, "The dejection on My persona is less to do with the loss of kingdom and more to do with the loss of Your company, My beloved. I assure You that these 14 long years will fly away like 14 short moments. Although I am physically leaving Your company, I will continue to stay in Your memory. I may walk away from Your presence, but I will carry You in My heart." Rama spoke these seemingly illogical words with extreme gentleness, knowing the present condition of Sita's heart.

Continuing in the same breath, He articulated His expectations of Sita, "After My departure, Bharata would be the king. You have to be ready to tolerate the change.[4] More than tolerance, You would have to learn to respect Bharata as a qualified ruler and serve him selflessly. If You notice any lapse on the part of Bharata and Shatrughna, You must ignore it, considering them Your sons and brothers.[5]

Sita, while I am away in the forest, use Your time to gain spirituality. Perform deity worship. An important, inseparable part of Your religious practice would be to serve My father and mother Kaushalya, who will emaciate in the grief of My separation like innocent grass burns helplessly in a forest fire. Exhibit unbiased equality toward

---

[4] Expressions of love may be illogical, but expressions of expectations should be logical.

[5] Showing sensitivity is difficult and being insensitive is easy; however, showing sensitivity when one is personally treated insensitively is too much to expect. Rama so easily demonstrates this with His words.

all My mothers who have so lovingly brought Me up."[6]

"Ha, Ha, Ha! You expect Me to laugh, right Rama? If anyone heard this, the natural reaction would be laughter!" Tears rolled down Her cheeks because Sita was in agony, but She pretended otherwise.[7]

Sita could not believe that Rama actually thought of leaving Her behind and departing for the forest alone. Separation from Her husband was unthinkable. Never in the last 12 years had she spoken this way to Rama; nevertheless, the thought of separation from Him invoked such strange emotions that She did not realize what words emerged from Her mouth. Aware that a focused Rama would not care much for emotions, She quickly put forth a logical explanation.

"Except for the wife, every relative of the man suffers or enjoys his or her own *karma* or actions. The special aspect of a husband-wife relationship is that the two entities suffer and enjoy each other's

------

[6] When one zooms in on the bad deed of a person, all the good seems nonexistent. As an artist, one may zoom in on one part of an image, but unless one focuses on the complete image, one will be unable to do justice.

Similarly, when one reminds oneself and recounts the numerous good deeds done by others, the bad aspects seem like unimportant details of the image, else those seem like the entire image.

[7] Only humans can camouflage the colors of their emotions. Laughing while actually crying and crying while actually laughing are two blends in the myriad colors. The secret to understanding deep human emotions is not through the face, but through the heart.

Sita was so hurt that She addressed Rama by His own name. In traditional societies, women did not directly call their husbands by their names. That Sita was hurt was evident from that one utterance. She realized Her mistake immediately and ensured that She never repeated this again.

fate.[8] My dear Lord, don't deny Me the privilege of suffering with you. For years, We have savored joyous moments together, why do You want to face Your sorrows alone? If You think that I will be an obstacle during Your exile, I assure You that I will be an asset. As You walk through the forest, I shall walk ahead of You, clearing the path of thorny grass. Having My feet pricked by thorns would be far more pleasant than treading the rosy soft flower paths of the palace."[9]

"A wife is called an *ardhangini* because she shares the joys and sorrows of her husband. She halves his miseries and doubles his joys."[10]

"My parents have taught Me all the etiquettes. You need not teach Me how to handle Your family in Your absence, because I, too, will not be here to handle them. My dear Lord, My loyalty to You will act as a repellent, keeping fears of forest animals at bay. Under Your protection, the gruesome forest will be like My cozy paternal

---

[8] A variety of tastes increases the pleasure of eating; a dull meal lacks this variety. When the tongue gets varied flavor bursts of sweetness, tanginess and fieriness, it feels euphoric.

Varied experiences make the husband–wife relationship exhilarating. Relishing the joys and suffering the sorrows together thicken the bond. Just as the sweetness of a confectionary heightens immediately after a bitter taste, the feeling of joy heightens after a suffering.

[9] When Sita tells Rama that She would walk ahead of Him clearing the thorny grasses, the exact words She used were *kusa-kantakam*. A deeper study reveals the true meaning of the words – *kusa* when split becomes *ku* and *sa*; *ku* means earth and *sa* means happiness, and, *kantakam* means obstacles, which are like thorns. She was actually saying that demons like Ravana are obstacles to the happiness of residents of the Earth. So She would walk ahead and pave the path for Rama to eliminate them.

[10] Without a husband, the wife is like a painting without colors and without a wife, the husband is like a smudge of colors.

home. When living a simple life of discipline, the only demand I will make is of more service to You. With You in clear water ponds filled with floating lotuses and gliding swans, the repugnant forest will transform into a congenial heavenly planet. You know that I will not demand anything extraordinary and that I will relish living on simple roots and fruits, so what are Your reasons for not taking Me with You?"

With Sita becoming more and more adamant, Rama decided to be more graphic in waking Her up to the realities of forest life. "Your flowery understanding of a forest is acceptable in dreams, but the stark reality is totally different. When one hears the roaring lions in mountain caves, the heart skips a thousand beats. The deafening sound of waterfalls in an otherwise quiet night makes it impossible to get a wink of sleep. With the days beset by lions' roars and the nights drowned by the noise of crashing waterfalls, how can a delicate person retain sanity for long? Even if You manage to find a quiet place at night, how can Your delicate body sleep on a hard bed of stones covered with forest leaves and flowers infested with slimy creatures?

As You walk the thorny forest paths, large wild animals will be waiting for easy prey. Your dream of ponds filled with lotuses and swans will turn into a nightmare at the sight of the yawning crocodile with razor-sharp teeth. Then, there are dangerous quicksands that even elephants cannot escape.

Even if You chose to remain on safe land, camouflaged snakes, creepy reptiles and scorpions could present poisonous surprises at every step. Insects, mosquitoes and flies that constantly buzz and bite will prove a perpetual annoyance.

Starvation and darkness are a human being's greatest fears. These can make even the sanest human act callously. A person who suffers with constant hunger is prone to anger.[11] A delicate fairy like You will be unable to withstand fasting. Fasting has to be performed according to one's stamina, Sita.[12]

Your delicate body cannot even handle the heat of the sunrays, how can it handle the harshness of the mountains? Just as stubborn ice melts in the heat of the sun, Your determination will also melt with the first experience of austerities and inconvenience. I speak for Your welfare, Sita, do not insist on accompanying Me. You will do Me a greater service by staying back here."

Sita spoke almost instantly, surprising Rama with Her repartee, "The heat of the sun, the fire and the mountains are insignificant compared to the heat of the fire of separation from You. The numerous disadvantages of forest life that You have painstakingly explained will turn into advantages if I put Your affection before them, because these hardships give me more and more reasons to be completely dependent on You and seek Your shelter.[13]

---

[11] A fasted belly and a fattened ego sometimes exist in the same body. Fake fasting to exhibit one's greatness grows cacti of anger instead of florets of tolerance.

[12] A camel and a cat can never compare themselves to one another. A camel drinks a lot in one go and fasts for long a period, whereas a cat drinks a little at a time and more often.

Conscious understanding of their respective needs and capacities is their secret of survival.

[13] The disadvantage of difficulties is the reason for taking more advantage of the shelter of God.

Where Rama pointed out difficulties, Sita only saw opportunities.

"You talk about fearful animals lurking around in the forest. Where else are animals supposed to stay? Their natural home is the forest, just as the natural home of a wife is wherever her husband lives. Just as animals disconnected from the forest cannot survive for long, a wife disconnected from her husband does not survive for long. The wildest of animals will fear seeing You, so why should I fear them when I am by Your side?

My dear Lord, if You are still not convinced of My sincerity, let Me tell You a story from My past that will shock You. Eager to know My future, My parents invited a woman astrologer. While studying the lines on My left palm, her forehead crinkled with anxiety. Shifting her gaze from My palm to My face, she began face reading. Those crinkles of anxiety on her forehead gave way to a smile on her lips. The shifting of emotions on her face, from anxiety to relief, caused a flutter in My parents' hearts. The astrologer realized that all eyes were on her, so she spoke her mind: 'This girl would be an abode of auspiciousness, a magnetic force attracting the attention of the Supreme Lord and a rain cloud distributing divine grace indiscriminately, but...'[14]

My parents' jaws fell and their hearts skipped many beats. It seemed as if until the woman finished uttering the words that followed the 'but,' time itself had to stop, the sun could not move and even the wind had to pause to listen.

---

[14] Different words spoken by different people in different situations have different impacts.

> When a surgeon says, "Sorry," it evokes fear.
> When a pilot says, "Mayday," it strikes panic.
> When a policeman says, "Stop," it causes anxiety.
> When an astrologer says, "But," it elicits concern.

She said something that shattered their dreams and broke their fragile hearts. According to My destiny, I am to go to the forest twice in My life. Ever since I heard this prediction, I have had My bags packed. I have been patiently waiting for destiny to open its palm and take Me through life's thrilling adventures. Today, destiny has unclenched its fist by opening Keikeyi's mouth; therefore, I say My Lord, whether or not You go to the forest, I have to." Sita was, in fact, full of enthusiasm just by imagining the exciting time She would have with Rama in the forest, but His cold expression punctured Her gusto and left Her in tears. The flow of tears created a wet patch on the ornate carpet below her feet. She now realized that Rama's diamond-like sturdy heart would not melt from the heat of Her sorrow. She needed a more powerful tool to bring about some change. She decided to use a tool She had never thought She would ever have to use on anyone, let alone Rama. *Insult!*

In a fit of helpless rage, Sita clenched Her fists, tightened Her body and raised Her voice:

Kim tvaa manyata vaideha
Pitaame mithilaadhipah
Raamajaamaataram praapya
Striyam purushavigraham

"I pity greatly the ignorant masses of Ayodhya, who consider You their hero and glorify You. If the caretaker of Mithila, My father Janak were here, he would have surely felt that he had mistakenly married his daughter to a woman claiming to be a man."

CAN NEGATIVE EMOTIONS BE TOOLS TO DISPLAY POSITIVE LOVE?

Was Sita right in insulting Rama? Can disagreements bring about agreements?

Sita represents a self-confident wife. Such a wife has the following four roles:

1. To compliment – She compliments Her husband for qualities He possesses.

2. To complement – She complements Her husband with qualities He lacks.

3. To care – She cares for him and His assets.

4. To correct – She corrects when He deviates from *dharma*.

1. To compliment another, one has to constantly meditate on the good qualities that person possesses and the good deeds that person does. Sita appreciated Rama regularly. The difference between flattery and appreciation is genuineness. Only a person who knows the value of appreciation can compliment another.

2. To complement another, one has to know one's own strengths. A person who complements has to be like a shadow. In the morning or during prosperity, the shadow follows you, because then you don't need any assistance; at noon or in the heat of challenges, the shadow lies beneath your feet, cooling the area where your feet stand. When you need that person, he or she is there; in the evening or during poverty, the shadow is ahead of you. Such a person makes your difficulties his or her own and assists you by taking the lead.

3. To care, one has to have experienced the care of another. In the *Ramayana*, there is no mention of the love between Rama and Sita shared before They left for the forest; however, there is an elaborate description of their love for each other during the years that they were in exile. The need for love and care is magnified during difficulties.

4. To correct another, one has to be intelligent and sensitive. Sita's expertise lay in using negative emotions to bring out positive love. Negative emotions are like poison in ayurvedic medicine. A drop too much or too little can kill instead of cure. This role should remain like that drop.

Her father called Her *dharmacharini* while handing Her over to Rama, indicating that She should assist quietly as Her husband followed the codes of *dharma* diligently, yet assert firmly if She saw an apparent deviation.

In Vedic times, when a man followed his *dharma*, such as doing charity, performing yajna, his wife had to be present and sanction his actions, only then could the duty be performed. The wife, therefore, had to be constantly by her husband's side. Here Sita is asking Rama how He could consider leaving her behind as He would be unable to perform any *dharmic* duties without Her. Would this imply then that for 14 years He would not perform any *dharmic* duties?

The duty of a man is to protect his wife, but if he were to live elsewhere, how could he protect her? Just to provoke Rama, she calls her father Mithiladipah, indicating that he was the caretaker of Mithila. She wanted to tell Rama that where Her father could take care of the whole of Mithila, Rama could not take care of even one woman. What would His father-in-law think of Him?

If the proportion of the four roles that the wife plays is close to perfect, then the relationship will be healthy. Only then negative emotions can be used as tools to show positive love. Only then, can disagreements bring about agreements.

Despite Sita's rant, Rama stood as firm and composed as ever. When He shut His eyes, Sita watched intently to observe the reaction that followed. Anyone else would have missed the disappointment in Rama's eyes, but not Sita. She knew that She had hurt the person She loved the most;[15] She also knew that Her only reason for doing this was to convince Rama to take Her along to the forest.[16] She would have 14 long years to make up for this one wound by applying Her soothing salve of love. In that one moment, Sita resolved to turn the 14 years of exile into years of continuous bliss for Rama through Her servitude and love.[17]

Intent on changing the sullen atmosphere in the room, Sita asked Rama a question that altered the course of His thought process.

---

[15] Hurting another is easy, but knowing when to hurt, whom to hurt, how to hurt, why to hurt is difficult.

[16] If there is ego involved in the hurting, then relationships break. But if there is service involved, gratitude will eventually manifest itself and love will increase.

[17] If you choose to hurt someone, be ready to undo the hurt through the hard work of love.

"Could You tell Me, My Lord, what is *swarga* or heaven and what is *naraka* or hell?"[18]

Rama was baffled because He could not predict where She was headed with this question. A minute ago, She had mocked Him, questioning His ability. Was She now going to hurt Him further by questioning His intelligence?

Sita answered the question Herself: "The definition of heaven and hell vary according to the mindset of the person being asked. If I am asked this question, My answer would be, heaven is hell without You and hell is heaven with You.[19] My definition of heaven and hell revolves around Your presence or absence. My Lord, I am dependent on You as much as Savitri was dependent on Satyavaan.

Difficulties that come in the path of serving You will be My greatest joys and the satisfaction of serving You will be My only asset. When I walk with You through the forest, every thorn that pricks My feet will feel like swabs of cotton. The rough gravel path will transform into a smooth deerskin carpet. Exhaustion from

---

[18] Heaven and hell are planes of priorities. The definition of heaven and hell actually depend on what we center our lives around. So naturally, because different people have different perspectives, they have different definitions for heaven and hell.

[19] For a person struggling every day to make a living, earning daily wages is heaven and not earning is hell.

For a healthy man, sickness is hell and cure is heaven.

For a student, an exam is hell and holiday is heaven.

For a stock investor, a bull market is heaven and a bear market is hell.

For a sage, heaven is focusing on the purpose of life and hell is attraction to material things.

For Sita, being with Rama was heaven and being away from Him was hell.

My service to You will feel like the comforting friend, whereas night sleep will feel like the enemy who puts an end to My days of service to You. The wild sandstorms will seem like a spray of fine sandalwood dust. The fruits and roots that You feed me in the forest will seem like the best delicacies in the world.[20]

Do not leave Me in hell My Lord, take Me to heaven with You. These one, three and ten[21] years of separation from You will be like visiting 14 hellish planets." Saying this, Sita embraced Rama, sobbing intensely.

The room fell silent, broken only by Sita's intermittent sobs. The tears flowing out of Her eyes were like water droplets falling out of two lotuses. Soon Rama's clothes were all wet. Rama gently lifted His arms to embrace Sita tightly. How could He even think of being away from His very life? How can the body move without the soul? Sita had won, and He had lost. In fact, in His defeat lay victory: He had won, and Destiny, which had tried to separate Them, had lost. [22]

---

[20] A living entity should offer this prayer to God.

Perceiving the opportunity to serve as assets and perceiving difficulties during service as opportunities to purify are the best dispositions to approach God.

[21] Rather than saying 14 years directly, Sita actually spoke about how She could be separated from Rama for one, three and ten years. Why did She break up the 14 years into three parts?

She did this to remind Rama about the purpose of their incarnation. The division of the 14 years is that for the one year She would be in Lanka, for the three years in Panchavati and the ten years in the Dandakaranya forest.

[22] Scriptures are like multilayered cakes. Each layer has a different flavor. Every character has multiple roles to play, and through each role emerges multiple teachings.

In this episode, Sita plays three roles – Sree *tattva* or the role of an eternal consort, *jiva tattva* or the role of a living entity and *madhyavartitva*

It was final: Sita was accompanying Him to the forest!

Rama drew the curtains on the last act of the drama by saying, "Time will soon prove that I can very well protect You. But how could I ask You to accompany Me to the wild, uncomfortable forest unless I knew Your real desire? Wouldn't people in future criticize Me for being selfish and having asked an unwilling, unprepared spouse to follow? From Your perspective, a wife's role is to share the joys and sorrows of a husband. But from My perspective, the role of a caring husband is to constantly meditate on the comforts and protection of His wife. Sita, I did not want to cause any discomfort to You just to address My needs. Now that I realize You are determined to stay in the forest with Me, I know that in Your loving company, forest life will soon become auspicious and enlivened."[23]

---

tattva or the role of a guru.

As Lord Rama's eternal consort, she is called *Sree tattva*; She cannot be separated from the Lord just as effulgence cannot be separated from the sun, fragrance from a flower and coolness from the moon.

As a living entity or *jiva tattva*, She teaches how a living entity should behave at the very thought of being separated from God – feeling lost and in misery without God's presence in our lives. The absence of God's memory in our lives should seem like hell and His presence like heaven. As a *guru* or *madhyavartitva tattva*, She shows that the primary responsibility of a *guru* is to correct a mistake and show us the right path.

[23] Just like jigsaws fit into each other's grooves to reveal a perfect picture, reciprocal care for what pleases one another reveals perfect love.

In a jigsaw puzzle, a perfect turn occurs when the multiple projections in a card are carved to accommodate or fit into multiple grooves on multiple sides. Similarly, in relationships, care has to be shared on many fronts to result in perfect love.

Rama and Sita were both sincerely trying to express Their care for one another. Rama's soft grooves willingly accommodated Sita's sharp penetrating projections. The combination then naturally revealed Their perfect love.

Rama asked Sita to part with all Her possessions and prepare to proceed toward the forest. Sita began distributing Her valuables immediately, until She was left with nothing more to give.[24] Rama smiled at Her eagerness to be with Him. But more than that, He was pleased with Her detachment to Her favorite possessions.[25]

Sita was beaming as She stood by Rama to proceed to the forest. Rama turned toward Lakshmana who had been watching everything quietly. Rama opened His arms to embrace him indicating that this was the final embrace before departing. Lakshmana was aghast. This meant that Rama wasn't planning on taking him along. A torrent of tears rushed down Lakshmana's cheeks and he fell at Rama's feet. "Why did You change Your mind? You had initially agreed to take me along. I cannot live without You, Rama."

Lakshmana's claim left Rama curious: "And when did I promise to take you along with Me?"

Lakshmana realized that this was his only chance to convince Rama, and he decided to give it his best shot. He spoke with extreme self-confidence: "You may not have promised me directly, but Your words had subtly indicated just that.[26] When You were coaxing mother

---

[24] Attachment always precedes detachment. Sita could detach Herself from so much because She was deeply attached to Rama. Keikeyi attached herself to wealth and the kingdom, so she could detach herself from Rama and from shame.

[25] Attachment is not a problem; what you are attached to defines the problem. When your attachment attaches you to your personal pleasures and detaches you from other's pains, it becomes a problem.

[26] Our choice of words is the harbinger of the subtlest of feelings that often cannot be self-deciphered. A selfless comrade with a microscopic vision can decrypt them for us.

Kaushalya to permit You to go to the forest, You used the plural pronoun to state that You would go to the forest. Since You were speaking to a superior person like Your mother, Your humility would not have permitted You to say 'We' when implying Yourself alone. In fact, my Lord, You did not use the *dvi-vachanam*, which implies two people, instead You used *bahu-vachanam*, which implies more than two people. You definitely suggested that Sita and I would accompany You.

Besides that, when You were conversing with mother Sita just now, You explained to Her about how to treat all Our family members in Your absence. You went to the extent of explaining how She should treat Bharata and Shatrughna, but You did not even utter my name. Does that not mean that You took for granted that I would be with You in the forest?"[27]

A smile threatened to appear on Rama's lips, but He suppressed it and spoke to Lakshmana. "More than a brother *(bhrataa)*, a companion *(sakhaa)* and a friend *(snigdah)*, Lakshmana, I have known you as an ardent follower of *dharma* who is ever attentive of His actions *(dharmatmah)*, a valiant hero who never gives up in any circumstance *(virah)* and an obedient nobleman who is ever willing to serve *(vashyah)*.

Without your presence, how do you expect Our father to survive? More importantly, how can our lonely mother Kaushalya handle so much sorrow? In following the instructions of superiors, there

---

[27] Through the simple words that Rama whispered, the intelligent Lakshmana decoded His deepest desires.

A shallow reading of the scriptures escapes such subtle lessons that demand attention.

is great merit. Understand the predicament, Lakshmana, and stay here. Ayodhya needs you!"

"As far as need is concerned, there is a far greater need for me in the forest than in Ayodhya now. Both You and Sita have packed Your bags, but who will carry them? Who will help You procure the roots and fruits? Who will guard You in the forest while You are asleep at night, and when both of You are immersed in loving conversations during the day? My dear Lord, You and Sita are not trained to do this. Let me accompany You both as a menial servant," Lakshmana said.

"Bharata is inspired by Your principles of morality and righteousness. He will ensure that equal treatment is given to all the mothers. There is no need to worry at all.

And as far as protecting and taking care of mother Kaushalya is concerned, a thousand villages have been granted to her and she can maintain not only herself but hundreds of Lakshmanas like me. She does not need me, Rama. Ayodhya does not need me. Nor do You need me.

As soon as water leaves the tank, the fish and blue lotus meet a waterless grave. You are the life-sustaining water for us, Rama. I am like a fish swimming in the ambrosial water of Your mercy. And Sita is like the blue lotus blooming happily in Your loving embrace. If the water has decided to leave the tank of Ayodhya, please let the fish swim along its currents. I humbly fall at Your lotus feet! Please, Rama, don't be cruel to me. Take me along!" Lakshmana fell at His feet gripping Them like a creeper clings to a tree for sustenance.

As Lakshmana lay sobbing at Rama's feet, he looked up at Sita with teary-red eyes. His eyes were pleading and She was his only hope.

Slowly, Rama released His clenched fist and extended His arms to gently and softly place His beautiful pinkish palms on Lakshmana's shoulders. Pulling him up in a welcoming embrace, Rama said, "Come with Me!"

THE TEST OF EGO AND THE TEST OF DEDICATION

Rama had lain two subtle traps to test Lakshmana:

- You are irreplaceable
- The world needs you

Lakshmana clearly saw through these two traps and responded with clarity. The first trap was the test of ego and the second was the test of dedication.

1. To think one is unique is an act of recognizing the greatness of God's creation; it leads to gratitude. But to think one is irreplaceable is an act of instituting one's own greatness; it leads to arrogance.

2. In the overwhelming pressure of trying to address the needs of the world, we often forget to address our priorities. Rama was pointing out to the needs of the world, but Lakshmana was focusing on his own priorities.

A living entity has to overcome two feelings to be accepted by God. The Lord tests us to see if we have any other priorities besides Him. Lakshmana clearly prioritized his relationship and service to Rama over everything else.

The role of the mother is to ease a father's sternness and accommodate a child's lapses; therefore, Lakshmana turned helplessly to the divine mother, Sita. Only She could mitigate Rama's sternness and accommodate Lakshmana's lapses. Her presence was his hope. Taking God's shelter through the divine mother is the formula Lakshmana is teaching us to gain favor with the Lord.

possessions shed to shower hope

Picking up the heavenly bows, the impenetrable armors, the quivers with inexhaustible arrows and the swords that were housed at Vasistha's abode, how happy Lakshmana felt serving Rama. How miserable he had been a few minutes ago at the thought of Rama not taking him along to the forest and abandoning him to suffer the comforts of Ayodhya! Lakshmana concluded that if the world could hear the thoughts running through his mind now, it would definitely consider him a fool. Who would consider the wealth of a kingdom without Rama to be dust and the dust of the forest marked with Rama's footprints to be more valuable than gold? Lakshmana smiled contentedly, as he ran back with the weapons to Rama's palace.

Lakshmana had also informed Suyojana, Vasistha's son, of Rama's desire to meet him before leaving. Suyojana, Rama and Sita were soon facing each other with folded palms. No words were spoken. Rama and Sita circumambulated Suyojana thrice clockwise. Soon piles of armlets, earrings, gems on a golden chain and bracelets were lying at Suyojana's feet. In addition, Rama offered Suyojana His elephant Satrunjaya, which was gifted to Him by His maternal uncle. He also gifted him a thousand surplus powerful elephants.

Sita gifted amulets adorned with figurines, pearl necklaces, a gold chain and a studded girdle to Suyojana's wife. She also offered her an ornate couch riveted with jewels.

With tears of gratitude, a heart filled with sorrow and lips pouring blessings, Suyojana accepted the gifts.

Next, Rama facilitated the maintenance, education and food of every learned *brahmana* and pure-hearted sage near Ayodhya. He ensured that all employees at His palace would be provided maintenance for the next 14 years, so that they did not have to struggle for their livelihood in His absence and could continue their job of maintaining the palace till His return. It was then the turn of His father's chariot driver, Chitraratha, whom He gifted amply, expressing gratitude for his life-long service to the family.[28]

Rama called upon the leader of Ayodhya's student community. Thousands of students studied the Vedas under the guidance of certified teachers. Each of these students was not only scholarly but also led a very austere life, craving neither for facilities nor riches. They often studied for days on end, not stepping out to beg or even to eat, to satiate their thirst for knowledge. Even great, learned men adored the commitment of these students. To facilitate their learning, Rama offered them 80 cartloads of jewels, 1000 bullock carts carrying rice, 200 bullocks for cultivation and 1000 cows for their nourishment.[29]

---

[28] Worrying about the security of dependents when personally experiencing insecurity is a sign of a care-filled leadership.

[29] A fenced farm that is watered and treated produces a good yield. Similarly, a student when provided with in an anxiety-free atmosphere, nourished by the water of basic needs and the manure of good teaching, produces the yield of wisdom.

Having given away all their possessions, Rama turned toward Sita and Lakshmana and smiled with satisfaction. It was time to proceed toward Their destiny.

Just as They started, a skinny, fragile-looking, impoverished *brahmana* wobbled toward the trio. Though he was shabbily dressed, with a cloth that barely covered his body, an air of purity coupled with a glowing effulgence around his persona left no doubt in anyone's mind that he was a great sage. Rama instantly recognized him as Trijata, a descendent of the great sage Gargi.

Trijata looked at Rama with love-filled eyes, grateful to have been allowed such easy access to the prince. He had just walked in through five gates and not a single guard tried to stop him. This was most definitely the result of Rama's training on how to welcome and respect sages.[30]

As he lovingly looked at Rama, he was reminded of his home and his heart filled with gratitude for his wife, who had coaxed him to seek Rama's grace. Just an hour ago, his emaciated wife had placed his distressed, hunger-stricken children in front of him and coaxed him to seek some charity from the kind Rama. Moved by his children's plight, the otherwise self-content Trijata instantly dropped his axe, spade and plough and took a walking stick to trot up to Rama's palace.[31]

---

[30] When there is love, there is no threat. Free non-bureaucratic access to a leader creates confidence in the follower.

[31] Trijata's wife had told him to seek charity for her and the children because he would not have bothered to ask anything for himself. But, in fact, she had actually wanted some facility to serve him, not really to end her and her children's suffering.

In artificial love, the focus of our desires and aspirations is inward. In

Rama's beauty left the poor sage speechless. He struggled before finally managing to speak out and request charity so that he could take care of his family.

Rama's eyes twinkled. Sita could see that He was up to something, but She couldn't guess what it was. Rama said, "All My wealth is for the service of the deserving *brahmanas*. But unfortunately, I have already given away all My possessions. The only possessions I have left with Me are a few thousand cows grazing on the other bank of the Sarayu river. I would be happy to hand them over to you, but on one condition."

As Rama spoke, Trijata's expressions changed several times like the weather in a hill station. When Rama said that all His wealth was for the *brahmanas*, Trijata's face beamed like the hills on a sunny day; when He said that He had already distributed all His wealth, Trijata's face became gloomy like the hills on a cloudy day; when Rama said that He still had a few thousand cows left, Trijata's face gleamed like the hills welcoming a burst of sunshine after rain; then again, when Rama put forth a condition, Trijata smiled and frowned like the hills during a sun shower, when there is simultaneous rain and sunshine! Rama smiled through Trijata's anxiety. Sita had no clue what Rama was up to.[32]

Rama extended His long arms toward the Sarayu river. "Standing here, you can take as many cows as you can throw this staff over."

real love, the focus of our desires and aspirations is turned outward, in the direction of the one we love.

[32] Like unpredictable weather conditions, our varied life experiences constantly change our expressions.

Sita stood baffled by Her husband's claims. A bewildered Trijata, too, shook his head. Rama stood casually with His hands on His hips and smiled. The distance was at least a few thousand meters from where they were standing.

It seemed cruel of Rama to place this condition. Even a much younger and fitter man could not have thrown the staff to the outer gate of the palace, let alone throwing it across the river over the thousands of grazing cows.

Surprisingly, Trijata removed the cloth covering his torso and tied it tightly around his waist. Determined, he picked up his staff, slowly at first, and then gradually picking up pace, he twirled it. Gathering all his strength, he placed his right foot ahead and flung the staff with all his might in the direction of the Sarayu river.

The staff whizzed past the entrances of the palace, past the gardens and lanes of Ayodhya, over the wide Sarayu river and beyond the thousands of cows grazing on the bank to land with a loud thud next to a bull, which jumped away in sudden fright.

"Bravo! Bravo!" Rama ran toward Trijata and embraced him, heaping praises. Soon Rama's jovial mood was replaced by His regular somber and self-composed demeanor. "All these cows will be delivered to your abode immediately, O Trijata! I am extremely sorry for joking with you in this way, please forgive Me. The only reason I did this was to show the world that a *brahmana* does not beg from inadequacy or weakness, but rather by begging, he gives an opportunity for the prosperous to serve. Wealth when shared brings joy in this life and fame in the next, but wealth when hoarded only causes misery. The real strength of a *brahmana* is unfathomable and accumulated by dint of his austerities."

FOUR GEMS

Through the story of Trijata, Rama has offered the world, four bejeweled lessons.

1. Who is weak and who is strong is not a matter of external analysis but of internal strength. Trijata was physically weak, but spiritually strong.

2. One should first deserve to desire. Nothing in this world should be available without effort. Rama made Trijata work to deserve the cows.

3. Human action supported by God's grace can possess unimaginable potential and yield inconceivable results. The combination of effort and grace leads to miracles.

4. Finding fault with your own thought process is an important aspect of growth, but seeking forgiveness for faulty actions is important for survival.

Rama first thought: "The reason I tested this man was because I thought that I am wealthy, he is poor, I am young, he is old; I am strong, he is weak." Instantly He sought forgiveness for such thoughts.

Rama asked Trijata if there was anything else He could do to serve him. Trijata blessed Rama and left blissfully, still trying to comprehend the full purport of Rama's test.[33]

---

[33] Having received enough, Trijata did not want anything more from Rama. Unhealthy greed gives you the fake confidence of walking in the sky but

hope slumps into nothingness

Dressed in a white, spotless silken saree, a confused Kaushalya found herself walking simultaneously toward her only hope and her only fear. Her husband was her only hope and Keikeyi her only fear. Today she was going to confront both.[34]

As she paced toward the palace, she prepared herself mentally. She wanted to know from Dasaratha what had really conspired. Crowning Bharata king was never a disturbance to her, because all four boys were equal in her eyes. All she wanted to know was for Bharata to become the king, why did Rama have to go to the forest? This seemed illogical and incomprehensible, but more than anything else, unnecessary.

Her racing mind went blank as soon as she stepped into the inner chambers. The monarch was lying on the ground – lifeless. A loud moan escaped Kaushalya's lips. It was all over now! She began beating her chest and wailing loudly.

The loud cry grabbed Vasistha's and Sumantra's attention; they burst into the room in an instant. Vasistha rushed to the king's side to examine his pulse. Life hadn't quite deserted the king. "Death is knocking," Vasistha stated grimly.

Gently, he brought Dasaratha back to consciousness by sprinkling cool waters on his face and tenderly massaging his chest. "O pious

---

satisfaction gives you the contentment of walking on the ground. Trijata was satisfied.

[34] When the source of hope and the source of fear come together, they give birth to the child of uncertainty.

king, Keikeyi is not capable of iniquitous acts. She will soon give up her desire. Do not be anxious."

As soon as he heard this, Dasaratha opened his eyes. "Before death claims me, I want to place the crown on Rama's head. Tell Him not to leave Ayodhya for the forest."

The pitiable sight of the King led the sage to turn toward Keikeyi, who stood indifferently, a little distance away, with her back toward them. "My dear daughter, give the kingdom to your son Rama and life to all of us. If Rama leaves Ayodhya, death will first claim your husband and then numerous others. The sin of exiling Rama is the same as waking naked without any shame. Clothe yourself in sinless glory by giving kingship to Rama and life to us. Acting like this…"

Vasistha was rudely cut short by Keikeyi's brazen and unexpected proclamation, "If the king's promise is broken, I will die that instant!"[35]

"What kind of a woman are you? Are you a demon? The ghost of desire haunts you and the proof of this is that you are ready to step on the dead body of your husband to establish your son on the throne. What good is the throne smeared with the blood of your husband? You have stooped so low that even before the king agreed or even uttered a word, you instructed Rama to go to the forest. Those were your words, but you proclaimed that they were the king's instructions…" Vasistha was so utterly disgusted that he decided to speak no further.

---

[35] Keikeyi loved Rama. But when her love for Rama conflicted with her ambition of making Bharat king, she chose to dislodge Rama and prioritize her ambition. It was not about Bharat, but about her ambition.

Sometimes love is dethroned when ambitions are enthroned.

Dasaratha continued from where Vasistha trailed off, "I have seen you for the venomous vampire you are, slowly sucking the life out of me. You are using the same string I wedded you with as an amulet to guard your son and a noose to strangulate me.[36] Have I actually wedded death instead of a woman? In the presence of my spiritual master, I declare today, that you are no more my wife, and I forsake your son if he decides to follow you. He will no longer have the right to perform my last rites."

Dasaratha broke down and collapsed yet again. The swoonings were so fast and frequent that the beleaguered king had no memories of the few moments he was actually conscious! As Dasaratha slumped into nothingness, so did Kaushalya's hopes. She had come to Keikeyi's murky palace looking for answers. The afternoon's events had revealed the answers: Dasaratha was the loser, Keikeyi the victor and her son the victim. And her? Alas! No words could describe Kaushalya's plight as she stood over the remains of her life, her emotions gushing out as a silent river of tears.[37]

drop of vicious joy in an ocean of forlorn tears

Rumors blazed across the city as uncertainty spread its tentacles across the whole of Ayodhya. Only one man could dispel all doubts, and his name was Vasistha. Was he really going to do that?

---

[36] The ghost of mad desires becomes a vampire that sucks the blood of others.

[37] Sometimes, we have no role to play other than to accept whatever life throws at us.

As the *acharya* walked into the coronation arena, everyone realized that he had a message to deliver. All hopes were pinned on whatever he had to say. Vasistha patiently waited for everyone to gather together before unleashing the lethal words battling in his mind. His eyes restlessly darted around to see if the most important of Ayodhya's citizens were around to hear him directly. The rest would know soon.

"Keikeyi has claimed the two boons she had been promised by the king years ago. One, she has wanted immediate crowning of Bharata as king; two, she has demanded a 14-year exile into the forest for Rama. We need not worry; Ayodhya will have its king soon."

As Vasistha walked away, countless kings and citizens fell to the ground, writhing and wailing in pain. His words had pierced their hearts like a sizzling hot iron shaft thrust into a fresh wound.

But not everyone was sad. Amid the sea of pain and tears, was a drop of wicked pleasure by a lone, maliciously happy person. The hunchbacked woman stood bent over her crooked stick, a wide smile spanning her face. The more she saw everyone suffer, the broader her smile became. Her strategy had nailed it. Manthara turned away from the wails, raised her proud chin, as high as her bent body allowed and walked into her tiny den of joy, far removed from the ocean of sorrow.

HOW CAN ONE EXPERIENCE PLEASURE WHEN OTHERS ARE IN PAIN?

Manthara had no one to love, no family to care for and took no responsibility toward people dependent on her.

An emotionally weak person attempts to grab security through acts of insensitivity.

The rapid spread of the terrible news triggered mass devastation and sorrow. Women began wilting like lotuses without stalks, their hair loose, ornaments scattered and eyes turned crimson with anguish.

Innocent children, too, began bawling, not knowing why. Birds, flowers and animals across the vast expanse of Ayodhya grieved like never before; even the death of their loved ones had not evoked such sorrow.

Flaming kitchen stoves were snuffed out, raging sacrificial fires were denied butter, ecstatic dancers were robbed of their smiles and wise philosophers were rendered speechless. The sad news had put an end to Ayodhya's happy habits.

Ayodhya's agony multiplied hundred-folds on seeing Rama and Lakshmana walk out of their palace toward Keikeyi's, shorn of the royal umbrella's shelter or the royal guards' protection or the chariot's comfort. Their sorrows brimmed over on seeing Sita walk along with Rama and Lakshmana, the Sita who was always so shielded from public gaze. Even the sun would consider itself lucky if it got a chance to spot Sita! Here She was, walking in full view of the people. When reality suddenly dawned on the citizens, Ayodhya went insane. The horror of suffering! Rama alone was not going to exile for 14 years. Sita and Lakshmana were, too.[38]

"Sheer injustice!" shouted one. The citizens felt uprooted.

Another agreed, "A city that does not respect love is like a forest disrespectful of roots. Let us this very instant desert Ayodhya and

---

[38] Agony manifests itself when things go against one's desires, but it magnifies itself when suffering befalls one's object of love.

turn it into a forest and embrace the forest and turn it into Ayodhya. Let Keikeyi inherit a kingdom devoid of people, riches and love, but brimming with silence, scarcity and contempt."

Hundreds cheered in approval. As Rama moved into the crowd, He walked steadily, determined and unfazed. No emotional rancor could unsettle Him now and nothing could sway His decision. Rama swam through Ayodhya's sea of sorrow to enter Dasaratha's island of misery.

Sumantra's moist eyes were the first to greet Rama. He stood at the threshold of Dasaratha's inner chambers. Rama requested him to inform the king of His arrival. Sumantra walked in, only to see the once-powerful sovereign sun in eclipse; a once-blazing flame reduced to ashes; a once-unfathomable lake now scorched. Dasaratha's obvious helplessness made Sumantra uncomfortable.

"Rama is here, your Highness. He has already handed over all His personal possessions and stands at the gate awaiting your audience." Sumantra tried not to let his voice betray his pain.

Dasaratha ordered, "Call all my wives! I will see Rama along with them."

Within moments, 350 women entered the room along with Sumitra and stood beside Kaushalya. Dasaratha hoped Keikeyi would feel remorse in the presence of all her co-wives, who had equal rights on him and his property, and perhaps relent.

Rama glided into the room, graceful as ever. Were it another day, Dasaratha would have spent a moment or two admiring this quality of his son. But today, he hauled himself up and ran toward Him hysterically, but began to go limp midway; it was the weakness taking its toll.

Dasaratha's slump set in motion thousands of anklets, which tinkled together as all but one of the queens rushed to their husband's aide. But they stopped when they saw Rama and Lakshmana rush to stop the falling king and managed to hold him firmly. The queens chorused, "Alas! O Rama!"

Rama gently led Dasaratha to a couch nearby and spoke. "O respected father, confer your kind permission on Me to enter the forest. Though I tried to dissuade them umpteen times, Sita and Lakshmana are bent on accompanying Me on this journey. Just as Lord Brahma, the lord of the universe, blessed his four sons, the Catur Kumaras, to enter the forest permanently, you, O Lord of this earth, bless your two sons to enter the forest temporarily. Your blessings will be Our armor."

A teary-eyed Dasaratha said, "Rama, imprison me and rule Ayodhya!"[39]

"Father, for the sake of My comforts, do not allow unrighteousness to prevail in your pure life. These 14 years will merely be a long walk for Me. I will be back soon to clasp your lotus feet and continue to offer a lifetime of service to them." Rama tried to comfort the guilt-ridden heart of Dasaratha.

Much to everyone's dismay, Keikeyi was shamelessly whispering something into the monarch's ears. Those within earshot were aghast. "Let Rama go! Don't waste time in these useless sentiments."

---

[39] What Dasaratha meant was "You break rules, but I won't." He tells Rama to do something that He would never do.

Dasaratha had great affection for Rama but an extreme degree of attachment to Keikeyi. This is the predicament of a spiritual aspirant: affection toward God is often coupled with attachment to sensual pleasures.

While Keikeyi was pouring hate and selfishness into one ear, Rama was pouring love and confidence into the other. In this confusion, Dasaratha said to Rama, "Deep in the forest lies Your path of advancement and welfare. Ayodhya is now a place of deterioration. Your mind is virtuous and Your decisions cannot be reversed by anyone. So leave Ayodhya, Rama! I pray that all auspiciousness grace Your journey.[40]

But Your weak father has one request. Stay back for one last night in Ayodhya's lap of luxuries before embracing a life of difficulties. Let me shower You with all material joys tonight. Let me envelope You with comfort before throwing You into the dark well of suffering. Forgive me, Rama, I was tricked into this by Keikeyi."

Rama spoke, "Father, a sorrow delayed can never become joy. I cannot wait here for another moment. I must leave.[41]

Let Bharata be seated on the throne of Ayodhya as I choose to sit on the throne of *satya* (truth). Pleasure lies in the pursuance of *dharma*. Seeking pleasure by chasing things that promise gratification only grants temporary joys."[42]

---

[40] When Dasaratha told Rama that "Your mind is pious," he also simultaneously meant "My mind is impious." When he told Rama that "Your decisions cannot be reversed," he also meant "You are unlike me whose decisions can be reversed easily." Dasaratha actually meant "Because my mind is not righteous, I changed my decision of crowning You."

[41] Inevitable sorrows do not become joys by postponement. Delay only aggravates the poignancy of grief.

[42] Myopia, or shortsightedness, is the inability to see distant objects. Those who seek short-term pleasures focus on the word **my** and hence, cannot see long-term consequences.

Rama's words of determination were followed by wails of helplessness. Grief engulfed every heart in the room except Keikeyi's, and all eyes became moist except her's. While the heat of her desires kept her left eye dry, the fires of envy kept her right eye dry.

On seeing Keikeyi's dry eyes, Sumantra flew into a rage, his eyes burning like twigs in the dry summer heat. All he wanted now was to bring some joy to his master, Dasaratha. He had to drive some sense into the heartless queen. Scowling, he hurled sharp words at her like poisonous arrows.

"You foolish, adamant lady,[43] your husband has taken care of you like a gardener nurtures a sweet mango tree. But little did he realize that he had cut down a sweet mango tree named Kaushalya and planted in its place a bitter neem tree named Keikeyi. Now, in the hope of growing mangoes on the neem tree, he is watering it with milk. No matter how much nectarine milk he pours on a neem tree, the fruits will always be bitter.[44]

Your inflexible obstinacy will only result in the death of your husband and destruction of the entire dynasty. Don't be foolhardy like your mother."[45] When Sumantra spoke these words, Keikeyi's

---

[43] Although Sumantra was a charioteer, his wisdom had led Dasaratha to appoint him the leader of ministers in his kingdom. Besides, because of his loyalty, he had the freedom to even call the queen a fool and a stubborn lady.

[44] In berating Keikeyi, Sumantra was also pointing out to Dasaratha each of their obvious faults.

[45] Sumantra was a *suta*, which means a charioteer. The word *suta* also means thread. Just as a thread can link different things, Sumantra had the ability to connect facts from different eras to present circumstances and provide solutions to complicated problems.

ears perked up. When she had ensured that no one knew of her dark secret, how did this man find out?"

Keikeyi felt squeamish as Sumantra went on to narrate the story of her mother.

"As you know, King Ashwapati, your father and the king of Keikeya, had an interesting supernatural ability a sage had once awarded him. He could understand animal and bird speech. It might have seemed liked a boon, but, in fact, it became a bane.

There was a condition for this benediction: even if he understood what the animals and birds said, he could not disclose the details of the conversation to anyone, because death would accompany the disclosure.[46]

All was well as long as he used his boon for entertainment and thrill by just eavesdropping on bizarre animal and bird conversations.

One day, as he was strolling in the garden along with his wife, he heard two mating birds conversing. Their discussion made him laugh inadvertently. His ever-suspicious wife had noticed him staring at the mating birds and wondered if he was laughing at the thought of some paramour. She badgered him to tell her the reason behind his laughter. Soon, he knew he was trapped.

Manthara gave bad advice and Sumantra gave good advice. The word *su* in Sanskrit means *good*. Both held deep secrets in their hearts and both revealed these only when needed. Manthara spilled secrets to create anarchy and Sumantra to create harmony.

[46] One should consider something a boon or bane depending on its practical use to society. Ashwapati's boon was ultimately useless. He could neither show it off nor use whatever knowledge he gained from it.
The source of his entertainment became the source of his misery.

He explained to her that despite him wanting to, he could not reveal to her the reason for his laughter, because he was bound by a condition. Her suspicions grew and she began nagging him to let out the secret. He helplessly told her that he would die if he did. To his dismay, even at the cost of his life, she remained persistent. She had to know the reason behind his laughter, even if it meant that her husband would die.

Although he loved her, Ashwapati decided to take a stringent step for the long-term benefit of his kingdom and banished his wife.

Keikeyi, do not repeat your mother's mistake. Let go of your stubbornness. The future of our kingdom depends on your willingness to be flexible. Unfortunately, unlike your father, Dasaratha will not kick you out for your obstinacy. He will tolerate it and allow the kingdom to suffer."

Sumantra and the hopeful Dasaratha searched for a change in her eyes, but were met with a frosty glare! Keikeyi was a block of cold, expressionless ice. If Sumantra's fiery words and Dasaratha's sweltering agony could not melt her, then nothing would!

Just as he was about to become delirious because of Rama's impending departure to the forest, Dasaratha decided to take one last shot. "Sumantra, let immeasurable amounts of riches, mountains of cereals, umpteen number of servants and multitudes of trained armies be sent along with Rama. Let Keikeyi live in a barren kingdom, enjoy void lands, deserted palaces and drained treasure troves."

Keikeyi was consumed by unbridled anger the moment she heard this. Her voice sounded alien to Dasaratha. It seemed as if a witch had taken possession of her! She spat out with a rage so venomous, a demeanor that contradicted her regal upbringing and her royal status. "Who would relish wine without spirit? Without strength, power and glory, a kingdom is nonexistent. I am not a fool to stand silently while smart ideas float in the air. Why is the Ikshvaku dynasty so surprised by the banishment of Rama? Hadn't King Sagara of our dynasty banished his son Asmanjasa? Why is it so difficult to send Rama away? Was Asmanjasa banished with all his wealth following him? Sagara just threw him into the forest. We have a precedent. Why make a big fuss now?"

Dasaratha winced at the comparison. The hapless Sumantra and Vasistha moaned as their beloved king bore insult after insult. Frustrated, one of the ministers, Siddhartha, bellowed, "Sagara banished Asmanjasa for his cruelty. He had tortured and killed innocent children for fun. Only an insane person would compare Rama with Asmanjasa!"

Dasaratha declared, "I have no reason to stay on in Ayodhya without my life. This city has become a mental asylum. I will leave along with Rama."

Rama stood unaffected by the commotion. He realized it was about time he spoke. "Rest assured, I have cheerfully given up the desire to rule this kingdom. When a person has given away his elephant, wouldn't he be called a fool to be attached to its heavy chain? After giving up the royal throne, what sense does it make to hanker for royal attendants, money or food? The forest will take care of My needs. As far as wants are concerned, answer this. Can a sieve ever be filled with water? Never! Similarly, the mind can never find fulfillment, no matter how many material things one acquires. I humbly request all of you to merely provide Me with a crowbar, a spade, a basket and garments made of tree bark."[47]

Keikeyi had already arranged for the garments and she gladly handed them over to Rama, Lakshmana and Sita. Rama began wearing the coarse garments given to Him. Lakshmana followed suit.

Sita, however, struggled with Her new rustic garments. She was so used to the most delicate and softest of silks and could not fathom how such rough clothes would stay on Her body. Every time She tried wearing it, it slipped off.

Noticing Sita struggle, Rama began gingerly helping Her into her clothes. Sita's skin was bruised by the rough material. To hurry things, Keikeyi forcibly wrapped the bark around Sita, causing Her much pain. Everyone with a heart in that room felt pierced by Sita's agony. Why did such a delicate, softhearted angel have to undergo such hurt?

Tolerance had reached its limit! Vasistha yelled at Keikeyi, "You and your perverse mind, Keikeyi! Have you decided to annihilate the noble Ikshvaku dynasty with your conduct? You trapped your husband into submitting to your desire, which was bad enough. But victimizing Sita is intolerable. You had not asked for Sita to be sent into exile. The delicate Sita need not face this hardship.

In fact, the Vedas assign to the wife the status of her husband's representative. Sita could indeed ascend the throne and rule on

---

[47] Wants are uncontrolled needs and needs are controlled wants.

When a fire is tamed, it is like a controlled want and can help cook a meal. But when untamed, the fire is like an uncontrolled need and can destroy a forest.

behalf of Rama until He returns. If Bharata is truly Dasaratha's son, he would never accept to be ruler at the cost of Rama's banishment and the anguish of millions of Ayodhya's citizens. If I know Bharata well enough, he would insist on sitting at Rama's feet rather than on an elevated throne.

Yet, even if Sita has decided to follow her husband into the forest, there is no requisite to make her wear the bark. She is after all Ayodhya's daughter-in-law. She should be decked with the most exquisite apparels, ornaments and garments."

Keikeyi, indifferent to all the banter, stepped away. Mistaking her indifference for allowance, Dasaratha ordered all kinds of ornaments, jewels and silken garments to be brought for Sita use. For Dasaratha, Sita was the goddess of fortune. How could he allow the goddess of fortune to be so poorly dressed?[48]

Realizing the succor it would bring her father-in-law, Sita decided to submit to his request. This would perhaps be his last request she could abide by. She went in and shed her simple clothes and returned modestly dressed – not too loud for the forest and not too muted to suppress her royal lineage.[49]

Realizing that everything that needed to be done was done and everything that needed to be said was said, Rama walked up to His father and requested Him to take special care of His mother

---

[48] The well-adorned Sita leaving Ayodhya implied that Rajya Lakshmi, the goddess of the kingdom, was leaving and with her was gone the fortune of Ayodhya.

[49] Sita was sensitive about not being attached to her opinion, but at the same time she did not take advantage of an allowance to enjoy here.

Kaushalya, who had never experienced such suffering in her life.

Dasaratha broke down. He introspected, "The fact that I am not yet dead despite such woe, proves that I must have been a hardened criminal in my previous birth. That I am undergoing separation from my sons definitely implies that I would have distanced some parent from his child previously."

He added sarcastically, "With changing times, the behavior of people changes. These days, in exchange for good behavior and dutiful dealings, parents reward their children with expulsion to the woods. Sumantra, take Them in a chariot up to the entrance of the woods."

Kaushalya walked up to Sita and tightly embraced Her, complimenting her on taking the bold decision of joining her husband in His struggle. She told Her how ordinary women show affection to their husbands only when their husbands provide them with sufficient resources and comforts, but how, at the first sign of discomfort and trouble, they become numb to their husbands' feelings. Not only do they harass them with acrimonious comments, but they also constantly remind them of their failures. She urged Sita to treat Rama respectfully, given the dire circumstances. "My Rama is already hurt, don't hurt Him more."

Her mother-in-law's words irked Sita, but She soon realized that these words were the result of love for her son than doubt toward her daughter-in-law. Rather than retaliate, Sita reaffirmed what Kaushalya needed to hear. "I will carry out your command, mother. But I am no ordinary woman. Being trained by glorious parents, I know My duties toward My husband. For a woman, there is a limit to how much her parents can do for her and there is a limit to how much her son can do for her, but there is actually no limit to how much a husband can do for her. Just like a *vina* without a string produces no music and a chariot without a wheel doesn't move, a woman without her husband is curtailed. I know My duties and I assure you that I will smudge My husband's sufferings with the colors of love and care."[50]

As Rama in all His humility offered His respects to mother Kaushalya and all the 350 queens, and asked forgiveness for all offenses or inconvenience He caused unwittingly, the queens were moved to tears. They were going to miss this gentle darling for 14 years![51]

With folded hands, Sita, Rama and Lakshmana circumambulated Dasaratha three times and bade the palace goodbye.

parting pangs

A lone golden chariot waited outside the palace. Two bows, quivers of arrows, spades, crowbars, bundles of clothing and boxes of ornaments were loaded onto the chariot one by one. Sumantra, an otherwise cheerful person, was sober today and his eyes were reddened because of constant crying. He stood a little away from the chariot as if not wanting to be connected with it or rather fearing it.

---

[50] In Sanskrit, the string and the *vina* are both of feminine gender and the wheel and the chariot are both of masculine gender. By using the same gender for both husband and wife, it is implied that life can be smooth only if both cooperate with mutual love and concern.

[51] Asking forgiveness is natural for those who think themselves imperfect and consider themselves prone to mistakes; however, it is more natural for those fearful of displeasing the ones they respect.

As the three figures emerged from the palace, pain ripped through the billowing crowd outside the palace. This was definitely Ayodhya's darkest hour. Even anxious horses and elephants seemed to cry in agony. Astrologers informed that the presiding star of the Ikshvaku dynasty, Vishaka, was enveloped by smoke and that four malignant planets were inching closer to the star, denoting disaster.

Only fools needed astrological predictions to confirm this when they could clearly see Rama and Lakshmana clad in plain tree bark and wooden clogs and Sita standing beside them. Disaster was distinctly visible!

Every step the trio took toward the chariot crushed the hearts of the countless citizens. What the old king was supposed to do, his young son was fulfilling. What people found difficult to accomplish in old age, Rama was doing at the peak of youth. Why was the prince renouncing everything when he ought to take up responsibility?[52]

The trio exchanged no words and quietly stepped into the chariot. Sita seemed almost gleeful when climbing into the chariot. Shouldn't the thought of going to the forest have caused her misery instead? Forest or palace, what really mattered was Rama's companionship.

The chariot sliced through Ayodhya's populace, leaving behind a trail of tears. The chariot raced farther and farther away, and with it went Ayodhya's hopes and dreams.

---

[52] Renunciation as a sacrifice when performed by the right person at the right time with the right mood generates the right gratitude, but as Rama was the wrong person demonstrating it at the wrong time, it was generating pain rather than gratitude.

Suddenly, all attention was pulled away from the moving chariot ahead to the static silence behind. For the first time since morning, the king had appeared outside his palace, not alone, but with his 353 queens flanking him. On a regular day, this panorama would have been compared to a full moon surrounded by shining stars. But today, it seemed as though they were witnessing a waning moon amid falling stars.

Dasaratha hurried down the stairs to catch up with the chariot. "Rama! Rama!" the king panted. Meanwhile, Queen Kaushalya wailed relentlessly, words failing her. The monarch was running behind the rumbling chariot like a dead body dragged by its departed soul. It was surprising that neither Rama, nor Lakshmana and Sita turned back to look even once despite Dasaratha's repeated entreaties.

Dasaratha ordered Sumantra to stop the chariot, but on hearing His father's command, Rama in turn instructed the charioteer to speed up. Sumantra was confused. Both were his masters – Rama the master of his heart and Dasaratha the master of his life. He felt like a mouse trapped between two heavy wheels, sure that he would be squished no matter which side he tilted toward.

Rama offered Sumantra a practical solution to this predicament. "Proceed at a fast pace. When you come back after leaving us, if the king asks you why you did not stop the chariot as per his command, you could say that the command couldn't be heard because of the noise of the crowd, the trumpeting of elephants and neighing of horses."

WHAT REALLY COUNTS AS TRUTH?

Could Rama be considered untruthful to have recommended that Sumantra tell a lie?

Was Dasaratha truthful to have sacrificed what he loved the most for siding with the truth?

The result of truth is not expected to be suffering.

If Sumantra had stopped the chariot as per Dasaratha's instructions, it would not have given any solace to Dasaratha, instead, it would only have increased his pain. Prolonging a painful situation is not advisable; hence, telling the truth at such a time would not be a correct decision. "I did not hear you," was the only reply that would be acceptable to Dasaratha.

In general when *punya* (piety) and *papa* (sin) are defined, helping another is *punya* and inflicting sorrow is *papa*. Such a necessary lie, though not be of any help to anyone would at least prevent harm and therefore would not inflict any *papa*.

In decreasing the pain in Dasaratha's life, Rama was not being a liar.

There are two types of truths in this world – relative truth and absolute truth. A relative truth may be a truth to someone and a lie to another. Such truths can vary. But absolute truth does not vary. It only refers to God.

To satisfy the relative truths of this world, Dasaratha gave up the absolute truth, Rama, thereby causing unlimited suffering in hundreds of people of the city.

Dasaratha's truthfulness, therefore, increased pain and Rama's untruthfulness decreased the experience of pain.

Old age and exhaustion together prevented Dasaratha from keeping pace with the fast-moving chariot; however, the able citizens of Ayodhya ran behind the chariot. The older and weaker ones fell behind, but their eyes continued to follow it.

In an attempt to give solace to their king, the ministers told him about the codes of conduct: If the king desired Rama to return safely, he should not follow Him a long distance to bid farewell. Understanding the wisdom of their words, Dasaratha abandoned his efforts to stop Rama. He watched longingly as the chariot sped away, even after it was no longer visible and the dust fanned by the wheels had settled.[53]

Dasaratha yet again collapsed in sorrow. Kaushalya and Keikeyi ran toward him to hold him. Just as Keikeyi placed her hands on Dasaratha's shoulders, he shrugged her away. "Don't touch me with your hands. I repudiate you as my wife today. If your son accepts the kingdom happily then I disown him as well. You will surely get the kingdom and I will give you the first gift – widowhood."[54]

With Kaushalya's support, Dasaratha silently walked to her palace. He told her that his eyes had gone with Rama and that he was now blind with grief. He began to caress Kaushalya's hands, smell them and kiss them repeatedly. These hands had fondled Rama for

---

[53] From this day, one of the names of Lord Rama became *drishti-chit-apahari*, meaning one who through His eyes steals the heart of the one who sees Him.

[54] A person whose dream is shattered always retaliates against the person whose dream is fulfilled. At night, many dreams together can be fulfilled, but during the day, fulfillment of one's dream may annul another's.

Connected to the dreams of leaders are the dreams of followers, thus, a single shattered dream causes a domino effect.

the longest time and were naturally the most intimate reminders of Him.

Slowly as the sun began to set, unknown fears began to well up inside Kaushalya's heart. Over the past three days, the setting sun had been hiding different colors of sadness. Beginning with Dasaratha's nightmare to Keikeyi's haunting boons to the ghostly desolation of Ayodhya, dusk had only increased the horror.

As Kaushalya sat on her soft bed, she began to sob, reminded that her son would have to sleep on hard stones. "How can I sleep peacefully when I know my son won't even have proper food to eat? The lioness Keikeyi has driven my calf into the forest for other animals to devour. How can a mother, to protect her own child, destroy another's child?"[55]

Sumitra, Lakshmana's mother and her co-wife, came to console Kaushalya with sweet words. She reminded her that Rama was a repository of divine virtues. He had not gone to the forest, but instead, entered the garden of righteousness. She reminded Kaushalya that a son who would go through such trouble just to prove the greatness of his father definitely couldn't be ordinary. The world may have seen him go without any fortification. But according to Sumitra, Rama had the armor of purity, the shield of virtue and the wealth of truthfulness. She reminded Kaushalya that Rama had an able servant in Lakshmana and a chaste partner in Sita. Being of such high character and in the company of people who loved him

---

[55] A woman is like the earth. When she bursts with compassion, clear water comes out, but when she bursts with envy, molten lava comes out.

But when both cool down, water and lava combine to create a mega-blast. When the same woman has extreme compassion toward one and intense envy toward another, the combination creates disaster.

more than their own life, Rama could not be unhappy.

Sumitra guided Kaushalya out of unhappiness to hope by telling her that she should assume her natural role as a brave woman, who wasn't impeded by personal calamities but provided comfort to the weak minded.

For the first time in the day, Kaushalya smiled. Both women then held hands and turned their attention to the crestfallen king.

Would the king survive the entire trauma?

Would those of Ayodhya's citizens who followed Rama manage to convince Him to return? Or would they return with shattered dreams too?

CHAPTER 6

A FOREST WEEPS

A vast ocean of adoration gushed toward the golden chariot. A million and more surges of affection trying ceaselessly to engulf the carriage as it made its way toward the mammoth gates of Ayodhya with their beloved Rama, Lakshmana and Sita. Today, it was not the daunting entry that blocked the chariot, it was love – deep, unrelenting, effusive love. Just as the unfathomable, water-filled moat surrounding the city walls always stopped enemies from making their way in, this ocean of people within the city walls were attempting to stop the trio from leaving Ayodhya's shores. And what an ocean it was! Born out of the countless salt tears shed by Ayodhya's hapless residents, this ocean of love had now surrounded the chariot, hoping to hold Rama back.

For Ayodhya's citizens, Rama was *Matsya avatar* that had once saved the world from the ocean of devastation. What was Rama doing now? Was He saving them from the ocean of devastation or throwing them into an ocean of desperation? He didn't swim in the ocean like the *Matsya avatar* this time, instead He sat on the boat and watched them drown haplessly. Had the beautiful incarnation become hard hearted like the beautiful queen of Ayodhya?

From high on the chariot, Sumantra could see Ayodhya reeling under the devastation of being ripped from Rama. The people, the birds and the animals, all frozen from sorrow, their eyes transfixed on Rama and tears streaking their cheeks, they stood so still that they seemed like lifeless etchings on a mega canvas named Ayodhya.

Sumantra blinked away his tears. Ayodhya now seemed like a colossal crematorium – every house resembled a funeral parlor and every remorseful citizen like a ghost. They consciously avoided eye contact with Sumantra, their messenger of death. It was almost as if Keikeyi had set every house on fire, and the sorrow-filled wild flames from the burning were so intense that Ayodhya's streams and ponds, which could otherwise douse any blaze, were now scorched pits instead! Every tree was bare; each had shed its purpose of living. At this point, Rama was like a green pot of celestial elixir, and every drop of nectar that dripped from His mouth could be lifesaving.[1]

Rama stood at a plane much higher than the citizens and much higher than Sumantra, not only physically, but spiritually and intellectually, too. As Rama stood watching the wailing crowd, He smiled, knowing full well that it was time to raise their plane of understanding.[2] This smile was not that of a grateful prince bidding goodbye but that of a loving father sharing knowledge.[3]

As soon as Rama's ruddy lips moved, the lifeless paintings began to

---

[1] Words of inspiration spoken by the wise are like lozenges. They have the power to soothe and rejuvenate a devastated heart.

[2] Alliance with air (that is accustomed to soaring high) elevates a balloon to the high skies. Without air, the balloon remains in the lower plane. Only those higher on the inner plane can elevate the lower ones.

[3] A king or leader has many roles to play: He is a friend, a well-wisher, a subordinate, a protector, and often a father, who has to educate and encourage his children.

breathe. "The love of followers is the best form of encouragement for a leader. The love all of you have for Me is evident through your tears. If you love someone truly, you should strive to please that person the way he/she wants to be pleased.[4]

The genuineness of your love for Me will be tested if you follow two things[5]: One is to make sure that the king does not suffer any agony because of your thoughts, words or actions, the other is to repose in Bharata the love and faith that you have in Me, because he will prove to be a very dynamic and caring king; he may be young in age (*vayobaalah*), but he is ripe in wisdom (*jnanavriddhah*); he is gentle in his demeanor (*mriduhuh*), but fierce in combat (*viryagunanvitah*). If you can do these two things for the next 14 years, I can assure you that you will please Me by showing your real love for Me."[6]

The more Rama glorified Bharata, the more the citizens felt drawn toward Him as their king. With every word, Rama captured every corner of their heart, leaving no room for anyone else. How could they explain this to Him?

The crowd's emotions notwithstanding, Rama signaled Sumantra to steer the chariot toward the gate. As the carrier edged toward the exit, so did the crowd. As was expected, the younger, fitter ones managed to push themselves close to the chariot and hence, in closer

---

[4] Love is not a passive monologue but an action-packed movie that ends with pleasing the beloved.

[5] Paradoxical leadership is about a leader having qualities that seem inconsistent and contrary, but which make the leader wholesome and accommodative.

[6] Today, people are unlike Bharata. They may be old in age but are children when it comes to wisdom or gentle in a fight but ferocious in mannerism.

proximity to Rama, while the not-so-energetic elderly staggered helplessly behind. In all the mêlée, an old *brahmana*'s piteous wail caught Rama's attention. The *brahmana*, addressing neither Rama nor Sumantra, said, "O horses! Come back! I beseech you to return with Rama to the city."

Rama turned toward the direction of the cry and spotted the aging, fragile frame of the *brahmana*.[7] Alongside him were many more such *brahmanas* whose hearts chorused the same words. He saw their heads trembling with weakness and age. Rama stepped off the chariot, followed by the angelic goddess and the faithful brother and walked toward the exit gate. The *brahmanas* offered the shade of the clouds to Rama as he walked toward the forest. The chariot didn't move toward the forest, it stood in oblivion, unnoticed by anyone.

When the city gates opened, Rama emerged like His ancestor, Bhagiratha, who had brought down the celestial Ganga. Just as the Ganga followed Bhagiratha, this ocean of citizens followed Rama; the only difference was that Ganga had flowed mirthfully behind Bhagiratha, but Ayodhya's sad souls flowed despondently.

As Rama walked on, His wife and brother behind Him, the citizens beseeched Him to return to the kingdom. Only silence followed the entreaties.

Ram's eyes were riveted ahead, His lips sealed. On realizing that all the imploring was futile, the people pursed their lips. But no

---

[7] Sensitivity of the strong is hope for the weak.

Sensitivity is natural for a delicate artist and insensitivity is inbred in a crude warrior.

Rama's display of sensitivity was not a politician-like gimmick to impress his vote bank, but the spontaneous action of a soft, caring non-scheming heart.

matter how much they tried, their eyes refused to comply – the tears were relentless. As they ambled behind Rama, they could feel warm drops on their shoulders. They looked up to find birds atop trees also weeping.

As the entourage ventured ahead for a few hours, each person had only one thought: is there anyone who can stop Rama from going into the forest?

As Rama walked on and the trailing crowd kept crying, almost as if trying to stall the Sun Prince's progress toward the forest, the Tamasa river transformed into a wall and the sun disappeared behind the mountains. The sun, too, wanted Rama to stay back in Ayodhya for one more night. Soon the sky turned as dark as Keikeyi's mind, the very mind Manthara had poisoned.

"Let's halt for the night here on the banks of the Tamasa." Rama instructed Sumantra, who was following them, riding the chariot alone. Sumantra released the tired horses to graze, as the citizens found their own resting spots along the banks of the river. For as far as one could see, there were humans everywhere – on sand mounds, on the river's *ghats*, in gardens, under trees and even on tree tops!

Rama chose to spend that evening fasting, sipping a little river water and doing what He had been wishing to do for 14 years: listening to great souls.[8] He sat at the feet of great sages, soaking in their sagaciousness.[9]

---

[8] When one studies great books, one gains knowledge; however, when one hears great souls, one receives wisdom.

Wisdom is knowledge digested by humility and realized by application.

[9] Rama began a new episode in His life by embracing humility and austerity. When one embraces humility, no embarrassment is awful.

At a scenic yet protected spot, Lakshmana and Sumantra prepared a bed of leaves and flowers for Sita and Rama. As Rama began to lie gratefully on the bed, He poured out His heart. "This is Our first night in the forest. Look at the birds settling down into the cozy comforts of their abodes. For 14 years, We will not have anything We can call Our home.

Back home, those who could not accompany Us must be miserable. I pray that father and mother don't become blind with all the crying. Only Bharata's kind-heartedness gives Me confidence. By coming with Me, Lakshmana, you have done a good deed. Your company will help Me handle this calamity confidently."

The weary Prince talked away to sleep and the worn-out Sita dozed off, exhausted from the extreme events of the day.

Lakshmana noticed that within seconds sleep had prevailed over the tired travelers.

But tiredness was not a luxury two people could afford. Lakshmana and Sumantra were all eyes and all ears as Rama and Sita slumbered in the distance under a giant tree. The two men sat watchful, revealing their hearts to each other. Lakshmana was all praise for Rama, glorifying Him profusely, utterly fascinated by each of his brother's gestures.

Before long, the topic drifted from Rama to the day's events. Lakshmana could now steal time to reflect upon his own life. All day long, his focus had been Rama and nothing else. Now that there was the mind space, his thoughts rushed back to the morning and to Sumitra's palace. He confided in Sumantra.

a mother sets free

Earlier, Lakshmana had tiptoed into the palace, as scared as a deer walking into a hunter's snare. Would the net of love entangle him and keep him away from his mission? Would he become entwined in strong emotions? Lakshmana had been in two minds as he approached Sumitra's palace. Should he be tender because this would be the last time he would meet his mother in private before leaving for the forest for 14 years? Should he be firm, considering she was the last obstacle that could prevent him from accompanying Rama? One mother (Keikeyi) had taken away the kingdom from Rama, goaded by affection for her own son Bharata. Will another mother (Sumitra) now take away service from Lakshmana, forced by her attachment to her son?

Lakshmana's mind had been pulling in opposite directions, torn by how his mother would react.

But even before Lakshmana had spoken, his mother had pacified him: "Today, what I desired for as I drank the celestial nectar is being fulfilled. Both my sons have found the opportunity for service toward their siblings – Shatrughna serves Bharata and Lakshmana serves Rama.[10] You are born to rule the kingdom of service, Lakshmana. No one can ever dethrone you from this one kingdom. Rule happily. Your subjects are your senses, your desires and your mind."[11]

---

[10] The position of service is devoid of any coveting, competition or conspiracy. It is filled with permanence, pleasure and protection.

[11] The only competition an assistant faces is from a questioning mind. The mind inspires competition by asking, "Don't you want to be master one day?"

Sumitra had continued:[12]

Ramamdasarathamviddhi
Maamviddhijanakatmajam
Ayodhyamathavimviddhi
Gaccha tat yathasukham

"O Lakshmana, from hereon, Rama is like your father, Sita like your mother and the forest, like Ayodhya, your home. And let your only source of pleasure come from following and serving Rama."[13]

Saying these words,[14] Sumitra had broken down.[15] Lakshmana had gone closer to her and held her gently for some time. As soon as she was steady, he had pulled away from her, touched her feet and run out of the palace.

As he had scuttled down the palace stairs, Lakshmana had breathed easy.[16] He had felt like a deer that had escaped out of the hunter's strong snare. But there was a difference: This hunter had let go.

---

[12] When the aim of life changes from pleasing the ego to pleasing God, it changes from egocentric to god-centric.

[13] Sumitra represents a glorious parent who inspires and instructs the child to live a life centered on discipline rather than indulgence.

[14] When duty clashes with love, most people compromise duty, using love as justification. Duty should use intelligence and love should use the heart.

[15] Sumitra used her brain to suppress her heart until she had made a decision. Once through with the tough part, through her tears, she allowed her heart to burst with love.

[16] Every family needs balancers who can prevent emotions from tipping.
    Lakshmana was emotional, but the cool Sumitra acted as the balancer. Kaushalya, too, was emotional, but a calm Rama acted as the balancer.

a wife lets go

Lakshmana had no idea what he was in for. As he had stealthily entered Urmila's chambers, he had ensured that no sound escaped, because this delicate fairy was always in her own dream world. And dreams break at the hint of a tinkle! Urmila, the beautiful wife of Lakshmana, was an exemplary artist. She immersed herself daily in painting canvases. No one except Lakshmana was allowed anywhere near her when she was in her painting frenzy.

She had been painting her favorite couple, Rama and her sister Sita, that fateful day. It was a rather serious depiction – the coronation of the most exquisite couple in the universe! In fact, she had just finished painting it. Urmila considered it her masterpiece and had planned to gift it to the royal couple as soon as they returned from their coronation.

KABOOM!

A clatter somewhere nearby had startled the sensitive Urmila. Her masterpiece had been ruined. The bowl of wet paint in her hands had splashed all over the painting, defacing it completely.

Angrily, she had turned around to see what had made her jump right into her priceless painting. Her anger had dissipated the moment she had seen her guilty-faced husband trying to gather vase shards.

"My dear Lord, look what just happened! I was painting Lord Rama's and Sita's coronation scene. This is an inauspicious omen. What do I do, my Lord?"

"You can now paint it 14 years from now, Urmila. Rama has been

exiled to the forest for 14 years, and Bharata will be king instead."
Lakshmana had said in an attempt to pacify his beloved wife.

"What? How could this happen?"

"You will understand everything with time. What you need to
understand now is that the delicate Sita will accompany Rama to
the forest. And… to serve Them both… I must go, too."

Urmila had grasped the situation and immediately gathered herself.
An awkward silence had followed. Lakshmana had nothing to
say. But, before the hush could stretch too long, Urmila had said
something that would remain etched in Lakshmana's heart and be
his beacon of hope through the next 14 years.

"Opportunities to serve superiors come unsought to ones who
yearn for them. Creating an atmosphere for another to serve in a
focused manner is also service. I would love to accompany you to
the forest, but I will not. My joining in would invariably come in
the way of your service to Rama. Your duty could be compromised
because of my presence.

The duty of a wife is to constantly be in the company of her husband.
But to fulfill my duty, how can I obstruct yours, my Lord? Performing
a duty serves its purpose only when the object of duty is pleased. If
I insist that I do my duty to you by accompanying you, you will be
displeased because the object of your duty, Rama, will be displeased
with your negligence. So, my duty now is to facilitate the perfection
you can attain in your responsibility by staying away.

The essence of your going with Rama is sacrifice. You are sacrificing
your comforts, your wife, your wealth, your opinion and your
pleasures. My Lord, following your example, I am sacrificing my

desires and my duties.[17] The real duty of a wife is to understand the mood[18] of her husband."

a brother stands by

Sumantra could not hold back his tears as Lakshmana narrated the incident. With her sacrifice, Urmila had captured his heart forever. Lakshmana was overcome with emotion. He could speak no more. He stood up and walked away. Sumantra reflected, "What kind of a family is this? Everyone tries to forget himself or herself and focus on what pleases the other. But, amid such illustrious people, how could a mind such as Keikeyi's exist? Strange!" Sumantra then stretched himself out for a short nap to prepare for the day ahead.[19]

---

[17] People follow rules and regulations to show the world that they are duty conscious. But often, we perform our duties and create hurdles for others and prevent them from performing their duties the best they can; therefore, more important than duties is the purpose with which one performs them. Urmila sacrificed her duties to serve her husband, but she rightly embraced the mood behind performing her duties.

[18] Mood management from a hedonistic principle is about making those you love understand your mood and comply.

Mood management from an ascetic principle is about striving to understand the mood of those you love and complying accordingly.

[19] It is interesting that the four brothers represent good qualities and their wives represent the process that has to be followed to achieve those qualities.

Lakshmana represents the quality of righteousness; Urmila represents the quality of faith. By being extremely faithful one attains righteousness. Urmila assisted Lakshmana by being faithful.

Rama represents the quality of perfection; Sita represents peace. To achieve perfection, one has to be peaceful in all situations of life.

Bharata represents auspicious desires; Mandhavi represents

Lakshmana leaned against a tree bark with his arms folded above; he placed his forehead on his arms and murmured to himself. "I am so fortunate to have such a mother and wife. I may be lucky to serve directly, but these two have the fortune of pleasing Rama through their attitudes."[20]

A silvery feminine voice startled him and dragged him out of his musings. "I have come to serve you, O hero. I am *Nidradevi*, the goddess of sleep. It is too late now, your body is weary. Let my magic recuperate your energy. This is my service to society."

Lakshmana raised his head and turned away from her. Raising his arms toward the moon, he proclaimed, "Today I take a vow, for the next 14 years I will not sleep a wink. All day I will serve my brother and all night I will stay guard protecting Him."

The goddess of sleep was aghast. She said, "How is this possible? I have to serve you. You cannot disobey nature's laws."

Lakshmana suggested, "Go to my wife, Urmila, who is in Ayodhya. She will accept your service on my behalf."

Nidradevi left for Ayodhya. Urmila consented, and for the next

---

enthusiasm. To fulfill the auspicious desire of seeing Rama one should cultivate eagerness.

Shatrughna represents wealth; Shrutikirti represents service. Wealth becomes meaningful only when used in service.

[20] Being members of the same family is not just about looking similar but having similar moods. A tiger and a cat may belong to the same family, but have different moods.

A family in which every member strives to motivate others into the best mood experiences harmony and satisfaction.

14 years, she slept during the day on behalf of Lakshmana and at night for herself.

IS LOVE CONFINED TO PHYSICAL PROXIMITY?

As the distance between two hearts increases, the repulsion between two bodies escalates.

It is better to be mentally close and physically away than the reverse!

Real separation is the distance in mindsets. To be physically far and yet mentally close requires maturity and mutual respect of purpose.

Lakshmana was engaged in serving Rama by forgoing sleep for 14 years and Urmila showed inertia in serving Lakshmana by sleeping for 14 years. But both focused on serving the one they loved. They demonstrate mental proximity unaffected by physical distance.

---

a prince slips away

The gentle rustling of leaves did not escape Lakshmana's sharp ears. As he raced back toward his treasure, Rama and Sita, several thoughts began rushing into his mind: Who could be moving at this late hour? Was it a hungry animal prowling? Or was it an enemy?

Relieved to see it was only Rama searching for something, Lakshmana ran up to Him and paid his respects. "What can I do for You? Do You need something?" he asked eagerly.

Placing His arms around Lakshmana's broad shoulders,[21] Rama said, "I was looking for you Lakshmana. I have just made a decision. A king's foremost duty is to relieve his subjects of the difficulties they bring upon themselves. The personal challenges a king faces should never be shared with his followers. The only thing a king can share is their difficulty. Weak is the king who puts his followers in trouble to get relief from his personal difficulty.[22] Dealing with difficulties strengthens a person.[23]

The citizens' determination shows that they would rather give up their lives than give up their resolve to follow Me. If their determination to put up with inconvenience is so strong, then My determination to prevent them from being inconvenienced is stronger. Let us depart from this place well before they wake up!"

With Sumantra's help, Lakshmana readied the horses while Rama woke Sita up. While it was still dark, the four mounted the chariot and crossed the shallow section of the river. Rama, Sita and Lakshmana then dismounted from the chariot. Rama instructed Sumantra to ride the chariot northward before re-crossing the river and to cleverly take the chariot back to where They were. Needless to say, Sumantra had to do it in a way that would make the citizens feel that Rama had probably returned to Ayodhya.

---

[21] The desire to shift your burden to another's shoulder is always foremost when the burden is heavy and the duration long.

[22] A leader's expertise is not about how adroitly he or she can offload his or her burden, but about how gratefully he or she can handle the load.

[23] Just as the struggle to push against a heavy weight strengthens the muscles, the struggle to hold the heavy burden of responsibility on one's own shoulder strengthens the leader.

But when one adopts deception compassionately to reduce another's burden, it is called deliberation.

Confused, they would have no choice but to return as well.

Soon the chariot was flying like the wind toward Kosala's borders.

Meanwhile, the trio was delighted at the sights and smells of the beautiful countryside, something they had not really experienced so often.

an entourage gives up

"Where is the chariot? Where are the horses?" shrieked the citizens as soon as they woke up in the morning.

"Fools, you are worried about the chariot? Where are Rama and Sita? Where are Lakshmana and Sumantra?" shouted some others as they ran helter-skelter desperately searching for their lost treasure. Soon thousands of people were running amok, trying to find the lost royals.

An old sage crouched on the ground and cried out slapping his head with his palms, "Great souls say sleep is an enemy. It is an impediment to progress. Today I realized this truth. I curse this slumber that caused us to lose Rama!"

"Sleeping is fine, but why weren't we alert in our sleep? Don't the great souls say that those who want to make advancements should sleep like a dog? Alert." expressed another.

Some said, "Don't waste time lamenting. Let us track the chariot by following its wheel marks. They could not have gone too far."

As they tracked the chariot's impressions, their confusion compounded when the tracks led them toward Ayodhya. Anxious and distressed, they returned to Ayodhya. Anxious because of the faint hope that Rama could have returned home, but distressed by the greater possibility that Rama could have given them the slip and ventured into the forest.[24]

"Where are Rama, Sita and Lakshmana? Why have you all returned without them? All of you are useless! We survived one night trusting your abilities to persuade Rama to return. Death will surely consume us tonight." The women shouted at their sullen-faced husbands.

Soon everyone realized that Rama had abandoned them. The towering gates of Ayodhya became a mourning ground. No sooner than they understood the truth, people slumped where they were and cried bitterly.

Ayodhya had lost its charm: Like the sky without the moon, the sea without water, a tunnel without an end, a tree without fruits, the city was left without joy. The miracle city was now a miserable city.

It surely was a black day in Ayodhya's history. Mothers who gave birth that day considered their children to be ill-starred; merchants stopped exhibiting wares; none ate or drank; none even cooked; even cats did not enter houses to steal milk; dogs stopped barking, they only whined and constant streams of tears brimmed over from the hapless eyes of countless cows in Ayodhya.

Discussions revolved only around their misfortune. One anguished citizen said, "The fish are really fortunate for they can't live for more

---

[24] Great souls trick for a great cause.

than a few seconds after being taken out of water. But we are so hard-hearted that despite no longer being in Rama's company for one full day, we don't seem to embrace death."

Another suggested, "So what if death does not come to us? Let us go to the abode of death ourselves. Just like dry logs are arranged to burn a funeral fire, let us all burn together in the fire of estrangement from Rama."

Continuing with the melancholy, another voice added: "If we don't allow our bodies to enter the fire of separation voluntarily, our egos will be pushed into the fire of frustration of Keikeyi's instructions. This city has transformed overnight from stark white to pitch black. Soon every person in the city will have unsettled minds and negative ambitions. Is it not said that every citizen mirrors the ruler? With Keikeyi in command, what hope is there for us? If she could abandon her husband and her children, why would she care for us at all? All of us will be handed over to Bharata like helpless animals to the slaughterhouse. King Dasaratha, if I understand him rightly, will not survive this ordeal."

To check the intensely negative atmosphere and the nauseating reeling of minds, a sensitive sage kindled some positivity by taking their minds back to the forest. "The forest, mountains and rivers are most fortunate. They will have the constant association of Lord Rama. Why should we live in this city? Let us all go to the forest! The men can all serve Rama and the women can serve Sita. Instead of thinking of dying, why don't we think of living in a forest, a place where even the name of Keikeyi will not enter?"

Just the thought of living with Rama instantly lit up the thousands of faces that were mourning. Every one remembered the last instruction that Rama had given them before setting out for the forest. Silently, they got up and went back into their houses. The darkness of the night embraced Ayodhya, putting an end to a day of distress.

a river teaches how

After crossing the Vedasruti river, the chariot blazed past the Gomati river.[25] One glance at the Gomati river and Sita was mesmerized by it. The name of the river was apt, considering the spectacular view it offered. Countless cows were grazing on the soft grass by the banks. Sita learned from this river that one should be true to one's nature and repute. And how fortunate she was to travel with Rama, who always lived up to His reputation of being righteous![26]

Sita's rapturous giggles lightened Lakshmana's sober mood. He had no idea what had made Her crack up under the circumstances, so he turned toward his Brother and Sister-in-Law, to find them watching a mirthful pair of mating geese. Lakshmana realized that the least this exile could offer Rama was privacy with Sita. Sita suddenly caught Lakshmana staring at Them and She blushed. This embarrassed Lakshmana, so he swore never to look at the couple together for the next 14 years and decided to guard them from a distance, allowing them Their privacy while still ensuring Their safety.

Rama drew Sita's attention to some farmers removing water lily pads from their farms to wild growth. What was a weed for a farmer was

---

[25] Go means cow, and Gomati means the one who constantly thinks about cows or the mother of cows.

[26] If you allow others to define your reputation, then you allow them to paint your character; however, if character defines your reputation, then your actions define trends.

beauty for a nature lover! Rama lovingly compared Sita's eyes to the exquisite blue water lily petals. She suddenly began pondering over what Rama had just said about weeds. Did that statement have a hidden implication?

Did Rama mean that even though the cruel farmer Keikeyi may have extracted Him from the field of Ayodhya, the nature lover Sita considered this Her fortune?

Many of Rama's statements mystified Sita, for they seemed loaded with some deeper meaning. But She never clarified, for She knew some things were best left unanswered.[27]

Suddenly, Rama started laughing loudly and clapping. He looked more attractive when He laughed so heartily. When She followed His gaze, She, too, burst into peals of laughter. Drawn by the clear waters of the Syandika river, a herd of buffaloes crashed into the water. Women who were washing clothes, half submerged in the river, jumped up in alarm and ran asunder in disgust and fear. Not just the women, but everything in and around the river was thrown into disarray – large fishes leaped out of the water, bees quietly drawing honey from the flowers on the banks, swarmed away from the flowers startled by the group dive. So much had happened in such little time that the couple seemed thoroughly entertained. Lakshmana and Sumantra smiled, too, happy that They were happy.

Sobering down, Rama told Sita that this river marked the southern boundary of the colossal Kosala province. Because He had reached

---

[27] Predicting the mind of God is like predicting the final picture after seeing one piece of the puzzle. Rather than decoding God's intelligence, one should begin relying on it.

the border of His motherland,[28] Rama reverentially saluted and paid His respects. Tears streamed down His cheeks with gratitude for what the land had done for Him and His family.[29] While leaving Ayodhya behind, the circumstances were such that He could not pay His respects to the glorious city, surrounded as He was by throngs of people. At least now He could cry in peace.

As the sun began its slow descent, Sumantra brought the chariot to a trot, touching the banks of the Holy Ganga. For thousands of years, these banks had adorned the dust of the feet of exalted personalities. Great kingdoms, monarchs, sages had come and gone, but the Ganga had gone on forever. The four paid their respects to the great river that embodied purity and culture. The river had gained fame as a sin slayer. As soon as one comes near this river, it forces you to contemplate on your sins.

MEDITATIONS ON GANGA

1. The distillation of the proclivity to sin that one acquires by regret is far more important than just the purification of sin that comes as a result of bathing in the Ganga.

2. Many objects in the Vedic culture such as the Ganga remind one of the results of one's actions rather than just being impressed

---

[28] Rama addressed his land of birth as motherland for accommodating and molding Him.

[29] A mother is duty-bound to serve the child without any expectations. And the child is free to express gratitude without any obligation. When the mother considers her duty to be a burden and the child considers the fulfillment of its desires to be its right, then both seal the doors of their hearts with locks of expectations.

by the vigor of the action. The flowing river forces you to stop and contemplate on your flow of deeds.

3. The river represents a blend of the temporary, fleeting nature of life and the eternal, consistent nature of legacy. Just as drops of water keep moving away but the river stays, in life, situations and people may move away, but the legacy stays. Leaders move on, but leadership stays; parents move on, but their love and guidance stays and teachers move on, but education stays.

4. Just as drops of the river may quench the thirst of many, but have a personal quest to reach their destination (the ocean), in life, one should serve as many but not forget one's personal quest for perfection (liberation).

5. The river also represents the need to change with the passage of time. Just as new drops replace old drops, new ideas should replace old ones; fresh innovations should replace outdated ones; clear mindsets should replace polluted ones and keep steady the integrated principles that stand the test of time just as the Ganga does.

As the effulgent Rama arrived, sages performing penance on the banks of the river ran toward Him like swans toward a lotus.[30] They chorused: "The final goal of our life has been achieved." They drank the nectar of Rama's beautiful face with their eyes. Some of the most serious sages, many of them hundreds of years old, began

---

[30] Sages are called *paramhansa* or great swans. Because they emulate the quality of a swan, their expertise lies in separating milk from water. They don't accept a compromised lifestyle no matter how lucrative.

to dance in ecstasy, swiveling their shawls in the air as a bemused Sita watched their delight.[31]

Rama and Sita then took a holy dip in the Ganga and offered their evening prayers. As soon Lord Rama's feet touched the waters, the water level rose, as if brimming with joy. Ganga was finally able to behold the same feet that were the cause of her descent to this world.[32] The river felt as ecstatic as a new bride.

a chieftain keeps vigil

After choosing to halt for the night under a huge fig tree on the banks of the river, Rama asked Sumantra to let the horses rest. Lakshmana quickly created the softest seat possible for Sita and Rama.

Just as they were settling down, a group of tribal people with

---

[31] Spiritual life isn't about forsaking enjoyment. It's about embracing a higher level of enjoyment. The sages had long forsaken attraction to beauty that deteriorates and had been eagerly waiting for the beauty of Rama that enhances with time. Rama, known as *aparyamrita*, is one whose beauty enhances with time.

[32] When Rama had earlier appeared as Vaamanadev to claim all the three worlds from Bali *maharaja*, He had raised His foot to cover the entire upper planetary system until His toe pierced the outer shell of the universe. The ocean of milk cascaded down the lotus feet of Vaamanadev and trickled down to the heavenly planets passing through Brahma's planet. Grabbing the opportunity to wash the feet of the Lord, Brahma poured waters from his divine pot. This holy water combined with the water of the milk ocean descended to the heavens and became known as Mandakini Ganga. And when the same river reached further down to Earth under the influence of King Bhagiratha, it became Mother Ganga.

resounding drums, glaring torches and ululating women surrounded them. Lakshmana steadied his bow, anticipating an attack. The caution alarm in his head turned off only when the most elaborately dressed among them, their leader, stepped forward with folded hands.

"Welcome to Sringaberapura!" Rama rose up and rushed to meet him.

"This is surely Guha, the *stapati* or king of the *Nishada* tribe. He was a great friend of My father," Rama said as he hastened forward.

The two embraced one another and exchanged pleasantries. The chief introduced Rama to all his ministers and relatives. While the two were talking, Lakshmana took time off his vigil to observe the attire and the personality of the chief.

The chief had a pack of dogs guarding him. His tightly wrapped leather garment was held together by a uniquely embroidered waist belt that was embedded with tiger nails. His muscular limbs flashed amulets and anklets made of stones. A necklace of colorful shells adorned his beefy chest. Long sturdy, strapped leather sandals concealed his robust feet. His shoulder-length curly hair was adorned by an ornate helmet made of multicolored cloth and vibrant plumes. A formidable, strung bow hung over one of his stocky shoulders and a quiver of arrows lazily slung across his taut torso over the side of his other shoulder.

Lakshmana was amazed to see Rama showering so much love on this tribal chief; an aristocratic prince being friendly with a subordinate tribal chief, a rare spectacle indeed![33]

---

[33] Specializations often metamorph into proud isolations. But Rama, despite being an expert at so many things, was *sausilya* or amicable.

Guha's voice was authoritative, but his demeanor docile when he spoke to Rama. "It is such an honor to see You here my Lord. I may be the lord of a thousand boats and the master of an entire kingdom, but I am the humble servant of Your father and Your divine self. I am sold to Your goodness.

When news of what transpired in Ayodhya two days ago blazed into Sringaberapura, I found it hard to digest the act of the righteous Dasaratha. It just showed that even the best people have flaws."[34]

The whispers Rama had heard all through His journey over the last two days were loud and clear now.

Guha continued, "Do not worry, Lord Rama, You may have lost Ayodhya, but You have gained Sringaberapura. From this day forth, this city is Yours. You may have lost many servants, but You have gained a slave dog named Guha who can do anything for You. Please instruct your bondsman."

Bowing, Guha tendered himself to Rama. No sooner than Guha finished talking, his people laid a spread of excellently prepared dishes. After supervising the display of all the dishes, Guha offered them all to Rama. "All these lands belong to Your kingdom; we are Your subjects now and to serve You is our life's purpose. Your comforts are my responsibility. The best of food, the best of drinks

---

Rama's extraordinary demeanor just as much touched ordinary people as it did the royals; his uncommonness was just as accessible to the common folk as to those who lived in palaces. God is impartial when raining His mercy, be it hard rock or soft grass, fragrant roses or obnoxious corpse flowers, tamed fields or wild forests.

[34] The environment you allow yourself to be in causes you to be good or bad. After dipping your hand in water, you cannot complain of wetness.

and the best of accommodations are at Your disposal. We entreat You to rule us."

Rama responded with deep gratitude, "Your hospitality is par excellence and is only defeated by your love toward Me. We are very honored to have such a respectable leader as yourself visit Us.

I am grateful for these wonderful arrangements, but I apologize as I must decline your offer. I am bound by My vow to be an ascetic, to wear robes of tree bark and deerskin and to survive on roots and fruits for the next 14 years. An untamed mind can only be restrained by *sankalpa* or vows.[35]

If you really want to serve, you can do so by supplying nutritious forage to the king's horses. These steeds are his favorite, and by feeding them you will surely gain the king's favor."[36]

As Guha set out to execute this order, Rama ate fruits and water Lakshmana had procured for him. Farther down the river bank, Sumantra sat hunched and was crying bitterly. What a calamity! The same person who had appeared as Mohini Murti and distributed

---

[35] The discontent mind can never reach a state of fulfillment when flooded with attraction to material things, just as a sieve can never be filled with water.

   Just as the rushing water of a river uproots the trees on its banks, the restless and unrestrained mind can uproot one's existence.

[36] Was Rama being sarcastic?

   Did Rama actually mean that by feeding Him, Guha would gain nothing, but by feeding the horses, he might stand to gain from Dasaratha?

   Or did Rama imply that now in Ayodhya animals are given more love than people?

   Should we thus conclude that when people become animalistic (thinking of their own needs), the sense of whom to love more is lost?

celestial nectar to all the demigods was now relegated to eating roots and fruits. He could not face Rama and Sita, so he stayed away.

Before long, the divine couple was fast asleep on the velvety green grass bed that Lakshmana had painstakingly prepared. Bordering the grass bed with fragrant forest flowers was the best Lakshmana could do to ensure their comfort under the given circumstances.

To shake the old minister off his despondency, Lakshmana hurled a question at him: "Why is this place called Sringaberapura?" An opportunity to serve the virtuous princes was the only thing that could haul the old charioteer out of his depression. He perked up instantly. "This place gets its name from the unique hunting techniques used by the tribal people here. They make a stuffed deer that resembles a real deer. Feeling drawn to the attractive stuffed deer, the real deer lingers around trying to establish an irrational contact. That moment of weakness is what the clever hunters wait for. Within moments, the deer finds itself struggling in a snare, startled and bewildered at the sight of the motionless, stuffed deer."[37] Lakshmana smiled as he learned his first lesson of forest life: survival of the cleverest!

Sumantra had spent the whole of the previous night struggling with his sleep, so he excused himself to make up for it. Lakshmana turned toward his sleeping brother and sister-in-law; he could neither stop tears from gushing out of his eyes nor prevent anger from gripping his heart. He battled with himself to shake off these feelings and do

---

[37] A dummy deer teaches that your mind may mislead you. It may make you imagine something far removed from the truth, what your mind makes you see may not be what you get; therefore, it is not worth giving up your life for. Mirages don't exist in deserts; they only exist in the mind.

his job: be on vigil. Lakshmana stood up, bow in hand, and began pacing around the sleeping Rama and Sita, maintaining sufficient distance to ensure that the rustling from his footsteps did not disturb the weary couple.

Nothing but the rhythmic shuffle of Lakshmana's footsteps could be heard through the night; until Lakshmana's sharp ears perked to the sound of a heavier set of footsteps nearby. Lakshmana lunged to catch the intruder unawares. It was the burly figure of Guha, with his bow in hand. Lakshmana was taken aback. Why would he come back so late at night? Deciding to confront him, Lakshmana emerged in front of the tribal chief.

An equally confused Guha asked Lakshmana: "Why are you still awake, sir? You are not used to the austerities of forest life. You are our guests, please go and sleep, I will guard Rama and Sita. I know the forest in and out and all the traps that could exist. No one can escape my scrutinizing eyes. Moreover, I have a great desire to serve Rama. He is my treasure; I will do anything to protect my wealth. Have faith in me. I am what I am because of Him."

Taking Guha for his word, Lakshmana replied: "Being in Ayodhya cannot be more secure than being under your protection Guha. But the reason for my not sleeping is not only because I have to protect Rama, but also because I am guilty of having been unable to prevent this mishap. How can I then sleep peacefully? As many days as I see Rama and Sita sleep on the hard ground, I will not allow slumber to overpower me."

Lakshmana's determination stopped Guha from persuading him. He walked some distance away from Lakshmana. Weird thoughts began to occupy his mind. Love and hate were all that he could see today. What was confounding was that those closest to Rama hated him and those whose existence seemed immaterial showered so much love. If parents could hate and not love, could much be expected from other relationships? His mind wandered further. Why was Lakshmana carrying a bow in the middle of the night even after he had been assured of the royal couple's protection? The stepmother ensured Rama's banishment, could the stepbrother come along to ensure that He never returns to the kingdom?

Rama and Sita slept on the grass bed, as Lakshmana guarded them, constantly circumambulating, to make sure that they remained protected. A little deeper into the forest, hidden from Lakshmana's view, however, Guha was guarding Rama and Sita from Lakshmana!

Guha's guards and soldiers watched as their master held his bow steady, stealthily pacing Lakshmana's movements. They began to worry, and even doubted their master's intentions. Could he be trying to harm the Princes and Sita? A safe distance from the vision of their master, the soldiers, too, began pacing to keep an eye on Guha!

Amid all this, Rama and Sita slept, blissfully unaware of the anxiety the responsibility of their protection was causing so many people.

The entire night passed with Rama and Sita sleeping in the center, Lakshmana circumambulating, Guha moving around in an outer concentric circle around Lakshmana and Guha's guards moving around at the periphery in concentric circles around Guha.[38]

---

[38] The most engaging aspect of mundane life (which is sleep) loses its appeal to one who is charmed by the beauty of God.

a charioteer bids adieu

"KoooKooo! KoooKooo!" the sweet melodious sound of a cuckoo stirred Rama out of his slumber. As soon as Rama opened His eyes and sat up, He saw a beautiful peacock perched on a branch of a stooping tree singing with its head held high. It seemed as if the peacock was trying to wake Sita up. Rama woke her up, and soon they were ready to proceed further.

Rama summoned Lakshmana and Guha. They had to cross the Ganga and continue Their journey. Thus far, They had crossed all the rivers on the chariot itself, travelling over shallow sections. But the Ganga was mighty. There were no zones shallow enough for a chariot to make through. So Guha instructed his chief minister to bring their finest boat and their best boatman to ferry the three exiles across the river.

"Stop, before going any further, we need to adopt the hairstyle of hermits. Guha, could you arrange for some latex of a banyan tree?" Rama's request shattered Guha's heart; Rama's soft cascading hair always reminded him of the Ganga itself. Although he could not bear to think that soon these soft locks would be replaced with dreadlocks, Guha silently handed over the bowl of latex to Rama and Lakshmana. Despite sobs resonating the forest, Rama and Lakshmana matted their hair and bunched them up into a conical crown on their head forming the traditional *jata* or dreadlocks sported by hermits. When Guha saw Rama's cascading hair coiled into a dreadlock, he was reminded of Shiva who had captured Ganga in the locks of his hair. In place of a crown was hardened, coiled hair! Destiny had indeed played a cruel joke on such sincere people!

Soon the boat was anchored, and Lakshmana made a soft seat of grass and flowers for Sita and helped her in. Once He made sure

Sita was comfortable, Rama walked forward to board the boat. As soon as He raised His foot to step into the boat, an anxiety-ridden, shrill cry stopped him midway. "Wait!" Rama turned to identify the source of the sound. Everyone assembled there was baffled. It was from the boatman who was to take Rama across the river. He wanted to prevent Rama from boarding the boat. Guha was embarrassed with his subject's act.

Ignoring the glares of Guha and his mortified ministers, the boatman spoke: "I cannot allow You to step into my boat. It is very dangerous for my life." Sita looked concerned, and Rama became inquisitive. "How is that?"

The boatman replied, "I have heard stories about the mystical influence of Your feet. It seems that there is some kind of power in the dust of Your feet. Whatever Your feet dust touches turns into a woman. You had once stepped on a stone and it had turned into a woman. What if my boat, too, turns into a woman? I am a poor, married man struggling to provide for my family. What will I do if this boat turns into a girl, too? No! No! I cannot allow that to happen. You cannot get into my boat!"

Rama smiled, knowing what all of this was leading to and glanced at a very confused Sita. He asked the boatman, "So what do We do now? I have to go to the other side of the river come what may."

The boatman said, "The only way I can let You step into this boat is if You allow me to thoroughly wash Your feet so that I can make sure that every particle of dust is washed off."

Rama consented with a smile, and the boatman eagerly brought a plate on which he asked Rama to place His feet. Taking water from the Ganga, he began to wash Rama's feet with devotion. Everyone standing around had by now understood the clever boatman's trick.

The boatman washed the Lord's feet multiple times, pretending to make them cleaner. This way He got the opportunity to wash the feet of Lord Rama for a long time. Sita was the only person who felt uncomfortable about the whole episode.[39]

The boatman[40] then collected into a container all the water from the washing and began drinking it with great relish. As he was drinking, he glanced at Sita and began to smile mockingly.[41] After he was done drinking, he began moving around and enthusiastically sprinkling the rest of the water on his family and members of the tribal community. The event turned suddenly turned into an impromptu joyous festival.

"Are you satisfied? Now can I get into the boat?" asked the tolerant Rama. Embarrassed for having troubled Rama to fulfill his selfish desire, the boatman hurried and helped Rama and Sita[42] into the

---

[39] More than the excitement of the boatman, this story marks the embarrassment of Sita.

[40] In his previous life, this boatman was a tortoise in the Vaikuntha planet and resided in the ocean of milk where Lord Vishnu slept on His snake bed. Once this tortoise lifted its head and mistook the pinkish heel of the Lord to be a closed lotus flower. With the desire to lick the lotus, the tortoise raised its head, only to be pushed away by a disgusted Lakshmi *devi*. She did not want her husband's feet to be touched by the tortoise. Because she was in control, the tortoise had to helplessly move away.

[41] But in this situation, the tortoise-turned-boatman had control over the situation as Rama and Sita depended on him to take them across the Ganga. Naturally, he took revenge; he not only touched the feet of the Lord to his heart's content but also washed it and drank the water. It was symbolic of a lifetime of embarrassment for Sita.

[42] Sita realized that if anyone hankered to touch the feet of Lord Rama, She should not push him or her away. A lesson She would soon have a chance to implement.

boat and then hopped in and took up the oars to perform his service.

Rama expressed His gratitude to Guha for arranging this boat for their travel and offered to reciprocate. After the incident with the boatman, the devotional mood had spread and inspired Guha to be direct in his request to Rama. He said, "My dear Lord, as per your request, I arranged a boat to take you across the Ganga. At the time of my death, my request is that you take me across the ocean of birth and death in the boat of Your lotus feet." Rama smiled, conveying a thousand words.[43]

Rama's smile enhanced Guha's confidence in the merciful nature of the Lord. He further requested Rama to allow him to come along to serve them. Rama stopped him and said, "My dear Guha, today after meeting you, I now know why My father sent Me to the forest – to meet you, my fourth brother. With you, we have now become five. You are our unknown brother. Stay here and rule your kingdom with the sole purpose of pleasing Me. Remember that Your people are My own people, by looking after them, You will get the same benefit as travelling with Me and serving Me. When I am on My way back to Ayodhya after spending 14 years in the forest, I will surely return to your abode for some time."

Guha was crying. Never had anyone showered him with so much love. With these few words, Rama had given him a purpose and a new direction to rule his kingdom. If he could just live to make these instructions his life, he would be able to contribute sufficiently to the society.

---

[43] Small acts of service done with a sincere heart are reciprocated in an unbelievable proportion by the Lord.

Sumantra loaded Rama's and Lakshmana's weapons and Sita's ornaments and garments into the boat. Humbly, he asked Rama for his next instruction because the chariot was no longer needed. Rama gently rubbed his shoulders and requested him to return to Ayodhya and serve the old king.

Sumantra could not hold back his tears. He cried his heart out to Rama. "After seeing what You are going through, I am convinced that studying scriptures, behaving gently and living righteously are a waste of time. Only the tough and bent trees survive a storm and the straight ones fall first."

To ease Sumantra's pain and to clarify to all those with similar feelings, Rama cited examples of great, virtuous heroes from the past. He spoke of five heroes whose lives were centered on the principle of truthfulness. To prove their determination to follow the path of virtue, each had to undergo tests that ordinary men would find impossible to complete. As a result, their names became epitomes of righteousness.

The five heroes were Kings Sibi, Harishchandra, Rantideva and Bali and a sage named Dadhichi. Each underwent trials to prove that they were ready to adhere to higher principles at any cost, even at the expense of their lives. Sibi sacrificed his body to save a pigeon. Harishcandra was ready to give up his entire kingdom and his life to keep his promise to a *brahmana*. Rantideva fasted for 48 days and was willing to forego his final meal and embrace death in order to satisfy the needy. Bali gave up his kingdom and even sacrificed his body to fulfil a promise he had made to the dwarf Vamanadev. Dadichi *muni* offered his bones to be used as a thunderbolt weapon to protect the demigods from annihilation.

"Sumantra, *dharma* has four pillars – austerity, cleanliness, compassion and truthfulness. Those who do not follow these sacred principles corrode these pillars by their actions, just as rainwater corrodes an iron rod. By following My father's instructions, I am getting a chance to support these pillars of *dharma* and make them rust proof."

With this appeal, Rama gave His final departing instruction to Sumantra. He said, "Do you know that you are the Ikshvaku Dynasty's greatest well-wisher? With that in mind, carry out every one of the king's instructions. Tell the monarch that We are healthy and will soon be home after 14 years. Reassure mother Kaushalya several times a day that My health is at its best in the forest after consuming forest fruits, breathing fresh air and drinking invigorating river water.

Ensure that Bharata returns from Kekeya and is crowned monarch immediately. The only thing I expect of him is that he will treat all his mothers equally and will please Our old father. Let this become the only goal of his life."

Sumantra knew that these were Rama's parting words and that he would not be in His presence for the next 14 years. He offered his respects to Rama and said: "In all these years of serving You, if I have ever committed any offense, please forgive my ignorance considering that I am elder to You or considering that I am a minister. You are my master, and I, Your ardent devotee.

If You order me to return to Ayodhya, I surely will. But how do You expect me to return with an empty chariot? You have taught me that truth should always result in more benefit than loss. When Dasaratha asked me to slow down the chariot, You told me to speed up and later tell the king that I did not hear his command. This was to ensure that he suffers less and for that, You encouraged me to lie. Keeping the same principle in mind, should I tell Your mother that I dropped You off at Kosala, Your maternal uncle's kingdom. This lie will save her. Or, should I tell her the bitter painful truth that I abandoned You in the thick forest and returned? This truth will surely kill her.

Why do You want me to go through this suffering, Rama? Please allow me to accompany You into the forest. I will serve all of You by warding off dangerous animals with my chariot. Even if I am not worth taking along, look at these horses; do You think they will ever agree to return without You?"

One look at the horses convinced everyone about the truth in Sumantra's plea. The mute animals were shedding tears continuously. In unison, they trotted up to the riverbank to present their appeal to Rama with their tear-filled eyes.

"A sinner is denied entry into Amaravati, the abode of Indra, similarly the performer of the wicked deed of abandoning Rama will never be allowed to enter Ayodhya. If You do not allow me to accompany You, I will not return to Ayodhya, I would rather consecrate myself along with the chariot into the fire of lamentation."

Though Rama's heart bled at the plight of Sumantra and the horses, He stayed focused on His duty. Hopefully, this would be the last time He would have to be hardhearted to someone He loved. Breathing in deeply, Rama said: "Satisfaction will come to Keikeyi only when she sees the empty chariot. Different things remind different people of different aspects of life. To the people of Ayodhya, the chariot may remind them of My absence and offer them suffering, but the same chariot when seen by Keikeyi will remind her of her freedom and offer her liberation from anxiety.[44]

---

[44] Different things remind people of different things. Reminders in life

Keikeyi will only be able to breathe when she sees the empty chariot, and her ever-suspicious mind will accept the truthfulness of My father. Nothing will give Me more pleasure than seeing her happy. I earnestly request you, please return to Ayodhya for My pleasure and for the pleasure of the king."

Not wanting to prolong this discussion, Rama signaled the boatman. Rama took a sip of water from the river and paying respects to it, He prayed for the journey ahead. The boat glided away from the bank. Cutting through the smooth waters of the river, it edged toward the other side.

Hardhearted tribal hunters, softhearted sages and broken-hearted Sumantra stood forlorn, all of them tied together[45] by the departure of their beloved. There was nothing left to speak. Their eyes followed the boat until it reached the opposite shore. They then went separate ways.

---

when perceived rightly allow one to remain actively moldable and not mechanistically rigid. The fluttering of the national flag boosts national pride and reminds one of one's commitment toward the nation. An ambulance reminds one of the transient nature of life. The police uniform reminds one of staying within the boundaries of law. The empty chariot will remind Keikeyi of the completion of her plan and the success of her son.

[45] River Ganga is blue, Yamuna black, Godavari white and Kaveri transparent. But when they all mix into the ocean, you cannot differentiate between them. Similarly, when people of different colors, habits, cultures and tastes come together to serve a higher cause, their differences dissolve in the waters of cooperation.

The sages, the tribals and Sumantra were linked by the common cause of service to Rama.

a boatman finds peace

The boat journey marked a special chapter in the lives of the trio. From hereon, they were on their own for the next 14 years. With Sumantra's departure went the last link to Ayodhya.

The Ganga echoed Sita's heartfelt prayer for the protection of Rama and His safe return to Ayodhya at the end of 14 years. She promised the river goddess a donation of one lakh cows, soft clothing and food for the holy *brahmanas*. She also swore to undertake a pilgrimage to pay respects to all the deities on her banks.

As they neared their destination, the boatman jumped off. Wading knee-deep in water, he dragged the boat to anchor it somewhere convenient and dry for Sita, Rama and Lakshmana to disembark. Once on land, Rama looked at the boatman with gratitude, and Sita sensed His discomfort. He was always used to reciprocating in kind. Now because He was a pauper, He could offer nothing but gratitude. Sita unhesitatingly removed a ring from her finger and handed it over to Rama. He held the ring toward the boatman. "No My Lord! What do I not have by Your grace? An opportunity to serve You is a million times more valuable than all the wealth in this world. I cannot take anything from You." He fell at the feet of the Lord and cried. Despite umpteen persuasions, the boatman refused to accept anything in return for his service.

a sage shows the way

Between them, Rama and Lakshmana decided that they would guard Sita very carefully by flanking Her – Rama in front and Lakshmana behind. The wilderness and the savage nature of the forest, where insecurity reigns supreme and where every animal and bird lives in the fear of a sudden, fatal attack, did not seem to stop Rama, Lakshmana or Sita from appreciating the beauty surrounding them. Rama kept pointing at the wild splendor that ordinary eyes could not perceive.

Rama pointed to Sita to a miracle in the distance – lion cubs frolicking with elephant cubs! How could they be playing together? Rama explained that childhood was a phase of innocence. "With age comes ego and the law of the jungle – the survival of the mightiest.[46] Cubs do not worry much about food because their parents take care of their needs, they are more worried about pleasure. When the need for food takes priority over the need for pleasure, the very things that once gave pleasure turn out to be the sources of satisfaction for hunger."[47]

As another peculiar scene caught Rama's attention, He pulled Sita aside and pointed out in the direction of the shrubs. Some black wasps that were flying unsteadily were being led by another wasp. He explained to Sita, "These tipsy wasps have overdosed on the nectar from the flowers and can't keep their eyes open. The sober wasp is guiding them with his buzzing. The woozy ones will reach home just by following the buzz of their leader."[48] Sita found it funny and began laughing hysterically.

---

[46] The strength and courage of innocent childhood turns into weakness and insecurity of a fearful adulthood. As the animalistic mindset grows, hunger grows. As hunger for more grows, innocence of sharing love fades.

[47] The hungry jungle is also home to evolved humans (the sages) who have outgrown this hunger by focusing on the availability of abundance rather than indulging in carnal competition in scarcity.

[48] Petty intoxication not only makes one lose one's vision but also makes one a follower of someone else's vision.

Rama, Sita and Lakshmana's walks were not just fun and adventure, there was somberness to it, too. Sita always avoided treading on Rama's footprints. She ensured embedding Her own footprints in between Rama's and never disrupting His. Lakshmana, who was behind the two, always made sure that he never stepped on either of Their footprints.[49] He sensitively kept both Their footprints to his right and constantly worshipped Them in his mind.[50]

Sages observed the walking trio with delight since the *Pranava* or *Omkara*[51] had materialized for them; the mantra they had been chanting for so many decades had incarnated in the form of these three effulgent personalities and walked into their lives to bless them.[52] Their entire life of austerities had culminated to experience this moment.

---

[49] Anything connected to the Lord is called *tadiya*. At one level, the footprints of the Lord are considered worship worthy and hence, sacred. But at another level, footprints represent ideologies, teachings and the very heart of the master. An insensitive disciple not only treads on the footprints but also the heart of the master, whereas an ideal disciple does not step over his or her master's ideas to replace them with his or hers, but respectfully follows them. One is allowed to express one's own ideas, but in harmony with the thoughts of the teacher.

[50] Innovation is fine, but not at the cost of replacement.

[51] The word OM is made of three syllables 'a', 'u' and 'm'.

'a' –The foremost syllable in a series represents the Supreme Lord. Because the first alphabet is 'a' it represents the Supreme Lord, Rama.

'u' – Represents the energy of the Lord. Sita is the energy of Rama and hence 'u' represents mother Sita.

'm' – Represents the spiritual master who personally serves and brings one close to the Lord and His energies. Lakshmana is the *adi guru* or original spiritual master, hence 'm' represents Lakshmana.

[52] Because Rama led, Sita walked next, and Lakshmana followed, 'a', 'u' and 'm', it seemed like 'aum' was walking by.

The entire day passed trekking through the thickets. As the sun settled, the trio, too, decided to rest under a large banyan tree. As day turned to night, Rama's smile was replaced by a sulk. He began to wonder about the happenings in Ayodhya post His exile. His greatest worry was mother Kaushalya's safety from the torture of Keikeyi. Unsettled by harrowing thoughts, Rama asked Lakshmana to immediately return to Ayodhya. He broke down like a child. "No woman should give birth to a useless son like Me. When she needs Me the most, I am too far away to do anything for her. Her pets, the mynah and the parrot are able to render more service to her than this useless son of hers. When the trickster cat comes to steal away the offerings meant for the holy deities, the mynah signals the parrot, which in turn swoops down and pecks the foot of the cat, thus saving the holy offerings.[53] What can I do from so far? If I can't even do what the mynah and parrot do for My mother, of what use is a son like Me? Wouldn't it have been better had she never given birth to Me?"[54]

With Rama so disturbed, Lakshmana rose from being an assistant to a counselor.[55] He held Rama close to him and very lovingly

---

[53] Rama is comparing Himself and Lakshmana to the mynah and the parrot and Keikeyi to the cat. With this comparison, He is conveying that just like the mynah and the parrot prevent the trickster cat from stealing the holy offering, He and Lakshmana should have ideally warned Kaushalya and protected the holy throne from being stolen.

[54] The cat can also be compared to the mind, the mynah and parrot to the alert intelligence and Kaushalya to the pure soul. Just when the mind ventures to seek forbidden pleasure, alert intelligence has to bite it and protect the soul from an embarrassing loss.

[55] Throughout the journey, Lakshmana upgraded and downgraded his role depending on Rama's needs. But whatever role he played, Lakshmana never forgot his goal of pleasing Rama.

explained to Him that there was no need to worry. Kaushalya was extremely capable of handling any impediment especially when she was surrounded by wise men such as Vasistha and Sumantra. Now that the king had understood Keikeyi, he too would be kind to Kaushalya. Lakshmana explained to Rama that he couldn't live without Him. Lakshmana's love allayed all of Rama fears.[56] He wiped away His tears and fell asleep.

The huge banyan tree shed more sap that night than any other time in its life. Who wouldn't cry if Rama expressed His feelings in their vicinity?

All through the next day, They trudged along the jungle path till They reached the confluence of Ganga and Yamuna at Prayag. The *ashram* of Bharadwaja *muni* was situated exactly on the confluence of the two rivers. This destination was going to determine Their future course.

A deerskin-clad ascetic with a coarse tree bark wrapped around his waist and a water pot (which sadhus called *kamandalu*) in one hand and the *tridanda* staff [57] of a *sanyasi* in the other hand was gazing at them constantly. Tears trickled down Bharadwaja *muni's* sunken cheeks at the sight of the trio. A hardened sage weeping was indeed a very unnatural phenomenon.

Rama bowed and offered the forest flowers at the feet of the great master. Bharadwaja *muni* embraced Him. Welcoming them into his

---

[56] If a role is constantly changing, it distracts one from the goal.

[57] A *tridanda* staff that a renunciant carries is three sticks tied together, indicating that one has dedicated three aspects of his personality to the service of God and society – his thoughts, words and actions. The stick constantly reminds the renunciant of this resolution.

hermitage, he offered them *madhupak* drink and delicacies prepared from roots and fruits.

Bharadwaja *muni* was indeed a unique person. As he sat in his ashram, he was surrounded by various birds and beasts – from ferocious tigers to timid monkeys and from savage eagles to docile sparrows, all seemed to be comfortable with him and with each other.[58]

The *muni* told them that he had already heard about Their banishment and offered to host them for the next 14 years. Prayag, he said was the holiest of all places.

Rama said: "It is not only the confluence of Ganga, Yamuna and Saraswati that makes it holy but also the confluence of the fourth river of knowledge and purity of your holiness. Such holy places turn into attractive tourist spots. My dear sage, that is why We cannot stay here. People from various cities will come to visit Us knowing that We are here. So I beg you to direct Us to a place that will delight Sita and at the same time will be sufficiently inaccessible."

Bharadwaja *muni* understood their predicament, "Sixty miles from here stands a mountain called Chitrakoot. Divine sages inhabit this mountain. It has an extremely charming landscape with fruit bearing trees, lakes, and birds of limitless variety, deer, elephants and black-faced monkeys with long tails. Any person who glances even once at its peak will be unable to sin again. Such is its purity. This picturesque location will be best for all of you."

---

[58] Peace exists when there is no fear. When you have nothing to hold or nothing to take away, you are fearless and so are people in your company.

Grateful to the sage for his hospitality and guidance, Rama, Sita and Lakshmana then decide to take some rest. As the sun set, the fears that Rama experienced the previous day began overpowering Him again, but this time it is for a good reason. As the sun set in front of Them, yet another sun set far away from Them!

a king meets death

The dejected faces said it all. Without a word, Guha's spies had conveyed so much. "There is no hope now. They have gone too far to expect them to return. With time, their determination will only increase. We have seen them go through so much suffering while trekking into the forest path, but they somehow have the mystical ability to be unaffected by pain. Even the delicate Princess did not complain. After stopping over at Bharadwaja *muni*'s ashram at Prayag, the trio has now begun Their journey toward Chitrakoot. They should be there soon." Guha sulked and Sumantra rode away. The common link between them suddenly snapped.[59]

Whatever little hope Sumantra had of Rama's return was now lost forever. He covered the entire distance between Sringaberapura and Ayodhya as if in a dream. Stony silence greeted Sumantra as he entered the city with an empty chariot. He wasn't used to such quietness. Every time he had entered into this city in the past, riding this chariot with the king, a pompous ceremony had ushered them in. Even more stupefied than Sumantra were the horses; they almost failed to recognize the city and refused to enter the gates.

---

[59] Physical pains are many times unavoidable, but mental suffering is always discretionary. When one voluntarily chooses the path of pain, he anesthetizes himself from mental suffering.

Suddenly, Sumantra heard a rumble of footsteps as herds of eager citizens ran toward the chariot, expecting their beloved Prince. The sight of the empty chariot left them empty-hearted. Every time they looked in the direction of the chariot, their eyelids slumped in anguish. Life seemed stale.[60]

Sumantra could feel the singeing heat waves blowing from every corner of Ayodhya's imperial palace. Every heart was burning with grief. The palace walls were melting with the unbearable temperature. The heat within the citizens' hearts seemed to escape through fiery words and hot tears. All he could hear was Kaushalya's misery and Keikeyi's barbarism.

Vasistha decrypted Sumantra's expressions and soon realized that Rama had not returned. The wise sage left the palace quietly. There was no point in staying to watch the wailing soon to follow. He did not want to seem weak to the entire dynasty that respected him as their *acharya*. It was better to cry alone.

Sumantra stood still before the king, his face downcast. Sumantra began to narrate every detail to Dasaratha and Kaushalya, their perked up ears resembling the beak of a *chataka* bird. But instead of sprinkling cool showers of assurance, he hurled a hot thunderbolt of catastrophe. [61] "After Rama, Sita and Lakshmana entered the dense forest on the other side of the mighty Ganga, the horses were just

---

[60] When Rama was in Ayodhya, the citizens were like tortoises, confident that the protective shell of Rama's presence in their lives would help them endure all kinds of difficulties. Without Rama, they felt as helpless as toppled turtles, writhing on their backs, feet up in the air.

[61] Like *chataka* bird waits all year long for the first drop of cool rainwater to enter into its parched throat through its beak, Kaushalya too expected some positive news; however, Sumantra's words struck her like lightning.

not ready to return. Constantly shedding tears, they kept looking back and glancing at the direction of their departure.

As I helplessly returned, I could see that it was not just the horses that behaved this way but every aspect of nature too. Trees were so sad that they stooped till they touched the ground. Flowers sprung off the trees, ending their life. Sap flowed out of trees as did tears from birds and animals. The animals lost their appetite, the birds lost their songs."[62]

As soon as Sumantra spoke about birds losing their song, Dasaratha let out a full-throated cry. "Aaaaagh! I can feel the pain King Yayati felt when he was falling from the heavens due to his own foolishness."[63] He embraced Sumantra as a drowning man grabs the only log of wood in the vicinity.[64]

Dasaratha was so disturbed that he began talking gibberish. He seemed to have lost his mental balance, which had a telling effect on his body: he tottered and collapsed, just to be held on time by Kaushalya and Sumitra on either side. Sumitra said, "O king, the only way your mind can become peaceful is if you understand what is happening to Rama in the forest. Now that Keikeyi is not amid us, you don't have to think before speaking, so go ahead and speak

---

[62] When the heart resounds with pain, can sweet music replace it with pleasure?

[63] As a reward for the many sacrifices performed by him during his lifetime, King Yayati ascended to the heaven. Indra received him most courteously and encouraged him to speak about his own meritorious acts. Yayati began to self-glorify and in the process unwittingly exhausted all his merits and was hurled right back to the mortal plane.

[64] Self-glory decreases one's merits, which is why the wise consider self-glorification suicidal.

out. Clarify your doubts with Sumantra."

Borrowing the confidence from his wise wife, Dasaratha asked the charioteer: "Could my sons adjust to the life of hermits? Did the delicate Sita repent her decision? Tell me exactly what was going on in each of their minds."

Sumantra revealed: "Not even for a moment had Rama deviated from the path of *dharma* inspired by His king. The exile episode was indeed due to the king trying to hold on to *dharma* despite his inconvenience." Dasaratha did not fight back his tears. Although sad, he was happy his Son was not blaming him and was able to appreciate his dilemma.

Sumantra continued, "The only thing the Prince expected from His father was kindness and fairness to His suffering mother. Rama has requested His mother to turn away her attention for the next 14 years from wrong that was done to her and focus on the positive contribution she can make. He has requested His mother to serve the deities of the Lord in the temple and the deity at home, her husband, with utmost devotion. Her devotion to her husband will only be comprehensive if she can respect and love all that her husband loved. Naturally, she should not treat other queens badly and consciously avoid any skirmishes with Keikeyi. Rama also expects His mother to treat the next king, Bharata, with the respect worthy of a monarch.

Rama has asked me to convey two things to Bharata – absolute, unconditional abidance to the king's instructions and to love and treat His mother Kaushalya as he would his own mother Keikeyi."

After a minor pause, Sumantra carried on, "I do not want to speak about Lakshmana's feelings, but I have to. Lakshmana was in a constant state of anger. He was unable to forgive king Dasaratha and felt that he had made the gravest mistake by allowing the ill-minded Keikeyi to dictate her terms. Lakshmana told me that the moment king Dasaratha gave up his kinship with Rama, he severed his kinship with Dasaratha."

Sumitra and Kaushalya felt helpless in the midst of the strong heat of emotions. Like a doe brushed by flames, Kaushalya suddenly spoke up: "Throw me into the forest with them. What do I get by staying here when I can feel the flames of hardship burning them? When Rama came to me seeking my permission before departing, my situation was like that of a snake having mistakenly caught a muskrat. Had the snake eaten the muskrat it would have died of poisoning, and had it let go, the muskrat would slit its eyes and blinded it. If I had held on and not let Rama go into the forest, I would have caused a fight within the family. I set Him free and now I am blinded by grief, unable to see Him.[65]

At least Rama is a rugged warrior and Vishwamitra has trained him well about the vagaries of forest life, but Sita is a delicate flower. She has not experienced hardship. I made sure that She never set foot on hard ground. She always sat on a bed, a soft seat, an ornate swing or my lap. I never asked Her to do any task, not even the easy ones like stirring the wick of a lamp. How will She now carry out the tough tasks necessary to live in the forest?

How can one expect a female *chakora* bird accustomed to living on

---

[65] Kaushalya's choice was between what makes her family unhappy and what makes her unhappy.

When one has to choose between two bad, people like Kaushalya forsake their personal happiness and people like Keikeyi choose their personal happiness, thus forsaking the happiness to others.

the nectarine cooling rays of the moon adjust to the glowering heat of the sun? If She could not handle the frightening painting of a monkey, how will She cope with the terrorizing realities of forest life? How can a swan used to gliding in sparkling waters be comfortable in a mucky quagmire or a saline ocean? Can a cuckoo be expected to find pleasure in a bitter-melon orchard after relishing the tastes of a mango orchard?"

Kaushalya's sad eyes led Sumantra to make a half-hearted attempt to please her. He wept and stuttered: "They are all happy in the forest. Sita is frolicking in the forest as if in a pleasure grove."

Sumantra then said that he remembered something Sita had mentioned about Keikeyi, but in a moment, he pretended to have forgotten it.[66]

Kaushalya had never seen the old minister so confused and fumbling. She understood that his mind was distracted by the departure of Rama, Lakshmana and Sita and their discomfort in the forest. She then turned to the root of all distress – her heedless husband.

"A woman relies on two men, her husband and her son. For me both have become distant. My husband is physically close but mentally distant. My son is mentally close and physically distant. You have not only taken away these supports of my life but also handicapped the kingdom and crippled the ministers with your injudicious solo decision. I congratulate you for achieving all these goals simultaneously. I am sure you must be proud."

---

[66] Sumantra realized that if he mentioned what Sita felt about leaving the kingdom, Kaushalya's hatred toward Keikeyi would increase manifold, so he preferred to lie about having forgotten what she said.

Kaushalya's taunts hurt Dasaratha. "I beg you not to hurt my wounded heart with your piercing words. I know I have blundered, but forgive me for I am your husband."

Kaushalya's anger evaporated when she saw the monarch's pitiable state and suddenly felt guilt. She placed Dasaratha's hands on her head and begged him, "Forgive me, My Lord, for speaking unpleasant words. Too much lamentation can make a person unreasonable." Their common sorrow helped bury the bitterness.[67]

Their sorrow drifted into slumber as daylight drifted into nightfall. Dasaratha woke up with a start in the middle of the night just as it had happened two days ago. He screamed vehemently, rousing Kaushalya: "Six days have passed since Rama left us and I am still alive. With passing time the ache is increasing. The reason I am still alive is probably because death is waiting for the pain to reach its summit. I need to reach the exact level of pain I had caused in the past.[68]

Kaushalya, a cloudy day from the past has clouded my mind. The price for the mistake I committed then (when I was young and blinded by overconfidence) is separation from Rama now. There is no escaping the law of *karma*. Feeling overconfident after successfully killing two animals by assessing their positions from sound alone, I shot a third arrow, and in one single shot killed three people. Although my arrow only killed an innocent boy, his blind

---

[67] Excessive lamentation is like trying to gulp hot tea. It results in a blistered tongue. One's lamentation for the past should not ricochet to destroy one's future.

[68] One has to bear the consequences of every action (good or bad), whether or not caused by ignorance.

and aging parents jumped into his funeral pyre, unable to bear the separation.

Before dying, the old parents told me that had I failed to report to them about my mistake, my skull would have cracked. And had I deliberately killed the boy, my entire dynasty would have been destroyed. But because I had unwittingly caused the death of their son, the sin of killing would not harass me, but the pain I caused them would. When I saw them dying in agony, I knew they were in pain, but I didn't know how much. Now I know exactly how much pain they were experiencing. They had told me that in my old age I would have to undergo the pain of separation from my son while dying. In the spirit of youth, I had brushed that aside because I wasn't yet a father then. But my past action has dogged me and now stands in front of me as a painful reaction.

Kaushalya, is this not the real reason for which I am suffering now? Am I foolish enough to send Rama, whom I love more than my life, into the forest? When a reaction is destined, even the wise act silly. How I wish I had reconsidered shooting that arrow! How I wish I had not listened to Keikeyi! How I wish I had not exiled Rama!"[69]

As he whispered Rama's name, Dasaratha began to breathe heavily. Almost as if in a yogic trance, absorbed in the memories of his son, Rama, Dasaratha left his body.

As soon as Kaushalya realized that Dasaratha had departed, she

---

[69] Destiny forces you to act in certain ways to shape your future. But isn't another term for destiny "past action." The law of *karma* is just and balanced. Like an impartial judge, it awards or punishes you according to your destiny (past action), not only in the quantity but also in the quality of suffering or joy.

let out a cry loud as the thunderbolt that had struck a habitat of
birds. A huge tumult followed, with all the queens letting out a
high-pitched wails, which sounded like panic-stricken birds flying
out of their destroyed homes. Soon more and more wails echoed
from every nook of the palace.

Kaushalya blamed Keikeyi for Dasaratha's death. She said: "The
king did not die from a disease or a weapon, for both these have
to enter a person to cause death. The king died from the pain of
separation from a loved object. His son's parting killed him. Have
we ever heard of anything that can kill because it has gone away?
It's called a son. I have heard how children bring death upon their
parents. It is true among crabs or scorpions. Now I see it in humans,
too." In her pain, she had no idea what she was blabbering. The
other queens sobbed incessantly.

As soon as Vasistha received information, he took charge of the
situation. Because there was no one to perform the last rites of the
king, he ensured that the king's body was preserved in a large vat
of oil.

The Big M had assembled by then and had expressed their concern
to Vasistha about the possibility of anarchy in the absence of an
authoritative king. A letter was drafted and sent to Bharata at
Vishala, the capital of the Kekeya. Five sensitive, confidential and
astute messengers were chosen for this task, Siddhartha, Vijaya,
Jayanta, Asoka and Nandana.[70]

---

[70] For lack of clear direction during emergencies, stability can be lost and
anarchy can prevail. The role of the Big M becomes most imperative during
such times. In Ayodhya, the Big M rose to the occasion.

Sumantra was ordered to take charge of the affairs of the kingdom till the next king was appointed. All hell broke loose when the citizens heard their king's demise. A few days ago they had to choose between Dasaratha and Rama to be their king, but now they had lost both. They could not fathom which way Ayodhya's (and naturally their own) future was headed.

a princess prays

With the rise of the sun, Dasaratha's sons woke up and prepared to proceed toward their new destination – Chitrakoot. After performing the ritual of scattering boiled rice on the ground to ensure their safe travel, Bharadwaja *muni* gave them directions.

From the confluence of the Ganga and Yamuna, he asked them to follow the Yamuna, which ran westward. After crossing the Yamuna, they would find a gigantic banyan tree named Shyam with bright green leaves. He instructed Sita to offer prayers under this tree.[71]

Two miles from there, They would find a beautiful forest filled with bamboos and *sallaka* and jujube trees. That forest would lead them to the Chitrakoot mountains.

Following the instructions of the divine sage, the trio reached the banks of the Yamuna on the other side of which they could see the mammoth banyan tree. Lakshmana quickly constructed

---

[71] Did Bharadwaja *muni* purposely instruct Sita to worship this tree called Shyam? Was it a reminder that Rama would soon appear as Shyam in His next incarnation and would reside on the banks of the Yamuna river? Why did he not ask even Rama to worship that tree?

a makeshift raft and beckoned Rama and Sita. Sita smiled as She observed the caring Lakshmana. He had prepared a soft seat for Her with branches of reeds and rose apple trees cushioned with leaves and flowers. The raft was small and could only accommodate two people. With Rama and Sita seated, Lakshmana swam along pushing the raft to the other side. With rapt attention, Sita prayed to the holy river for the safe return of Her husband. On reaching the banyan tree, as instructed by Bharadwaja *muni*, Sita performed an elaborate worship of the sacred banyan tree called Shyam. Each of Sita's prayers was oriented toward Rama's safety and His quick return to Ayodhya. It seemed as if She had no desire of Her own.

As the day morphed into a beautiful night and the hot sun gave way to the cooling moon, the tough forest path finally merged with the heavenly mountain. The first sight of Chitrakoot caught the trio off guard. With the crescent moon mounted elegantly on top of the mountain, Chitrakoot was indeed a picturesque abode. Admiring the beauty of the mountain, the trio spent the night at the base.

Will Rama, Sita and Lakshmana actually be able to enjoy the beauty and peace of Chitrakoot and live there? What will happen to the disturbed city devoid of a king? Will Bharata decode the cryptic message?

CHAPTER 7

TEST OF INTENTIONS

The horses galloped past forests, across gardens, over roadways, around mountains and through rivers. The surrounding scenery was neither noticed nor appreciated. Racing rapider than the horses' hooves were the minds of the riders, mentally traversing the infinite distance between them and the city they had left behind a hundred times over. Caught between the glorious past and a fretful future, their minds ached too much to even register their distraught present – there was no time for food, no time for sleep and no time to even answer the call of nature.

Choosing to take the shortest and most torturous route had been painful, but wise – the messengers were rapidly approaching Girivrajapur in the province of Kekeya.[1]

"Don't tell Bharata about the death of the king or the exile of Rama.

---

[1] When one focuses on a valuable ambition, the body happily tolerates and transcends pains and inconvenience as much as an unpolished diamond tolerates rubs and cuts.

When one focuses on comfortable participation, the body grumpily churns excuses and complains as much as a lazy farmer complains about his seemingly unproductive and barren land.

Look cheerful; shower him with these extravagant gifts of silk and ornaments. Inform Bharata that his presence is needed in Ayodhya urgently." These etched instructions from the *kula-guru* Vasistha kept replaying in their minds.

The weary horses at last managed to sprint into the sleeping city of Girivrajapur. Yet, the mission was far from accomplished. It would be completed only when Bharata returned to Ayodhya with them. The night demanded patience because it had something in store for them.

a telling dream

"A ghoulish shrill laughter shattered the night's silence. I was running up a steep cliff to save my father. I could see the helplessness in his eyes... or was it fear? His body looked soiled, hair disheveled. He seemed as lackluster and hopeless as his black attire. I was running toward him, but either he could not see me or he did not want to see me. As I was about to reach the clifftop, he fell into the valley all of a sudden... or was he thrown off? I looked into the valley and was aghast to find the honorable king struggling in a slushy pond filled with obnoxious slush. The king was unable to bear the insult, but he was laughing hysterically. His mad laughter echoed through the valley. The entire atmosphere appeared to be ridiculing his wretched condition.

The moon shuddered and fell off its orbit and lay shattered on the ground. The all-pervasive darkness made the earth look like a woman stripped of honor. The king of elephants appeared near the pond shedding tears, his pride shorn because of his splintered tusks. The breeze stopped all of a sudden, and the colossal ocean evaporated within moments. The mountains in front of me whirled into a dust storm and disappeared.

My father had by then emerged out of the pond. But to my utter dismay, he began eating rice seasoned with gingelly seeds and drank from a bowl of oil. It was heart-wrenching to see him plunge his face into the bowl of oil.

Suddenly, a rusty-complexioned ghastly demoness appeared out of nowhere. She was laughing raucously as she dragged the king toward a chariot drawn by jackasses. The profanities that she spewed were interrupted only by her ghoulish laughter. After adorning him with a hibiscus garland, she harshly smeared red sandalwood paste on his face. She then pushed him onto the chariot and urged the jackasses to trundle southward.

The clippity-clop of the jackasses and the morbid laughter of the demoness still ring in my mind.

With so much dissonance within, how do you expect me to hear anything outside?" So saying, Bharata had gotten up and walked away from his surprised friends.[2]

Bharata had woken up feeling melancholic. His dear friends had tried their best to entertain him since morning. They had put up exciting dramas, shared rib-tickling jokes, held story-telling sessions and organized soothing musical concerts, but to no avail. When they cajoled him into explaining his morbid mood, his bizarre outpour caught them off guard. They patted him lovingly, trying to enhearten him.

---

[2] If one allows the booming noise of negative thoughts to dance like ghosts in the cemetery of our minds, where would one find the bandwidth to hear the positive notes of soothing flutes in our lives?

"Do you even know what such a dream means?" he asked them. Without waiting for any answers, Bharata continued, "It means the early funeral of either myself, Lakshmana or perhaps, our father Dasaratha's." Saying this, he glanced out the window toward the direction of Ayodhya, unsure of what to do or say. Little did he realize that the ominous dream that had wrecked his mental peace foretold many shattered dreams.[3]

rushed goodbyes

Upon the arrival of royal messengers from Ayodhya, Bharata and Shatrughna rushed into the courtroom of their grandfather, King Ashwapati.

One glance was enough for Bharata's keen intelligence to decode both the gross and subtle messages transmitted by the messengers. From the hundreds of millions worth of ornaments and silk presented to the king and the tens of millions worth gifted to his uncle, Bharata knew that the highest royal authority had sent them.

From the messengers' nervous posture, twitchy eyes and the short message of urgent return Bharata understood that they were withholding some information that could not be revealed here.

To put his doubts to rest, Bharata began asking them pointed questions: "My father is fine, I hope? And are the heroes, Rama and

---

[3] Through many foreign languages, destiny teaches us the ABCDs of preparing for inevitable change. Dream is the name of one such esoteric, less-understood language.

Lakshmana fine as well? Is goddess of virtue personified, Kaushalya, the fortunate mother of Rama, hale and hearty? Is *dharmadarsini*, the one who has clear vision of righteousness, the mother of two dedicated heroes, Sumitra, doing well? And how is my self-loving (*aatmakaamaa*) and irate (*sadhachandi Krodhanaapraajanmanee*) mother Keikeyi? What did she say?"[4]

One of the messengers, still uptight but not wanting to avoid the questions said: "All those you just inquired about are well. How else can they be? Be assured that the goddess of fortune awaits you with a lotus in her hands. We humbly request you to leave for Ayodhya right away. The *acharya* wants you to return instantly for an important task."

Bharata knew that they would never actually reveal anything without being instructed to; the only way he could unravel the mystery behind their strange behavior and the foreboding dream would be by actually reaching the center of all action: Ayodhya.

Bharata respectfully bade his dear grandfather and uncle goodbye. With a blessed sniff of his bowed head[5] and a loving pat on his back, the elders gushed that Keikeyi was extremely fortunate to have a son like him. As parting gifts, they offered him 2000 gold coins, 1600 horses, elephants from the Indrasira mountains, well-trained mules, massive dogs as ferocious as tigers and hundreds of attendants.

---

[4] Our surroundings can at the most influence our behavior but cannot be held solely responsible for it. Responsibility ultimately rests on the doer and not on the surroundings that influence the action.

[5] In ancient India, the traditional greeting of tender love was neither a hug nor a kiss but a smell of someone's head. The Upanishads suggest that fathers ought to sniff their child's head thrice the way a cow sniffs its calf, to insure its long life.

The happy gifts notwithstanding, Bharata's mind was churning, preoccupied as he was with disturbing and intrusive thoughts that were simply irrepressible.[6]

The retinue embarked on the long voyage to Ayodhya straightaway.

painful truths and evil schemes

It took them eight arduous days from Kekeya to reach Ayodhya. For the messengers, the return was longer because they had traversed to Kekeya in half the time. No doubt the route was fraught with more danger, but it was the only way to ensure speedy delivery of their message. Besides, it was just them and a few boxes of gold and silk. This time, however, there was a whole lot more.[7]

Bharata wanted to break away from the group and rush to his destination, but he patiently stayed with them for it was his responsibility to ensure that everyone safely made it through the several enemy territories on the way. On the seventh day, however,

---

[6] The human mind is like a restless bird that cannot settle peacefully on any of the umpteen branches that promise mythological happiness.
When calmness replaces restlessness and contentment replaces hankering, every opportunity fills the birdlike mind with factual joy and stability.

[7] The messengers from Ayodhya were like bees that go out empty and return loaded with honey. They had travelled from Ayodhya light but on their way back, they were loaded with gifts.
Light baggage ensures hassle-free travel. In the journey of life, one should not carry the baggage of preconceived notions, boastful self-praise, bad habits and judgmental diagnoses.
A light traveler should gather nectarine qualities from every flower in every orchard and return to share the nectar with like-minded people.

no sooner than they entered the friendly Kosala province, Bharata sped ahead, leaving Shatrughna in charge of the entourage's safety.

As Bharata's chariot galloped into the precincts of Ayodhya at the dawn of the eighth day, he noticed the eerie elements of his premonition all around him – crows, jackasses and jackals were crying in an evil sonata. Bharata found the pandemonium unnerving.

He turned to his charioteer who had abruptly stationed the chariot a little away from the city entrance and shared his discomfort: "Have we reached the wrong destination? Is this the Ayodhya I had left behind? Why does this city appear like a ghost town? Why is there such morbid silence? Why don't we hear the excited chatter of men and women? The gates seem bereft of eminent people eager to enter the city. Parks and gardens seem like ruins, as if no gardener or citizen has ever cared to visit this place. In fact, from this distance, the entire city appears like a forest to me!

The familiar sights, sounds and smells of Ayodhya are gone. So are the leaves on those sad trees, even though winter has yet to set in. Listen and you will notice, that gone are the songs of birds, too. And the uninterrupted soothing music, which was so unique to Ayodhya, has ceased. Why can't I smell the invigorating fragrance of sandalwood and aloe incense? I fear that something has gone terribly wrong with my kinsfolk."

The gatekeepers at the Vaijayanta gate bowed reverentially, hailing the prince as his chariot entered the city. Tears dripped on the ground from their lowered eyes; they were avoiding the confused gaze of Bharata. The main street was desolate and appeared like a dried river bed. Bharata disembarked from his chariot and began to walk toward his father's palace, absorbing every minute detail of his surroundings. Every house was unkempt and no embellished flags fluttered on their rooftops. Every few steps, though, some famished-looking voiceless citizens glanced up at him and paid him their respects, but they just hurried away. Temples seemed as if they had been deserted for weeks and the deities were left unworshipped. No trade and commerce seemed to exist in Ayodhya any longer.

As a very apprehensive Bharata entered his father's palace, he noticed rust on the hinges of the entry doors. Unable to find his father after searching all over, he went to the next most obvious place – his mother's palace.

Keikeyi sprang up from her golden couch the moment she heard that her darling son Bharata had just entered her palace. She ran toward the entrance to receive him. Her blissful and happy countenance surprised Bharata. He became curious; while the whole of Ayodhya was like a bed of lotuses covered by icy frost, Keikeyi seemed like a tribal woman who had kept herself warm by setting fire to an entire forest. Bharata touched her feet, but his mind was muddled by these confusing thoughts.

She gently embraced him and tenderly sniffed his head. "You have come from my father's house, which is like my heaven. I am excited to know how my father and my brother are doing. I am sure your stay there was happy. When did you leave to come here? You must be exhausted, let me arrange for your rest and refreshment."

Bharata interrupted her as she hurried to make arrangements, "Everything is fine at Kekeya. Grandfather and uncle have sent us loads of gifts that Shatrughna is bringing along. I raced ahead to find out the reason behind the urgency of *guru* Vasishtha's message. First tell me, what's wrong in Ayodhya? Why does the city look so forlorn? Why is there fear in everyone's eyes? Where is the king?

He doesn't seem to be in his palace. Besides, every guard and maid there seemed to be consciously avoiding my gaze. Is he here or is he in mother Kaushalya's palace? I am eager to seek his audience and blessings after such a long time."

"*Yagatisarvabhutanam, tam gatimte pita gatah.*

Your father has gone to the same destination that every animal reaches one day – the abode of death." Keikeyi's acerbic words sent shivers down Bharata's spine. He collapsed like a Sal tree struck by a thunderbolt, whispering, "Alas! What misfortune!" His mother's nonchalant dismissal of such a painful event just added to his shock.[8]

Very casually, almost dramatically, Keikeyi spoke to Bharata. There was rehearsed coldness in her lecture. "The wise don't grieve for that which is inevitable. There is no point lamenting about that which is perishable. The body will be destroyed at some point in time. Tears should be shed only if they can undo something. But no matter how much you cry, will your father come back to life? Stop crying and get up."[9]

With tears trickling down his cheeks, Bharata said, "I thought that the urgency was for Rama's coronation, and I was expecting father

---

[8] Insensitive persons living agenda-driven lifestyles do not measure the temperature of their words. When their words spill out, they blister the pathway from the ear to the heart.

[9] Philosophy can act as a salve or as a burning knife, depending on when it is spoken, by whom it is spoken, to whom it is spoken and with what intention it is spoken.

    When Krishna spoke these exact same words to Arjuna in the *Gita*, they acted as a salve. When Keikeyi spoke them, they penetrated like a burning knife into Bharata's heart.

to surprise me with that news. But he seems to have stunned me by going away. How fortunate was our father to have a son like Rama by his side as he breathed his last and who could at least have the satisfaction of performing the last rites. With the departure of the father, the eldest son takes on the role of guiding and directing. From now on, I am a natural instrument in the hands of Rama. But mother, I am curious. What could have caused the monarch's unforeseen departure? Was he suffering from some ailment? A great soul lives on through his words of wisdom and words of instruction. O mother, kindly tell me my father's last instruction for me. Also, please tell me the last words the great soul uttered before leaving this mortal world."[10]

"O Rama, O Sita, O Lakshmana! These were the last words of your father. Before departing, he expressed that those who would see them return were the most fortunate." Keikeyi's words enraged Bharata with fear. With eyes bulging out of his sockets, he glared at Keikeyi and demanded to know where the trio had gone in this trying situation.

Maintaining her icy cool demeanor, Keikeyi explained that Rama,

---

[10] Lakshmana claimed to be a servant of Rama, and Bharata claimed to be an instrument of Rama. The choice of whether or not to serve the master is not an option in either case. While the servant can choose how to serve the master, the instrument cannot.

Lakshmana told Rama how he wanted to serve Him, but Bharata acted as an instrument completely dependent on Rama's discretion. This mood is called *paratantriyam*. For Bharata, unlike Lakshmana, personal proximity was not as important as obedience.

The fourth son, Shatrughna, displayed *bhagvataparatantriyam*, which is complete dependence on Bharata, who in turn was a great devotee of Rama. Shatrughna, thus, represents distant assistance to Rama by assisting Bharata.

Sita and Lakshmana, dressed in tree bark and deerskin had entered the forest of Dandaka.

Bharata's head began to reel – first the death of his father and now the exile of his father-like brother. As always, bad news had to come in multiples! Bharata stared at his mother, the harbinger of such negativity. Little did he know that she was not just the conveyor but also the conductor of all the negativity surrounding him.[11]

"What was the magnitude of Rama's misconduct? Was He held for stealing off a *brahmana*? Was He held for harming a man of virtue? Or worse, had He longed for the wife of another? What did my saintly brother do to be expelled from the spotlessly pure and righteous city of Ayodhya?"[12]

She explained indifferently, "None of these. Rama can never do these things. His character is impeccable. The fact is that the king had decided to coronate Rama. To make *you* king in place of Rama, I redeemed an old boon the king had given me. Fulfilling my wish,

---

[11] The cuckoo that sings sweetly pecks harshly; the bee that sucks honey tenderly also stings sharply; the cat that carries its kitten lovingly also bites fatally.

A good mouth that is the harbinger of good to many becomes the harbinger of bad to some.

[12] Bharata is compared to a deep ocean into which unique rivers called supreme ethics flow. He was ready to let go of the best of relationships if values were compromised. If Rama had compromised on principles, Bharata would have let go of his relationship with his brother.

Instead of holding on to rock-steady principles, people like Dasaratha give up principles and try to hold on to moving emotions. He was ready to let go of Rama (principles) to satisfy Keikeyi (his emotions).

Bharata wasn't ready to compromise his principles for any relationship, but Dasaratha was willing to trade any principle for a single relationship.

he banished Rama and agreed to make you king. When Rama went away, the king just died, unable to tolerate this separation.

Now, my dear son, all obstacles preventing you from ruling this kingdom have been removed; come and take charge. I did all this only to ensure this end. It is not the time to be sad. Be courageous and rule the kingdom. Get up and instruct Vasistha and the other sages to crown you immediately," she said, going closer to Bharata to help him stand up.

Bharata shrugged her hands off and bellowed, "Aarrgh!" Keikeyi staggered away as she was caught off guard. The entire palace reverberated with Bharata's agonizing roar. His grief erupted like a volcano.[13]

Bharata paused for a moment; he turned to the direction of the Dandaka forest, closed his eyes, touched his folded hands to his forehead and offered a deep prayer of forgiveness to Lord Rama. The very next instant, he was screaming like a wild animal cut loose from shackles. Flames shot out of his breath; blood oozed from his eyes; his cheeks fluttered and his entire body trembled with anger.

"What happiness does a scorpion have when it has shred apart its

---

[13] Like an owl searching for rats, satisfied in its solitary existence inside a hole and short-term pursuits, Keikeyi searched for a position that would give her security and found satisfaction dreaming of the honor and respect she would receive as the mother of the king.

In the process, she conveniently overlooked her long-term responsibilities as a wife and a queen glaring upon her like the sun at noon. By focusing on her solitary existence, she became blind to the reality of the death of her husband, the suffering of her step-son, her resultant life of infamy and the mistrust she had subjected her own son to.

mother's belly? What happiness is there in ruling a kingdom after being the cause behind my father's death and my brother's exile?" Bharata spat out at his surprised mother.[14]

"By killing my father and turning my brother into an ascetic, you have slashed my body with two grievous wounds. And now by spouting drivel, you are sprinkling pepper on those wounds. I died the moment you revealed the hellish events that took place in my absence. Any hope for living on has abandoned me entirely. How do you expect a corpse to rule a kingdom? Dead people can't take any responsibility and neither can they enjoy any facility.

You are a sorceress whose only wish is to destroy our race. My innocent father thought that he was embracing a sandalwood log, but little did he know that he was embracing burning charcoal!

Only a fool cuts down a tree and waters its leaves or drains out a pond to keep fish alive. I am a leaf and a fish. I need the nourishment from my root-like father and branch-like brother to survive. No matter how much you water me, it will never be enough to sustain me while I stand alone. I need the natural cooling environment of Rama's presence and father Dasaratha's presence to survive the harsh heat of this world. Otherwise, I will thrash and flail like a fish out of water.

As soon as I accept the kingdom, the sin of murdering my father and exiling my brother will transfer from you to me. What will the world say? That I have managed to kill my father and expel my brother cleverly through my mother? My mother has given me a

---

[14] When one flaunts the fortune earned by stabbing innocent hearts, one experiences mental disenchantment instead of contentment.

rare gift of infamy. I ask you, why did you do this to me?[15]

It is impossible for pious, simple people to live with crooked, cunning ones. How can the virtuous mother Kaushalya and mother Sumitra bear your presence? Rama loved you more than His mother, and Kaushalya always loved you like a younger sister. Even you had such love for Rama. You were called *Sumukhi* because your mouth would be constantly chanting Rama's name. You were called *Sulochani* because you wouldn't look at anything else without seeing Rama first thing in the morning. How have you become *Kumukhi (vulgar mouthed)* and *Kulochani (casting negative glances)*? Now like a snake, you bite the very hand that feeds it milk. How can a mother not understand her child at all? What made you think that your schemes would make me happy? Don't you know that devotion to my brother is my greatest wealth? I am like a calf, how do you expect me to cope with the weight only giant bulls can handle?[16]

Even if I had the ability to handle the kingdom, I would not. I will just do the reverse of what you had planned. I will make sure that none of your wicked desires are fulfilled. If only Rama did not love you so much, I would not have hesitated to throw you out of Ayodhya. A person with such perversion does not deserve to stay in this holy city."[17]

---

[15] To the degree that one loves the white cloth to that degree one is conscious of even one black spot on it.

Being conscious of infamy is the contraception to wrong action.

[16] Honest knowledge and acceptance of one's capacity is the prerequisite to optimal performance. Bharata was honest about his limitations.

[17] Bharata did not allow his mood swings to affect his decision-making. Even in extreme anger, he did not throw Keikeyi out of the kingdom, but rather contemplated on what would make Rama happy.

Decision-making should be regulated by the consideration of how

Keikeyi was visibly shocked at the turn of events. She had convinced herself that she was doing all this for the welfare of her son. And now her son was systematically destroying the castle of assumptions she had built in the air.[18]

"The Ikshvaku dynasty has been following the holy tradition of crowning the eldest in the race. Why just Ikshvaku, even Kekeya follows the same tradition, doesn't it? The very name Kekeya comes from the *koo-koo* sound that the abundant peacocks there make. Don't you know the natural truth of a peacock family? Only the first-born has a natural feather crown on its head. All others that follow are devoid of that special crown. Rama was born first; this truth cannot be reversed, and the natural outcome is that only Rama deserves to be crowned in Ayodhya. I will make this happen, come what may.[19]

What kind of a mother are you? To secure a kingdom for your son, you have heaped insecurity on the life of mother Kaushalya's son. The heart of one mother should know how the heart of another beats. Even animals know it. Vasistha's *Kaamadhenu* cow once observed a farmer torturing two young oxen from morning to noon by making them toil in the heat. When the oxen fell in sheer exhaustion, hot tears rolled out of the cow's eyes. Those were not her own calves, but she experienced the pain of a mother.

God will view the decision made rather than allowing it to be swayed by personal likes or dislikes.

[18] To ensure living in one's own castle of assumptions, one does not mind even if it is built on the foundation of pulverized relationships, bricks of unverified facts, agenda-tainted windows and a roof of exclusive self-belief.

[19] Selfishness morphs the simple truths of life.

How can you be happy seeing another mother's child going through pain? And how can you be happy making another mother cry? I will not allow mother Kaushalya to cry. I will replace Rama in the forest and cast you into the ocean of tears.

Unconsumed poison has no power to kill. Similarly, since I have not accepted the kingdom, sin cannot accrue on me and I will be blameless. If there is any sin I can be accused of, it is that of staying in your sinful womb for so many months. And I will purify myself of that sin by performing severe austerities. As far as you are concerned, I recommend that you enter a fire or a forest or hang yourself to death."

After trying to drive sense into his mother, Bharata lost all bearings. He rolled on the ground in pain like an elephant pierced by a javelin and simultaneously dug by a spur and stung by a snake. From where Keikeyi stood, all she could see was a body in pain, some disheveled clothes and scattered ornaments.

This was déjà vu. Keikeyi could not bear to see this and tears welled up in her eyes. Not many days ago in this very house, she had flung herself onto the ground in exactly the same way, and her ornaments were scattered in the same fashion. Her act had caused much pain to Dasaratha, and her son's display of grief was causing her the same pain. She could clearly see how her own past actions had been responsible for her present misery. Keikeyi broke down for the first time in so many days and wept piteously. Bharata's agony and Keikeyi's sobbing attracted the attention of all the housekeepers. They rushed to inform the ministers about the chaos.[20]

---

[20] One punishes without punishing when one makes another realize and repent for the gravity of the mistake committed.

proof of innocence

As Bharata screamed innocence and begged forgiveness from the prominent people of Ayodhya, he could see in their midst, a shattered Shatrughna. Shatrughna had heard about it all and was completely distraught. The crying brothers embraced each other, unable to fathom how to undo what was done. Shatrughna suggested that they first take Kaushalya into confidence, pacify her and assure her of their innocence.

Soon, they were in front of the weeping Kaushalya. They ran and embraced her, the tears merging into rivers of sorrow. The sight of the three crying left every helper present in the room teary-eyed.[21]

Suddenly, Kaushalya shrugged the two off and stood aside. Her tears disappeared and her face turned fierce and strict. "It's time for you to rejoice. Your ruthless mother has done what no other mother has ever done. I am sure that you were well informed of the plan and I wouldn't be surprised if you were part of the plan, too.

My only question is why did you not send me to the forest with my

---

Bharata made Keikeyi realize her mistake by himself offering to go to the forest and replacing Rama. Bharata's decision woke Keikeyi from her slumber of ignorance.

This was the first time Keikeyi lost her self-control and burst into tears. She had not cried even when Rama left for the forest, or when her husband died.

[21] The prominent *rasa* or mellow in the Ramayana is *karuna rasa*, which means crying in compassion for others. The unique feature in this epic is that no one cries for himself or herself, everyone cries for the suffering or inconvenience of others.

son? Did you want me house-arrested in Ayodhya to ensure that my son does not attack the kingdom? I can assure you that I will pose no hindrance for you to rule happily. Even if Rama were here, He would have proved no hindrance either. O king, I request you to at least arrange for me to be sent to my son in the forest. I will be happy to leave this insubstantial city and carry with me the body of your father and the sacrificial fire in the house. Do you have at least this much compassion left to fulfill this desire of mine?"

His stepmother's words pierced him like sharp needles thrust into the gruesome wound created by his mother. He wailed and fell at her feet, wetting them with his tears. He begged her not to doubt his integrity. To put all fears to rest, he took a series of vows in the form of negative affirmations. These negative affirmations were a series of deviations, which, if performed, would result in severe reactions to the performer. By making these affirmations, Bharata was convincing her that he was ready to face the consequences of these sins if he was in any way responsible for the banishment of Rama.

the four sins of irresponsibility

Essentially, Bharata spoke of four categories of sins of irresponsibility; sins of irresponsibility that an accountable leader has to face, a *dharmic* follower has to face, a social pillar has to face and a judicious householder has to face. According to Bharata, if any of these sins were performed, it was disastrous for that role.

Sins of irresponsibility for an accountable leader at various levels are collecting taxes without ensuring protection, breaking the traditional codes of warfare, fleeing from a full-fledged battle, attempting treason against a loving fatherly king, imposing heavy labor on an employee without sufficient remuneration.

Sins of irresponsibility for a *dharmic* follower are going back on the promised remuneration to a priest, eating food without offering it first to God, disrespecting teachers, sleeping during both twilights and mechanical study of scriptures overlooking the subtle message taught by the spiritual master.

Sins of irresponsibility for a social pillar are falsifying the hopes of destitute beggars, setting fire to another's house, polluting drinking water, poisoning another's food, disappointing a thirsty person in spite of having sufficient water, kicking a sleeping cow and distributing gifts to the undeserving.

Sins of irresponsibility for a judicious householder are courting another's wife while disdaining his own, neglecting the request of a chaste wife to have a child, deceiving a friend, avoiding gratefully serving parents and abusing them, letting out a secret shared confidentially by others, eating delicious foodstuffs without sharing while being surrounded by family and servants, abandoning his dependents and maintaining dependents through a sinful occupation.

Bharata's vows pacified Kaushalya. She realized that he was as innocent as a calf. She walked up to him, cupped his mouth and stopped him from taking more such vows. She so appreciated Bharata's loyalty toward Rama that she said, "The moon may emit poison through its rays, the snow may emit fire, aquatics may give up their watery abodes and spiritual practices may stop eradicating errors, but Bharata will never turn hostile toward his brother Rama."

For the first time in the day, Bharata smiled weakly. Kaushalya embraced him and Bharata slept on Kaushalya's floor in lamentation. Although lamenting, he was at least happy that he was able to convince one person in the kingdom of his uprightness.

SIX SOLUTIONS TO SUCCESS

This chapter offers six solutions to overcome obstacles hindering your ambitions and goals in life. Each of these solutions is preceded by a test, which questions and challenges your aspiration to achieve the goal.

With every test, Bharata proves that his goals are carved in stone and not on shifting sands.

MISSION TEST 1 – CONFRONTING CRITICISM

When Bharata heard Kaushalya criticizing him and doubting his mission, he asked himself three questions that teach us how to face criticism rightly.

1. Why is she criticizing? Is she criticizing for personal profit or from personal pain?

2. Is the criticism from a personality I respect?

3. Is criticism her habit?

When he asked himself these questions, Bharata realized that she was hurt and feeling helpless and that although the spotless Kaushalya never criticized anyone, uttering these words were her way of dealing with this trauma.

Bharata dealt with criticism by taking a series of affirmations. By taking these affirmations Bharata did not solve Kaushalya's problems but gave her a strong demonstration of his sincerity. The seriousness and implications of the affirmations were so strong that Kaushalya immediately accepted the gravity of his mission and developed faith in the possibility of his accomplishing it. As for Bharata, taking such affirmations steeled his resolve.

three coins

"Lamentation that causes prolonged inaction is actually irresponsibility at an individual level and leads to chaos at a collective level. Every individual constantly carries three coins in his pocket. Each coin has two sides; and the side that is upfront indicates the dominant quality in his life at that moment.

The coin of hankering has hunger and thirst as its sides. The coin of experience has joy and sorrow as its sides. And the coin of existence has birth and death as its sides. Every person at every given point in time faces one of the sides of the three coins. It's not so painful if only one of the coins has a side that we detest. But if all the coins have sides that we detest, we call it calamity. Now you may have hunger, sorrow and death facing you. But that does not mean the sides of the coin will never turn. Don't lament for that which is unavoidable. Life cannot come to a standstill forever. Prince Bharata, get up and perform the last rites of your father now," Sage Vasistha instructed his pupil on the dawn of the next day.

Gently the body of the king was taken out of the vat of oil. The king's face seemed serene, as if in deep slumber. A mild golden hue diffused from his body. With great respect, the body was placed on a bejeweled couch.

The grim-faced Bharata began to sob uncontrollably. Vashistha intervened and asked the attendants to carry the body in a palanquin. As the palanquin exited the palace, an uproar emerged from the clamorous thousands waiting below. As their illustrious king made his last journey, the sad citizens scurried ahead, scattering along coins of silver, gold and precious cloth.

When Bharata set fire to Dasaratha's funeral pyre, hundreds of gathered citizens showered fragrant sandalwood sticks and essences into the royal pyre, bidding their dear king farewell. With a clay pot filled with water, Bharata circumambulated the pyre thrice. Each time, the clay pot was struck with a stone, which made the water leak; and after the last round, Bharata dropped the pot behind him on the ground. To the accompaniment of pure chants of *Sama veda* hymns recited by trained priests, the three queens circumambulated the pyre in counterclockwise direction thrice.

As the sun dipped below the horizon, the mourners along with their prince and queens took a dip in the holy Sarayu river for a purification bath.

The only sounds that could be heard from every corner of Ayodhya for the next 12 days were moans of sorrow and dismay. On the twelfth day, Bharata performed *shradha* for his father and doled out hundreds of goats and cows, large quantities of cooked rice, cloth and other presents to the *brahmanas*. On the thirteenth day, Bharata and Shatrughna collected their father's ashes from the funeral site and immersed it into the Sarayu river to mark the completion of the funeral ceremony.[22]

---

[22] All rituals, except those related to death entail circumambulation in clockwise direction. Funeral rituals require counterclockwise

gilded devil

For the first time in weeks, the two brothers found the time and space to sit together for some uncluttered thinking. The situation and the feelings that had consumed their lives at this point of time seemed so unique that they couldn't think of a third person who could empathize with them.

Thinking aloud, Shatrughna said, "I wonder why the prudent Lakshmana did not stand up and oppose all the nonsense... why did the heroic Lakshmana allow our father to be influenced by an evil-minded woman?"[23]

When they were seriously pondering over this, they heard a jarring tune and the off-key clanking of anklets and bracelets. They became curious. How could someone be so positively happy when the entire city was in mourning? This bliss seemed gravely insensitive to the plight of Ayodhya.

What they saw disgusted them. At another time, they would have

---

circumambulation, indicating that it was now time to unwind attachment to that body.

The pot filled with water symbolizes life within a body, and cracking the pot suggests that life has now escaped. Dropping the pot behind indicates that now there was no point preserving the body or looking back.

Twelve days are kept for mourning to allow the attached relatives to sufficiently remember the loving relationship they had and express gratitude for it. At this time, the identification with the body is extreme, so doing anything connected with the holy deities is not recommended because the focus would be the body and not the worship.

[23] When prudence combines with competence, it demands apt action.

been convulsing with laughter at this sight. But today, humor was not just unwelcome, it was forbidden.

Draped in the costliest of silks, bedecked with stone-studded gold ornaments and sandalwood paste daubed all over was the hunchbacked maid of Keikeyi appearing out of the eastern gate of the palace. With gold chains all over her hunchback and heavy cosmetics applied on her face, Manthara resembled a female monkey tied with golden ropes. She was totally out of sync with the city's sentiments. While everyone was sad and disturbed, she was cheerful, singing and dancing ecstatically.[24]

As she sang and frolicked about peculiarly, the doorkeepers caught her by her neck and began dragging her. She started hurling abuses and curses at them, swearing to ruin their lives because of her influence on Queen Keikeyi. Handing her over to Shatrughna, they said, "Here is the sinful and cruel woman who directed the events leading to the death of your father and exile of your brother. Instigating the innocent queen with her convoluted mentality, this woman has meticulously executed the doom of Ayodhya. Now do what you may with her."

Anger seized Shatrughna and he erupted by screaming at her with the ferocity of a lion. He caught her hair and began to drag her forcibly along the ground, yelling that he would make her taste the

---

[24] Being happy for no reason is a sign of naivety.

Being happy for others prosperity is a sign of maturity.

Being happy for others misery is a sign of malignity.

While the whole city was lamenting, Manthara was rejoicing. All her life, Manthra had no relationships of her own; because she had never experienced love, she could not comprehend separation either.

Refinedness in sentiments is the by-product of a tender heart.

bitter fruits of her cruel harvest. Manthara howled in excruciating pain as Shatrughna dragged her mercilessly. Her companions ran away in fear and decided to take the shelter of Kaushalya, lest the brothers harass them too.

Manthara's strewn colorful ornaments made the dark floor seem like an autumn night's sky bedecked with stars, and the gold-covered maid resembled a comet being dragged across the sky.

Keikeyi came rushing. Afraid, she begged her son Bharata to pacify Shatrughna, so that he would let Manthara go.

Bharata shocked his mother by saying, "If I was sure that Rama would not be displeased, I would have killed Manthara long ago. My brother, it's a great sin to kill or even harm a woman. If Rama comes to know that we have harmed this woman, even if we justify to Him that she was the one who brought so much harm to Ayodhya, He would still not be happy. In fact, He would refrain from talking to us."[25]

Convinced of his brother's argument, Shatrughna let go of Manthara. She staggered and fell at Keikeyi's feet, breathless and sobbing; like a gasping crane strangled with a noose, set free just when it was about to die. Keikeyi hugged her and calmed her frayed nerves.

---

[25] Bharata means one whose **bhava**, *raga* and *tala* was to serve Rama. He knew Rama's, *bhava*, *raga* and *tala* and could thus serve Lord Rama rhythmically. Essentially, this meant that he understood the mood and mission of Rama perfectly and was ready to align his life's priorities according to them.

barren throne

The blowing conch ripped through the early-morning silence. A slow-paced rhythmic drumming joined the steadily increasing pitch of the conch. Added to this was melodious intones of auspicious hymns. As the combined effect grew louder, Bharata sat up on his bed covering his ears and yelling, "I am not the king! Stop all this music!"

Silence followed. Bharata looked sadly at his brother resting close to him and said, "Just see how much harm Keikeyi has done. The kingdom without a king is like a stray boat without a rudder." As the brothers expressed their sadness to one another, Vasistha, who stood unnoticed, smiled. He had set up this subtle test to assess Bharata's innermost desire. The smile indicated that he had a satisfactory answer. Vasistha walked away content.

MISSION TEST 2 – CONFRONTING SUBCONSCIOUS DESIRES

Sleep is the most vulnerable platform to test one's subconscious desires. The mind plays with desires all day and what it cherishes the most it plays with it all night also.

Vasistha arranged for a sleep test to examine and confirm Bharata's real mission and his innermost desires. If he had the slightest desire for the throne, he would react positively to the kingly treatment.

Bharata dealt with his subconscious desires with alertness.

> When one decides to accomplish an impossible mission, alertness is not optional. The difference between dreamers and achievers is that achievers act even in dreams, while dreamers are wrapped in reverie even in action. Even at the subtlest levels of the subconscious level, Bharata desired only to fulfill his mission of bringing Rama back to Ayodhya and thus, he alertly stopped all the kingly treatment.

The brothers hurried to the courtroom, apprehensive of the happenings. This was the first full-court day after so many weeks of mourning and chaos in Ayodhya. As they entered, everyone arose; the brothers were then respectfully ushered to their seats.

"Fortunately, by the grace of the Almighty Lord, the kingdom has not lost its glory, even though King Dasaratha is no more and has left for the heavenly abode, and even though Rama and Lakshmana are no longer around and have departed to the forest. That this glory will continue cannot be a permanent assumption," Ayodhya's best-known well-wisher and royal *guru* Vasistha spoke.

"If a *brahmana* or intellectual visionary, who is ignorant of the Vedas, abandons his duties to pursue pleasure-seeking endeavors, it is a pity. It is a pity if a *kshatriya* or administrative governor who lacks knowledge of governance does not love his people more than his own life. If a *vaishya* or merchant is miserly and inhospitable despite all his wealth, it is a pity. It is a pity if an expert *sudra* or skilled laborer is arrogant about his expertise and is disrespectful toward others and hankers for honor. If a disciple breaks his vows and does not obey the orders of his spiritual master, it is a pity. It is a pity if a householder forsakes the path of duty out of ignorance. If a renunciant forsakes austerities and develops an attachment to luxuries and comforts, it is also a pity. O Bharata, but more pitiable than all these is a kingdom without a qualified king.

O noble prince, the king has surely gone to a higher realm because of his pious life. Don't lament anymore for his departure. Focus now on pleasing him by following his words. The king bestowed kingship upon you before departing. Make his words come true by accepting the kingship. Nothing was dearer to the king than his words. He was ready to bear separation from his beloved Rama and was willing to give up his own life for the sake of the word he gave his wife. By executing your father's command, you will follow in the footsteps of Parasurama, who held the words of his father so sacred that he killed his own mother.

Don't you know the story of Yayati who was once cursed by sage Sukracharya to become old and infirm in the prime of his youth? After countless mercy pleas, the sage allowed him to exchange his old age with someone else. The first four of his five sons flatly denied the ridiculous request for personal sacrifice. Puru the fifth and youngest son conceded and exchanged his youth for his father's old age. The result was that after a few years, when Yayati had his fill of enjoyment, he returned his youth to Puru, but he also awarded the kingdom to his son for his selfless sacrifice. Bharata, today you are like Puru, although younger. Dasaratha has awarded you the kingdom, and no sin will accrue on you by accepting the kingdom that has been awarded by choice. Come and accept the throne. Give security to your people."

Bharata could no longer rein in his emotions. Vasistha's constant pelting of stones guised as words ripped his heart. What followed was a torrent of tears; Bharata's body convulsed as if he was ordered to consume poison. But he closed his eyes and focused only on Lord Rama; gradually, he began to feel stable. If mere remembrance of

Rama could stabilize a person, wouldn't His presence stabilize the government? Bharata spoke in a logical yet fascinating manner to the august gathering.

"First, just as ornaments are useless on a naked person, questions asked without any intent of following the answers are useless; just as an abundance of resources for enjoyment is useless for a diseased person, chanting *mantras* is useless for a person not devoted to God; just as a handsome body is useless without the presence of life, all that I possess is useless without Rama!

Second, the kingdom and I belong to Rama. How can one property own another? The relationship between two properties is through the owner. My connection to the kingdom is through Rama.

Third, only a virtuous man should grace the throne. How can I rob the throne from someone far more superior? Be it learning, self-control, performance of duty, administrative ability, kindness or any other virtue, Rama stands on a loftier plane. The moment you install a sinner, such as myself on the throne, the earth will sink to its lowest depths. How can a sinner replace a man of virtue?

Fourth, you refer to Puru who sacrificed his youth for his father. But to install me as king, my mother sacrificed my father. What glory will a son like me find by sitting on the throne tainted with the blood of my father and the tears of millions?

Fifth, I say that if any great upholder of *dharma* present in this court considers my mother's act to be *dharmic*, then surely *Kaliyuga* has intercepted *Tretayuga*. This is not *dharma* speaking, this is the voice of ignorance borne out of affection.[26]

---

[26] The codes of *dharma* are not inscribed with sticky attachments but with stern principles.

Even if all wise men of the entire universe tell me today that my becoming king is absolutely in tandem with *dharmic* principles, I will not accept it."

Saying this, Bharata folded his hands and circumambulated the ingredients kept for coronation and said, "If anyone must become the king of Ayodhya, it should be Rama, and I will ensure that it happens. I will undo my mother's deed and replace Rama in the forest. I invite the whole of Ayodhya to travel with me to the forest. With folded hands, we will supplicate the principled Rama to return and rule the kingdom rightfully. I will take all these ingredients to the forest, coronate him there itself and bring him back with royal honor."

Vasistha's old cheeks were wet with tears. His training had not gone in vain. Bharata was the perfect disciple, and his decision today was the most perfect *guru dakshina*.

Bharata's words spread happiness all around. Ayodhya's citizens had tears of joy. After all, righteousness hadn't deserted the city. Bharata instructed Sumantra to mobilize the army to start constructing roads and pathways to the forest.[27]

For several days, Ayodhya's citizens had been aching from the venom of separation from Rama. Bharata's wise words became the *mantras* that had the potential to be anti-venom. His comments brought the kind of rejuvenating joy to Ayodhya's citizens that peacocks and *chataka* birds feel on hearing a thunderclap.

---

[27] The bumblebee not only lives knowing that its wings cannot handle its body weight, but it also deals with it through determination.

Similarly, Bharata did not simply live with the situation that his mother created, but he also dealt with it with determination.

A happy citizen spoke, "Bharata, you are the personification of love for Rama. It is, therefore, no wonder that you exude such words of love."

Another continued, "The foolish man who hates you because of your mother's wickedness shall reside in hell for millions of years with millions of his past generations."

Yet another elderly wise gentleman said, "Just as the gem on a serpent's head is unaffected by the reptile's faults and is instead, used as the antidote to the venom, you are the jewel that will extract the poison that your mother has spread."

The courtroom was buzzing with animated discussions and soon the joy spread far and wide across Ayodhya. Ayodhya's womenfolk were delighted with this news and urged their husbands to join Bharata's entourage and bring Rama back. From every home in every direction, smiling men began to emerge with bags on their shoulders. They were on a mission: Bring Rama back as the rightful king of Ayodhya.

MISSION TEST 3 – CONFRONTING CONFUSING CHOICES

When Bharata realized that Vasistha was testing his determination by offering him the choice of an easy path, he, in turn, tested the capacity of his choice muscles by adding four weighty questions to his choice bar. Bharata did not want to follow an easy path but rather the right path.

1. Am I gauging my choices logically or am I gauging them emotionally?

2. Am I evaluating my choices responsibiy, which means am I gauging the choices against higher standards or only against comfortable standards?

3. Will the result of my choice be a risk or a gain for the larger welfare?

4. Am I willing to face public scrutiny for my decision?

When Bharata asked himself these questions, he realized that he wasn't emotional at all, but had logically evaluated his options against the higher standard of the scriptures, which naturally meant that the choice would result in the greater good. And the proof that he had made the right choice was visible in Vasistha's tears and proud glance and the overwhelming joy on the faces of the citizens.

Bharata dealt with confusing choices turn by turn, placing them on a measuring scale with weights of longer-lasting impact and the scope of the greater welfare as counter measures.

He saw the obvious result with a vision to accept the responsibility of the outcome. Good choices are an outcome of deliberation and not desperation.

Hundreds of skilled people joined hands to set off on the colossal road-building task. The task force comprised excavators, mechanics, level string holders, plasterers, carpenters, road menders, woodcutters, supervisors, tent layers and many who were probably not high on skill but were high on the energy, courage, enthusiasm and compliance needed to do what they were told to.

Before long, the road to Rama began being laid. Shrubs were cleared;

rocks were pulverized and used to fill wells and low-lying areas on the path. Trees that stood on the way were felled and new ones planted along the sides. Sweet-water ponds were dug at regular intervals to help thirsty itinerants. Bunds were built along river banks to store rainwater and overflowing river water for irrigation and fill up ponds with fresh water. The sturdy roads were flanked by fragrant, flower-laden shrubs. At regular intervals, tents were erected to host the weary travelers.

Soon, a spectacular roadway stretched all the way from the city of Ayodhya to the banks of the Ganga.

hope march

The epic march began with 9000 elephants, 60,000 chariots with archers, 10,000 cavalry men and thousands of citizens led by Bharata and Shatrughna's chariot with a flag bearing the insignia of a *Kovidara* or purple orchid tree[28] fluttering high. All ministers and sagacious counselors were present. The queen mothers were gracefully carried in ornate palanquins.

Treading along with the dignitaries were the commoners of Ayodhya. Potters, ivory sculptors, perfume vendors, blanket weavers, tailors, dancers, washer men, fishermen, artificial stone workers, fumigators, *brahmanas*, mercantile men and those blessed with love for Rama joined this journey. A single thought strung all of them into a garland of assorted personalities, "When will we have that first glimpse of the magnanimous Rama for our sorrows to end?" Like thirsty

---

[28] Purple orchid signifies luxury, beauty, long lasting impact and stability.

elephants rushing toward fresh water, they were running toward Rama to quell their angst.[29]

Golden memories of past positive experiences in Ayodhya rushed through their minds. As their feet surged ahead, their minds raced behind. Amid this push and pull between the past and present, all movement stopped. Way ahead, right at the front of the entourage, Bharata's mind, too, had been racing, but into the future. He was trying to imagine the kind of life his brother must be leading. Then it struck him that his brother must be traversing the uneven forest terrain barefoot, and here he was riding a bejeweled chariot on a smooth road. No sooner than the thought crossed his mind, his chariot came to a halt and his feet auto-descended to the ground. Soon, the brothers were walking alongside their empty chariots.

The brothers' gesture motivated every accompanying citizen to step out of their conveyance and walk along. They immediately felt close to Rama and admiration for Bharata. Only one person was uncomfortable with the change of pattern and consequential change of speed. Kaushalya ordered her palanquin carriers to rush forward to catch up with Bharata. Seeing the palanquin hasten quickly, the crowd parted, allowing it to slice through the thick of Ayodhya citizens. Reaching his side, Kaushalya peeped out of her curtained palanquin and spoke. "My dear child, if you walk, the whole party will follow suit. They are already weary from sorrow, why do you want to tire them further by making them foot such a massive distance. They are physically and mentally unfit to handle

---

[29] Just as pearls are strung with a string, diverse humans with individual shortcomings are held together through the thread of a higher pursuit.

Just as the string covers the hole and exhibits the shining surface of the pearl, the thread of higher pursuits plugs our shortcomings and binds us together to achieve excellence.

444

44444444

this rigor. Besides, how we reach Rama is not as important as when we reach Him. In this situation, time is more important than means. I request you to mount your chariot and expedite the journey."

Bharata and Shatrughna bowed down to her wisdom and remounted their chariot. The journey continued; it was a silent one – no words were exchanged, no whispers shared, no music played and no heads turned. If it wasn't the movement, the entourage would have been mistaken for a painting on a wall. Despite the external silence, within every heart were loud incantations and resounding prayers, "Let our Rama come back."

On reaching the river Ganga, Bharata decided to halt at the village of Sringaberapura. As tents were being erected and people were offloading their baggage, Bharata went to offer his oblations in the holy river, especially for his departed father.

secret saviors

A hundred pairs of eyes watched as the army set up its camp on the opposite bank. Not a single movement on the river bank across went unseen. In a hushed yet firm tone, Guha spoke to his men, "More than the extent of this army is the extent of my determination to serve and protect Rama. The *Kovidara* tree insignia implies that this is definitely Bharata's army. Why would the newly-crowned sibling approach his exiled brother with an army? The only natural conclusion is that he has evil designs.

I am ready to lay down my life to protect my friend, and I hope all of you are ready to sacrifice yours for the sake of your master's mission." When all heads nodded in approval even as their eyes remained riveted to the army ahead, Guha continued: "Don your armor and get ready for a blood fest. Arrange 500 boats in such a way that this bank is inaccessible to them unless they penetrate through our phalanxes. With 100 youthful hulks on each boat, how will it be possible for that army to penetrate it without being thwarted completely?

Their first hurdle is the swirling river, which will be impossible to cross. Even if they did manage to, how could they cross this formidable army? With the double buttressing, victory will definitely be ours!" The fiery pep talk from their master pumped up the squad, which grinned in anticipation of the action.

On a more thoughtful note, Guha added: "All this action will be needed only if Bharata is actually inimical toward Rama. If he is favorably disposed, we will use these same boats to help them cross the Ganga safely. I will go to Bharata and test his love on the touchstone of friendly disposition. Neither hatred nor love can remain disguised from my sharp eyes. If I even get the slightest hint of his malicious intent, then his army of rats will be consumed by the snakes of Guha."[30]

condemnation and commendation

With deliciously prepared food and freshly extracted honey as offerings, Guha reached the now-settled encampment. Sumantra

---

[30] When one is completely consumed by anger, sober discriminating ability staggers like that of a drunk walking.

A good leader prudently stops an overdose of anger from entering his system like a healthy man consciously avoids overeating.

observed the tribal chief advancing towards them and informed Bharata about Guha's arrival. On learning about Guha's close friendship with Rama, Bharata became eager to meet him and believed he may be able to provide Rama's exact coordinates.

The first vision of Bharata convinced Guha that he couldn't have malice in his heart. His facial features closely resembled Rama sans the eternal smile. He had dark circles under his eyes from the constant crying and he seemed exhausted from his struggle to live. Guha assumed his natural humility and spoke, "I am reporting to You on behalf of Your subjects. We are Yours and everything we have is Yours." Saying this, he offered all the gifts he had carried with him.

After thanking him for his hospitality, Bharata right away asked Guha the question that had been plaguing him from the time they reached the river Ganga. "Dear friend, just tell me one thing, how do we reach the *ashram* of the great sage Bharadwaja? Is there any other route which does not require us to cross this massive river?"

Guha nodded and smiled, "Only mother Ganga can lead you to the abode of saints. But there is nothing to worry about. The river appears formidable only to those who have not taken complete shelter of her. For the fishes in the river, she is their home. And for us boatmen, she is the mother who maintains us. I have 500 boats that will assist your army in crossing safely. Not only will my men help you cross the river, they will also carefully guide you and your army through the forest, which they are so familiar with. But before I help you, you need to clarify a burning doubt I have."

Guha was contemplating whether he should adopt the diplomatic approach or the direct approach to test Bharata. Had he not seen the sullen face of Bharata, he would surely have acted diplomatically. He grimly asked, "Is your intention to attack Rama? The innocence on your face tells one story, but the extent of your army communicates another." When the color of Bharata's face changed, he added, "You must excuse me for so bluntly expressing my fear. My love for Rama veils my shame and clouds my intelligence."

Bharata became morose. The good feeling was suddenly replaced by a feeling of self-disgust. He felt like a tree burning from within. His stomach coiled and he covered his face with his palms. "You have stabbed me with a blunt knife Guha. Why did you suspect me? Why does everyone suspect me? Rama is my elder brother and now He is like my father. How can I harbor any ill will toward Him? I have set out to undo all the wrong that transpired in my absence. I intend to take Him back and rightly install Him on the imperial throne of Ayodhya. Please do not doubt my intentions, O friend."

With moistened eyes Guha said, "Blessed are you, Bharata! You are one in a million! In fact, you are the only one – no one can be like you. What Rama did is not as big as what you plan to do. He abandoned the kingdom because He was asked to do so. In order to remain an obedient son to His father and stay compliant with the rules of *dharma*, He took to a life of austerities. It is easy to forsake tasty food taken off your plate, but it is extremely difficult to resist the temptation of something that is available within your legal reach.[31]

You gained a kingdom without any effort. Who would blame you for ruling a kingdom that has come of its own accord to you? Your

---

[31] Bharata could have said that he was following the footsteps of Rama by being obedient to the father's decision and silently accepted and ruled the kingdom. Guha pointed out that what was obedience for Rama had become a temptation for Bharata. Thus, both reacted differently and perfectly.

decision to retrieve Rama and restore Him to His rightful place is indeed epochal. Your glory will spread faster than the light of the sun."

As much as blame made Bharata despondent, praise made him miserable. He somehow maneuvered the conversation in another direction.[32]

MISSION TEST 4 – CONFRONTING BLAME AND PRAISE

Guha's initial accusation for the mishap in Ayodhya and the subsequent praise for the decision to renounce kingship in Rama's favor, caused Bharata to mentally deal with both blame and praise by getting to the root of the two attitudes. He realized that they are actually two sides of the same coin. He prodded his intention with three questions.

1. What is the source of my conviction and willingness to take risk?

2. Do I rely on others' praise to judge if I am right and others' blame to decide that I am wrong?

3. Do I really have a self-reliance quotient or am I happy to be like the helpless log in an ocean pushed and pulled by others' opinions?

Bharata dealt with both blame and praise by ignoring them. Because anyone who dares to stand apart is criticized, he guarded himself against anger by maintaining a calm, detached spirit.

---

[32] The coin that has blame as one side and praise as another has zero value for a humble soul.

Negative attitude toward blame and positive attitude toward praise, he realized, are worse than blame and praise themselves. Every blame convinced Bharata about the urgency of his mission. He saw any praise as the benchmark that had to be achieved rather than having already earned it. Instead of defending himself or correcting others, he decided to patiently wait for time to prove his genuineness and integrity.

As night set in and Bharata lay in his tent, he found it difficult to traverse the distance between hitting the bed and going off to sleep. As he tossed and turned, his mind drifted to the night he dreamt of the impending disaster in his life. But that dream was nothing compared to the reality he woke up to. That nightmare had indeed foretold the shattering of dreams.

Bharata's grief was as formidable as the Himalayas. The sweat wrought by woe that trickled down his body was akin to the melting snow subjected to the fierce heat of the sun. Bharat's sighs and groans were like minerals squeezed out of the mountains because of pressure. The array of forlorn deliberations of his sad state was like a dense forest of trees on the mountain. His sorrow and lassitude touched Himalayan highs, and through the night, he drifted in and out of swoons.

Accepting defeat at the hands of his sleep-devoid destiny, he rose and exited his tent. Outside he found Guha sitting and staring up at the dark sky and a little way ahead, he saw his brother Shatrughna pacing back and forth. With darkness now shrouding his entire life, Bharata did not need to look at more darkness. He wanted the light of grace and knowledge. He requested Guha to describe the visit

Rama, Lakshmana and Sita made to this very spot not too long ago. He felt that would provide some much needed solace.

Guha described everything to the minutest detail, including the emotions that played out, from the time of their arrival to the time they rested for the night. Then he elucidated on the dialogue he had with Lakshmana, who was reluctant to take rest that night. He also told him how he, too, had remained awake to guard Rama and Sita.[33]

The next day, as they were departing from Sringaberapura, he explained, Rama and Lakshmana matted their soft, silky hair and set forth, leaving Guha heartbroken. When Bharata heard about his brothers' upgrade of renunciation, he swooned. Shatrughna ran up to him and managed to cushion his fall.

After regaining consciousness, Bharata was eager to see the exact spot Rama and Sita slept that ill-starred night.

When his eyes fell on the bed of grass, they almost fell out of their sockets. How much more pain would these eyes have to bear? The dead body of a father, the self-denial of a brother, the helplessness of a stepmother and the arrogance of an over ambitious mother were all equally excruciating to behold. Kneeling next to the bed of grass, Bharata sobbed, "Today, I am able to appreciate the power of

---

[33] Guha is known as *gahana-gochara*, which means a deep man, the meaning of whose words are not easy to decipher. But Bharata is known as *aprameya*, which means his sharp intellect can decode deep secrets.

When Guha said that he himself had stayed awake all night, Bharata reasoned that Guha had stayed up all night with Lakshmana because he did not trust him.

Bharata deciphered that for Guha, Rama was his most precious treasure and that he had to guard Him even from Lakshmana and Bharata.

time. The one who was used to such luxury is today reduced to such penury. Even today, the kingdom of Ayodhya is secure despite all its systems collapsing, the gates always being open and the absence of a king. This is only possible because Rama is mentally protecting it. The one who can protect the institution even in his absence cannot protect himself from destitution. How else can one explain this enigma, except by attributing it to the invincible time factor?"[34]

Indeed, Lakshmana and Sita are most fortunate to at least be sharing the burden of Rama and constantly basking in His loving company. After seeing this bed, how can I enjoy any luxury or comfort? Today, I take a vow that I will not sleep on soft bedding till Rama returns; I will sleep on coarse grass like my austere brother. I will abstain from palatable delicacies and dine on roots and fruits like my self-controlled brother. Shedding soft cloth, I take a vow that matted locks will crown my head and crude bark will cloak my skin like my delicate brother. For the next 14 years, like my uncompromising brother, I will not reside in a palace, let alone a city."

By this time, hundreds of Ayodhyavasis had congregated; word of Bharata in agony spread around the camp. As Bharata completed his vow, somebody collapsed behind the crowd. Keikeyi hadn't expected things to turn this bad. Her perfect master plan was honeycombed with imperfections. Every pain she caused was coming back to her in greater magnitude.[35]

---

[34] Time seems like a deranged pilot who puts passengers in a turbulent flight to an undesired destination. But in actuality, it is a seasoned pilot, who just follows the instructions of destiny verbatim as ordained by higher controllers.

[35] In the drama called *karma*, the first and the last scenes are the same, but with reversed roles; therefore, *karma* is actually the infallible dramatic instrument of *dharma*.

Caring friends took Bharata back to his tent. Now, even the desire to sleep had gone. But the remembrance of his glorious brother had pacified his perplexed heart.

As Bharata exited, the men and women of Ayodhya who had tagged along with him on this voyage, edged toward the spot where the divine couple had slept a few days earlier. With great remorse in their heart, they paid respects to the spot and circumambulated it clockwise. Crying and confused, they cursed Keikeyi, praised Bharata, lamented the loss of Dasaratha, expressed concern for Rama and blamed fate for their plight. No one except the sun slept.[36]

near yet far

With sunrise, Bharata walked up to Shatrughna, who was immersed in thoughts of Rama and Lakshmana. Bharata instructed him to seek Guha's help in crossing the river. Soon, the river was teeming with 500 large boats and one mammoth-sized boat, carrying the sign of a huge swastika. This special boat was covered with white canvas that was splendid and tastefully embroidered. As everyone clambered into their allotted boats, Vasistha, all the *brahmanas*, Bharata, Shatrughna and all the queen mothers boarded the regal one.

---

[36] The place where holy people perform holy actions becomes holy. And holy actions are not so much about taking as much about giving and forgiving.

Rama and Sita slept on a bed of grass by ungrudgingly sacrificing Their comforts for the welfare of others. This place thus, became one more holy place, forever reminding humanity about living a life of gratitude and forgiveness.

Once everyone was aboard, the make-shift tenements from the previous night were removed and every trace that this was ever a resting place was cleared for security reasons. Everything was left just as the entourage had found it when they decided to camp there for the night. The last thing anyone needed was an enemy tracking their movements by following the trail of tenements as they proceeded ahead.

Those that could not be accommodated in the boats sat on rafts fashioned with logs tied together. Some floated using the buoyancy of empty earthen pots and yet, others bravely swam across. Elephant hordes that swam across the river resembled mountains in motion.

They soon reached the opposite bank. It felt as if everyone had managed to cross the ocean of miseries. In a short time, the entire army reached Prayag within *maitra* hours.[37]

Bharata, who was now clad in bark and had matted his hair, chose

---

[37] According to the Vedic science, the day is divided into 30 *muhurtas* of 48-minute duration each. These are listed as *rudra, aahi, maitra, pitra, vasu, varaaha, vishvadeva, vidhi, sutamukhi, puruhuta, vaahini, naktanakaraa, varuna, aryamana, bhaga, girisha, ajapaada, ahir-budhnya, pushya, ashwini, yama, agni, vidhaatra, kanda, aditi, jiva, Vishnu, dyumadgadyuti, brahma* and *samudram.*

Each *muhurta* represents a quality or *guna*, which may or may not be auspicious depending on many factors. Depending on the muhurta of events that happen in life, it is possible to determine whether the event will be auspicious or not.

Interestingly, Bharata and his army arrived at Prayag in *maitra muhurta,* which was a very auspicious one and according to the modern timescale, it would be about 7.38 to 8.24 a.m.

The most auspicious time of the day is considered to be the *brahma muhurta* that extends from 4.24 to 5.12 a.m. Most spiritualists aim to begin their practice at this time.

to walk barefoot because it was a forest path and even chariots would tread slowly. He reasoned that if Rama had walked barefoot, by virtue of being his servant, he should have walked on his head. But because he wasn't capable of doing that, the least he could do was walk. By the end of the day's journey, the soles of Bharata's feet had blistered. Those who saw their prince suffering felt compassion. They could see that the blisters glistened on his feet like pearly dewdrops that crystallize on a lotus bud. But for Bharata every blister was a form of his repentance and he was oozing tears of atonement.[38]

Not wanting to spoil the serene atmosphere of Bharadwaja *muni*'s *ashram*, Bharata instructed his army to rest and he trod ahead with Vasistha and his ministers. He had already discarded his regal attire and jewelry, he now kept aside his weapons, too, and walked toward the *ashram* with no possessions.[39]

As Bharata reached the precincts of the hermitage, he left his ministers and walked in, with only Vasistha for company. Anticipating their arrival, Bharadwaja *muni* was already waiting with the traditional welcome fare. After the formalities, he embraced Vasistha and inquired about his welfare. He took care not to ask about Dasaratha, knowing what had transpired. The next moment, Bharadwaja *muni* tightened his face and spoke words that pierced Bharata like a dagger to the chest. "I hope you have not come to harm Rama in the forest."

---

[38] Atonement is like the fire that burns away past sins to ashes, which act as manure for new crop of hope to grow. But sincere tears of repentance are like water that nurtures the crop of devotion.

Atonement without repentance is hope without transformation.

[39] When one walks to the abode of his superior, one has to cast away the clothing of ego, the ornaments of skills, the crown of position, the weapons of defending one's belief systems and walk alone without any "yes men."

Losing his balance for a moment, Bharata said, "O venerable one, you are the seer of the past, present and future. If you question me like this what can I expect from the ignorant. Let me assure you that I don't have any malintent. It was my mother's mistake, foolishness rather, and I have come to rectify it. I am here to take Rama back with us to Ayodhya. My preceptor Vasistha will vouch for my intention."

Vasistha reconfirmed what Bharata had just said. Now visibly relaxed, Bharadwaja *muni* told Bharata: "You are indeed an apt descendent to the celebrated Ikshvaku dynasty. Gold dust that falls off from the gold block is certainly as valuable as gold itself. I knew your intentions, but I wanted to reconfirm directly. In fact, I wanted my doubting disciples and the world to see your love and ascertain your true glory.

I know why you have come to me, Bharata. You want me to point out the exact whereabouts of Rama, don't you? He has made the beautiful mountain range Chitrakoot his abode. I will definitely show you the exact location, but it is already twilight now, rest here for the night and tomorrow morning I will personally direct you to your brother."

MISSION TEST 5 -- CONFRONTING ACCOUNTABILITY

It is easy to say anything in front of amateurs and get away with it. But it is very difficult to say anything in front of experts. Bharadwaja muni was not merely an expert, he was a seer of past, present and future. When he asked Bharata about his real intention of coming to the forest, Bharata looked around and realized that the *muni* had created an environment that tested the accountability of his mission. He was in front of a person who could read minds, on the banks of the most holy river Ganga that demands transparency and in front of sages who were lie detectors personified.

Bharata dealt with this accountability test with self-confidence.

The conviction of a self-confident person inspires others to believe him and create positive change in their lives. Self-confidence is a by-product of trusting God with our problems. When personal ambition overshadows our vision, self-confidence may transform into overconfidence.

To prevent this from happening, a sincere leader invites a moral authority to inspect his motives. Such proactive transparency is far superior to the defective method of self-inspection; thus, combined with self-confidence in his intention and Bharadwaja *muni's* inspection of his intention, Bharata cleared the accountability test.

Bharata concurred with him; Bharadwaja *muni* then asked him to bring along his entire army. Bharata was surprised at the impractical proposal for the *ashram* did not seem large enough to host even a couple of guests, leave alone hosting thousands. Besides, Bharata did not want to spoil the sanctity of the place by imposing thousands of co-travelers upon the *ashram*, not to mention the chance that water bodies would be polluted, trees uprooted and inmates harassed for constant favors. But Bharata knew better than to argue with an illustrious sage. Anything was possible with such sages. He had heard beguiling tales about his own teacher Vasistha, including his bewildering King Kaushika (who later became Vishwamitra) by feeding thousands of his disciples. He silently walked up to his army and instructed them to follow him to the *ashram*.

goal unswayed

A gush of fresh breeze infused with the fragrance of *kadamba* flowers brushed their faces. The next moment there was a shower of millions of flowers of never-before-seen colors, textures, fragrances and varieties. The tired faces burst into smiles. This was unexpectedly rejuvenating.

In the few moments that Bharata had gone to fetch his army, Bharadwaja *muni* had invoked the presence of Vishwakarma, the heavenly designer to transform the rustic *ashram* into a divine theme park. He had wanted to provide the mentally and physically exhausted travelers a de-stressing experience. As Vishwakarma executed the instruction to perfection, Bharadwaja *muni* smiled shrewdly – a virtually stimulated entertainment test this would be! He resigned himself to an unnoticeable corner as the army entered to be welcomed with more flower showers.

Celestial dancers of exquisite beauty emerged pirouetting from behind every tree. Dressed in the most dazzling of silks, the dancers twirled and twisted to the song and music. Bharata could not believe that a replica of the heavens had replaced the rural ashram. A gorgeous shining meadow formed the dance floor. The jaws of the mesmerized soldiers dropped to the floor and went down on their knees absorbing the sights, sounds and smells.

As the spellbound army watched the performance, an impressive palace appeared out of thin air, right behind them. Two rivers of celestial drinks flowed alongside the palace. The trees along the pathway to the palace were laden with rich clothes and bejeweled ornaments instead of leaves and fruits. As the singers and dancers lured the hypnotized soldiers into the palace, the trees began shedding the ornaments on the necks of each passing soldier. The revelers were beside themselves and were too stupefied to comprehend what was happening to them, leave alone express it. They wondered, if such ecstasy was just outside the palace, how much more there would be inside! With great anticipation, they danced their way into the palace.

Inside, the chief musician of the heavens, Tumbura, lead an orchestra. The celebration touched euphoric heights with the singers, musicians and dancers performing like frenzied spirits full of implausible energy. The people of Ayodhya had by now joined the rave party and were beyond care – sometimes laughing, sometimes jumping, sometimes twirling, sometimes rolling on the ground, sometimes howling, sometimes dancing with gay abandon.

Nymphs carrying trays of mouth-watering delicacies and glasses of heavenly intoxicants sashayed into the palace. Soon every person was completely intoxicated and was staggering helplessly. The nymphs encouraged them to eat and drink more, and none of the people could refuse because of the love with which they were being served. Some of them blurted, "We don't want to go on, neither to Rama nor to Ayodhya. We are happy here; this is our destination. Eat, drink and make merry. What else do we need?"[40]

Despite the raucous mayhem, Bharata was sober. Celestial attendants had escorted him to the center of the palace to an imperial throne. They implored him to take seat and participate in the celebration.

---

[40] The first sacrifice at the altar of temptation is loyalty.

Succumbing to temptations has become the essence of life and its consequences reduced to superfluous details. Just as a rat focusing on the cheese neglects the trap or a fish focusing on the worm neglects the hook, a human focusing on indulgence neglects the outcome.

On either side of the throne were beautiful attendants holding yak-tail fans eager to please the one on the throne.

The throne reminded Bharata of his brother Rama. He closed his eyes and imagined Rama on the throne. With hands folded in supplication, he began to circumambulate the throne in reverence. He then sat nearby and began fanning the seat, imagining Rama on it.

From behind an ornate pillar, Bharadwaja *muni* smiled satisfactorily and walked away, leaving the crowd to make merry all night long.

MISSION TEST 6 –CONFRONTING IRRESISTIBLE TEMPTATIONS

When Bharata found himself suddenly in the virtually stimulated environment of irresistible temptations created by Bharadwaja *muni* he asked himself a series of questions that teach us how to deal with temptations that distract us from our mission. Though momentarily bewildered, his intelligence rang an alarm in the form of these questions.

1. Am I walking too close to the edge assuming that I won't fall? Are my secondary priorities overtaking my primary one?

2. What would Rama think if I succumbed to this temptation? Am I not accountable to Him?

3. What image do I want to send to my followers through my actions?

4. Am I fascinated by the wonders of God or God himself?

5. Am I honest about my weakness or do I allow ego-gratifying things to sway me?

6. Am I constantly evaluating my commitment to my mission?

When Bharata asked himself these questions, he realized that if he succumbed to temptations, it would mean that he was overconfident of his self-control. It would imply that although he set out with the right intention, in between the mission, comforts had become his priority. He realized that this would definitely upset Rama and set the wrong standard for His followers.

He contemplated that if the energies of God were so wonderful and fascinating, how much more wonderful would God be. So he accepted the fact that though he was weak, he should not allow even an inch of indulgence to come between him and his mission, lest he be misled from his goal.

Bharata dealt with temptations by being sober and not being carried away by the gush of pleasure that takes you high but leaves you dry. Instead, he chose to remain sturdy like a tortoise within its meditative shell till the transitory storm of temptation receded. He chose to fly like an eagle on the higher altitudes of remembrance of his mission and dedication to Rama, out of reach of the inferior storm of temptation.

uphill task

When the intoxicated eyes opened the next day with sunrise, it wasn't inside a luxurious palace. There were no dancers, no music, no carpets, no throne and no gardens either. They were all just lying on the bare ground in the middle of the forest. Disbelief, confusion, shock. Did all that really happen last night or was it a collective dream? The only tangible proof of what had happened, besides their vivid memories of it, was the fact that they could see faded garlands strewn all over the place.

Shrugging off the lovely memories of the previous night, they got up and dragged themselves toward the river and freshened up. Meanwhile, the ever-sober Bharata walked up to Bharadwaja *muni* and paid his respects. The now-satisfied sage embraced Bharata to his bosom; he had tested the young prince twice. With folded hands Bharata graciously thanked him for the hospitality he had arranged for his army and asked him for directions in his life and for directions to his life. "Your life and your words of wisdom are enough to show direction in my life. But I also want you to show me direction to my life. At the moment, I am like one of those mystical jinns who deposit their lives in parrots. My life is hidden in the blessings of Rama and until I don't retrieve it, I will be a lifeless ghost. Please show this lifeless body direction to reclaim its soul."

The sage directed him to travel 28 miles toward the east of the hermitage until he reaches the river Mandakini from whose banks rise the extremely beautiful Chitrakoot mountain range. Revealing that Rama, Sita and Lakshmana had chosen these picturesque mountains as their home, the sage urged him to proceed as directed. Bharata could imagine the sage actually seeing them on the mountain through his yogic powers. With smiles of hope, he took the sage's leave.

Just as he was turning away, the three queen mothers walked in and reverentially went around the sage and one by one proceeded to touch his sacred feet. Looking at the queens, the all-knowing sage purposely asked Bharata, "Could you introduce the queens to me, O Bharata?"

Reverentially pointing out to Rama's mother, Bharata said, "This lady who has become a bag of bones by constantly fasting is mother Kaushalya. Having given birth to the king among humans, Rama, she shines like Aditi the mother of King Indra and Lord Upendra, the dwarf incarnation of Vishnu."

Turning his gaze to Shatrughna's mother, he continued, "The one clinging to the left shoulder of mother Kaushalya is mother Sumitra, the exalted mother of the heroic and selfless brothers Lakshmana and Shatrughna. Her grief has made her resemble a withered *Karnikara* tree, bereft of flowers."

And without even looking in the direction of his mother and pointing toward her with his left index finger, Bharata spoke with eyes closed and tears streaming down: "And here is the one who has successfully achieved what no other woman in the world has. With one devious move, she has managed to kill her husband, the king of Ayodhya and banish two sons, Rama and Lakshmana. Although she is irate, impudent, arrogant and power-hungry, she perceives herself as exquisitely beautiful and believes that her beauty aids her intelligence. I wouldn't introduce her to you as my mother but as the mother of all my miseries."

Bharata broke down, sobbing and hissing like a restless snake. Bharadwaja smiled. This was precisely what he was waiting for. He wanted to help Bharata handle his emotions in a balanced way. Bharata's love for Rama was well founded, but his hatred toward his own mother was unwarranted. What she did was wrong, but his relationship with her was not. He had already punished her enough for her mistakes, and by cradling hatred, he was not only hurting her but also hurting himself. His heavy breathing and sighing were the symptoms of hatred. Hadn't Bharata asked for direction in his life, too?

"Your mother's act was definitely cruel, and you have undone it with your timely action. But bearing hatred in your heart is like carrying burning coal in a cloth. It is bound to make an unmendable hole in your heart. Let go of the hatred Bharata, forgive your mother. By forgiving her, you are not excusing her behavior but are not allowing her past behavior to destroy your present peace of mind. By your actions, you have clearly established that you hate her act of going against the principles of righteousness and are ready to take any measure to rectify it. You don't have to repeatedly show that you hate her. Forgiveness is a virtue that makes great people greater and hatred is a vice that makes weak people weaker.[41]

You should also know that your mother has unwittingly become an instrument of greater good to the world. From sunset emerges the moon, similarly even from negative actions can emerge constructive good. The temporary setting of the sun of Ayodhya will result in the rise of Ramachandra, the soothing moon of hope for the world. Rama's exile will bring ultimate joy to the world and the extermination of dark forces."[42]

Seeing sense in the wise sage's advice, Bharata wiped his tears and paid his respects to him. He then embraced his mother, who had finally found someone who could help bridge the gap between her and her son. Keikeyi had long understood her foolishness and had sincerely prayed for someone who could at least get her son to forgive her. She gazed at the sage with renewed respect and gratitude.

As the army marched southward, birds and animals began to fly

---

[41] Forgiveness is the fragrance that the sandalwood tree leaves on an axe that cuts it, the stone that grinds it and in the smoke that burns it.

[42] Hopelessness is not just sign of atheism but also a conclusive confirmation of it.

away from their path. Toward the second half of the day, the terrain became extremely beautiful – rising from along the banks of a lush river was an exquisitely beautiful mountain. Convinced this was Chitrakoot, Bharata excitedly ordered his soldiers to search for Rama.

When the searchers spotted a plume of smoke in the air, they hastened and reported it to Bharata. He immediately began walking in that direction along with Shatrughna and Dhriti, his spiritual preceptor.

As their leader went ahead, the soldiers' hearts throbbed in anticipation. The possibility of meeting their beloved Rama seemed near.

With his gaze fixed on the smoke, Bharata began to climb the mountain of hope.

Climbing up the mountain of hope was easy for Bharata, but would he be able to convince Rama to climb down the mountain of determination? Would love win over duty or duty win over love?

CHAPTER 8

WHEN LOSING IS WINNING

"What a luxury! Look at all these wonderful fruit-bearing trees; cashew nuts, mangoes, rose apples – all at arm's length! Who would not want such indulgences?" Sita smiled, not so much at Rama's style of diverting her attention from all the discomforts of living in a forest mountain, but on seeing Her ring on His fingers.

Rama had quietly kept Her ring from the time She had given it to Him to reward the boatman ferrying them across the Ganga. She could not understand why Her husband wanted to keep Her ring. She did not even consider questioning Him, because She knew there was always a mystery behind each of Rama's thoughts, words and actions. Most of Her questions about these mysteries had no immediate answers. But every time She saw that ring, it made Her giggle. She was always flooded with sweet memories of the time She spent with Rama in Ayodhya.

Sita recalled that late evening Rama had returned exhausted after a long day in the courtroom with His father, meeting people, inspiring them and performing multiple chores as Prince.

Sita, eager to relieve Him of His exhaustion, offered to massage His tired legs. Rama had always refused such servile proposals, but today He relented. As Sita was about to apply the massage oil, she suddenly screamed and threw the ring off Her finger. Rama was taken aback. He immediately sat up and held Sita protectively. He asked Her what had made Her shriek that way and throwaway Her ring.

Naïvely, she explained that before marriage, she had heard stories of how Rama had placed His feet on a stone and it had transformed into a maiden. Sita justified Her flinging off the ring, saying: "What if the stone on My ring turned into a maiden? How would I handle a co-wife?" Rama had almost rolled off the bed with laughing. All His exhaustion had disappeared without the massage! She could never fathom why He had laughed so much that day neither could she understand why He had worn Her ring but never returned it to Her. No matter why, She was sure of one thing: Rama did nothing without good reason.

She was still lost in Her thoughts when Rama shook Her out of Her reverie and pointed out to honey dripping from a honeycomb on a tree. His eyes sparkled with joy as He showed Her stones of different colors. Sections of the Chitrakoot mountain were silver, reddish, yellow and a whole range of colors. Precious stones were strewn all over, almost as if Mother Earth had carpeted her.

Suddenly Rama became silent and pulled Sita aside just in time to avoid embarrassment for a bubbly *kinnarra* couple absorbed in each other. Watching the couple frolic around Chitrakoot, Sita and Rama exchanged smiles. Rama looked intently into Sita's amber eyes, which reflected the early evening sunlight. "With such beauty why would anyone lament?"[1]

---

[1] When you focus on things that you have gained, you become grateful. When you focus on things that you have lost, you become hateful.

Sita shied away from His glance. Did He refer to Her beauty or that of the mountains? Again, she reached the same conclusion: Do not analyze Rama, just love Him.

Rama continued speaking to Sita, "The mountains have given Me two levels of happiness – one, that I am free from the debt that I owed My father, and two, that I have filled Bharata's life with joy."

On a more reflective note, He asked Her, "Sita, are You also happy here with Me?"

She smiled and said, "I do not need too many things to make Me happy. The only criterion that makes Me happy is Your smile."

Rama pulled her along saying, "Let Me show You My favorite part of the mountains. I love that heavenly scene, and this is the perfect time for it." His exuberance made Sita wonder how time had transformed the sober prince into a spontaneous forest-dweller!

Sita soon found herself standing behind Rama witnessing the most beautiful sight She had ever beheld in Her life. Rama was facing away from Her, standing with His feet touching the sparkling waters of the Mandakini river. The sky had turned a bright orange with streaks of gold; it was apparent that the sun was in the third phase of its setting. Naturally, the waters reflected the golden tinge of the setting sun. Fragrant flower trees lined the banks, their branches leaning into the river, almost kissing the branches of trees from the opposite bank. Thousands of fragrant flowers dropped from the trees into the cascading waters of the Mandakini river. Exalted sages

---

To create armors of positivity that can shield you, focus your cognizance on gratitude rather than on hatred and on gain rather than on loss.

and *siddhas* stood knee-deep in the glistening waters, offering their respects to the holy river. The floating army of flowers first gathered around the sages and having touched their bodies, further glided and paused at the feet of Lord Rama. Then silently, the flowers began their downward descent along with the river toward the ocean.[2]

As She stepped ahead to stand next to Rama, She noticed that Rama had closed His eyes, but His lips were murmuring something inaudible. He had assumed His natural sober mood, and that isolated moment of the animated mood from a while ago had vanished. He opened His eyes and whispered to Her: "This Mandakini river is Sarayu for Me and Chitrakoot is not different from Ayodhya." Sita smiled, nodding in silent acceptance.

As the couple turned Their backs toward the river to ascend the mountains, They saw a blissfully happy Lakshmana rushing toward Them. As he neared Them, he was panting, but still couldn't contain his joy: "Your house is ready! Even the ingredients to perform the purifying rituals are in place. Come and occupy Your abode! Finally tonight You will not have to sleep under the stars."

Patting his back, Rama smiled and asked him to lead Them. On Their way up to Their new home, Sita expressed a doubt: "Why do saints never say anything straight? Why do they speak in a language the less intelligent cannot comprehend?"

"What are you referring to Sita?" Rama asked.

---

[2] *Manah* means mind, *su-manah* means a pure mind. *Sumanah* also means flowers. In this context, the sages, who had pure minds, were offering their minds through these flowers to Lord Rama.

"When we reached here almost a month ago, we had asked from Valmiki *muni* where we should dwell. To such a simple question, he started telling how You should dwell in the hearts of people who constantly remember You and chant Your names, in the hearts of those who are devoid of anger, envy, pride, greed, hypocrisy and deceit and in the heart of those whose heads bow down to You in reverence. Having said that, he pointed out to the place where Lakshmana has built Us a house. What does all that mean to Us?"

Rama's answer was as clear as Mandakini's waters: "Where there is dependence, there ought to be reassurance, where there is responsibility, there ought to be flexibility and where there is a need, we ought to be there in deed. Greater than the power to fight the wrong is the need for the power to let go of attachments.

Valmiki, the great sage, was hinting that We are not supposed to reside comfortably in one place, but rather live wherever there is a call for help. So Sita, We are surely going to enter Our new house, but how long We will stay there, We do not know. We can stay only till We get a desperate call from someone in need."[3]

Sita smiled at the simple truth. She hadn't come to the forest to stay comfortably but to serve Rama contently. She could not think of anyone from both Their families who only lived to enjoy, they all lived to serve.

The couple entered the new house, detached yet excited. A house could not be a binding for them anymore. Their lives of selfless

---

[3] Just as rigid bones and flexible muscles make a human body, rigidity in following principles and flexibility in extending compassion make a body human.

service would always be like the gift of freshness the forest offers.

false accusations

After performing the purifying rituals, Rama and Sita began appreciating the intricate details of Lakshmana's service. The hut had been built in alignment with the principles of *vaastu shashtra*.[4] The floors were plastered with vermillion. The walls were studded with gems and jewels fetched from the river and mountain caves and everything was designed so intricately that Sita could not take Her eyes off them.

In Their private room was a canopy made of peacock feathers and leaves. It would have taken Lakshmana ages to make this canopy. She could barely fathom how many nights Lakshmana must have spent constructing it and how many days he must have needed to gather the material needed to make every part of this house spectacular. The happiness on the face of Rama and Sita was worth a million words to Lakshmana. It meant a lot to him that They appreciated every aspect of his creation.[5]

After admiring every corner of the house, Sita looked at Rama questioningly. Rama gave a knowing smile and said: "Yes, in spite

---

[4] *Vaastu shashtra* is the ancient science of architecture and construction. Mentioned in the Vedic scriptures, these are principles, design and layout outlined for any dwelling place, including houses, towns, cities, etc.

[5] The signature of love is drawn through millions of dots of contemplation, lines of selfless action and curves of forgiving accommodation.

The excellence of love is judged by the intricacy of details to express that love.

of having such a spectacular house, if the need arises, We will leave it and go." Puzzled, She turned to see how Lakshmana would react. After all, he had toiled for so long to make this house, wouldn't he be attached to his creation, even if he had no plans of staying in it? Lakshmana smiled and said, "Mother, don't You understand that it will give me an opportunity to serve You yet again by making another house elsewhere. My brother has taught me that we ought to perform our duty not for the sake of reward or appreciation but for the sake of duty itself."[6]

What kind of people were these brothers? Did they ever think of their own interests? How can people be so selfless? As Sita pondered, Rama asked Lakshmana: "I have come to the forest with the selfish agenda of gaining fame for keeping My father's words. And because of my selfishness, you have to go through so much pain. I am indebted to you for everything. By the way, where did you learn these skills of making boats and houses?"

Lakshmana replied with a bashful look, "All the pain that I experience in Your service is the source of my greatest joy. While You learned to become a master, I focused on learning to be a good servant." Rama smiled at Lakshmana's sincerity and sat down to eat the fruits and roots that His brother had gathered.

Suddenly, they heard pandemonium outside the hut. The quiet of the sunset was suddenly disrupted by the mayhem of hundreds of trumpeting elephants, roaring lions, screeching birds and hundreds of fleeing animals. Instantly, the brothers were out in the open with Sita standing nervously at the doorway.

---

[6] One should focus on devotion to duty rather than hankering for appreciation of result.

They noticed animals and birds fleeing from the foothills of the mountain deeper toward the jungles. Something or someone surely was scaring them away. Looming in the distance was an enormous dust storm. From their high mountain post, they had the advantage of a clear and far view. They could also discern the sounds of a moving army. Rama asked Lakshmana to quickly climb up a tree and scan the area to ascertain if it was actually the army of a king on a hunting expedition or was it something else?[7]

Lakshmana nimbly climbed a *sal* tree and looked toward the direction of the dust storm. What he saw in the far north gave him goose bumps! "It can't be," said his heart. "Why not?" taunted his mind. So many "can't-be things" had already transpired in Ayodhya. This could be just another addition to that list.

"Extinguish the fire! Tell Sita to hide in a cave behind the hut. Brother, don your armor, string your bow and mount your quiver. Get ready for a blood-curdling fight! An army is headed this way." Lakshmana screamed all charged.

Rama coolly asked him: "Whose army do you think it is, Lakshmana?"

Without a word, Lakshmana slid down the tree. Like a restless fire emitting heat, he shot back sarcastically. "An army is on its way with a gift. The mother has already given us the sweet gift of banishment, and the son is now on his way with the sweeter gift of death. The

---

[7] Holistic vision means seeing what your eyes can see and also what they can't.

Rama wanted Lakshmana to not only see from a higher perspective, but also comprehend from a higher perspective.

Seeing from a higher perspective means having holistic vision.

overambitious son of Keikeyi is on his way to kill us and make *his* Ayodhya free from future enemies.

Even from this distance, the *Kovidara* tree insignia fluttering on the flag of Bharata's chariot is as clearly visible as is his evil intention, which seems to be flying even higher than the flag itself. Power corrupts, and absolute power corrupts absolutely. But for the first time, I can see it happening right in front of my own eyes. Bharata was such a noble person that many compared him to You in nobility. After succumbing to the gross pleasures of the senses and subtle mind, he seems willing to go to any extent to achieve more and do anything unrighteous.[8]

Bharata's devotion to Your lotus feet is well-known. But the day he stepped into Your shoes as king of Ayodhya, he transgressed all boundaries of love and entered the forbidden zone of covetousness. Like a sly fox, knowing that You are helpless in the forest, he has come to reassert that the Ayodhya pie is his and his alone. If my assumptions are wrong, why would he come with such a vast army? Why should we blame Bharata for his actions? Anyone with power is undoubtedly corrupted.

Has the world not seen the moon god molest his guru Brihaspati's wife? Have we not seen Nahusa, who became a temporary king on behalf of Indra, force weak *brahmanas* to carry his palanquin? Have we not seen King Vena torment his subjects to insane levels? His torture increased to such an extent that the sages had to kill him with a *humkara mantra*. When all these powerful personalities

---

[8] The desire to enjoy sensory pleasures at any cost and the desire to have dominance and control over others are like the two stones tied to the legs of a swimmer, which ensure drowning of nobility.

could not handle power properly, how can we expect Bharata to be an exception?

O brother, prepare for a fight! A fight, the world has yet not seen! Bharata may have made his calculations, but he did not calculate one thing: My anger! It is because of him that You and Mother Sita are going through so much trouble. I will annihilate him and reestablish Your rule. Don't worry about sin Rama; no sin accrues on killing an aggressor. From today, the roles will reverse. Keikeyi will be the one crying and mother Kaushalya will be the one smiling. After I kill Bharata and his brother, I will surely terminate Manthara, the source of all evil in Ayodhya, and her first victim, Keikeyi, thus freeing Ayodhya from all evil influences.

Today, Chitrakoot mountain will change its color. Blood will flow as profusely as the waterfalls after the rains. After I discharge my debts to my bow and arrows, heaps of bodies will lie across the mountain. There will be no enmity among animals for there will be no scarcity of flesh. The mountains will become a slippery dance floor for ghosts and hobgoblins. Any human who sees this mountain tomorrow will faint in fear, seeing arms, heads and legs float down the rivers of blood from the mountain."

An incensed Lakshmana then rushed into the hut and wore his anklets, donned his armor, tied his dagger to his waist, wore his quiver and took up his bow in his hands. He turned to run out of the house and almost bumped into his elder brother who was blocking the doorway.

As soon as he saw his brother standing like that on the doorway, Lakshmana realized something was up. He hated Rama for being too overrighteous. Why does his brother have to be so perfect? Why does his brother have to tolerate all the injustice and suffer?

He loved Rama and could not bear to see Him suffer a life of inconvenience.

Rama said: "Lakshmana, what you have said about the flip side of power is true wisdom. Indeed umpteen rulers in the past have succumbed to the temptations of the power matrix."[9]

This was Rama's style of correcting, and Lakshmana recognized it from the first sentence. First Rama found something appreciable in what he had said and whatever followed was His rectification. Lakshmana was mentally preparing himself.

"The intoxication of power becomes overwhelmingly compelling for those who do not have a canopy of saints over their heads. But for humble rulers such as Bharata who willingly submit themselves to the scrutiny and able guidance of wise men, power cannot intoxicate the same way just as few drops of sour substances cannot split an ocean of milk.

Let Me tell you how much confidence I have in the integrity of Bharata. I wouldn't be surprised if darkness swallows up the noon sun or sage Agastya who drank the entire ocean drowns in water collected in a cow's footprint, or Earth gives up its forbearance or even if mount Meru is blown away by the wind emanating from the breath of a mosquito. But Bharata being intoxicated with power and losing his balance will really take me by surprise.[10]

---

[9] The power matrix is when one considers power to something that has to be grabbed and enjoyed.

The empower matrix is when one considers power to be a service that is awarded and shared.

[10] Power is like a swift breeze that flips over light paper. To be saved from

Lakshmana, be assured that this world will always be a combination of evil and good. But great people like Bharata are like swans, internally equipped with the mechanism to separate milk from water. They are programmed to easily separate good from evil.

When such a Bharata is coming Our way, why do We need to lift Our weapons? Or, Lakshmana, do We have some evil plans against him? If I ever want to rule a kingdom, it is only for the sake of protecting and giving pleasure to My brothers. My mind is unattached to the pleasures of the kingdom, but is attached only to abiding by righteousness. What benefit will I gain by obtaining even Indra's kingdom by unrighteous means?

If you are wondering why he is coming to Chitrakoot now, let me assure you that he is coming out of concern. Out of extreme anger at his mother's decision, he must have mobilized the entire Ayodhya to fetch us back. Lakshmana, don't accuse such a noble soul before you know his real intentions. I would go to the extent of saying that if any accusation is made against Bharata, I would consider it an accusation against Me."

By this time, Lakshmana had dropped his bow and was recoiling into himself. But the worst was yet to come.

Rama continued: "Why does one who is in trouble think of solving his problems by throwing others into trouble? That is the way the animal kingdom functions. I can never think of killing my brother and father simply for the sake of a kingdom. I do not want Bharata to hear any harsh words from your lips. Why do We find

---

the flip side of power, one has to be protected by the heavy weight of right company.

that people, who are supposed to love each other abusing each other? Lakshmana, if you speak all these words in aspiration for the kingdom, just let Me know, and I will request Bharata to hand over the kingdom to you. He will happily do so in a moment."

Lakshmana had already shriveled with shame and was on his knees, his hands folded, begging for forgiveness. Suddenly they heard the loud trumpeting of an elephant. Lakshmana found his excuse to escape the scrutiny of Rama and the uncomfortable ambience the discussion had created. "I think our father Dasaratha has also come mounted on his royal elephant Shatrunjya."

Rama understood that Lakshmana was feeling ashamed about his explosive nonfactual judgment of Bharata and was sheepishly looking to change the tense atmosphere between them. He played along and said: "The monarch is soft-hearted and must have definitely come after contemplating that Sita is unequipped to handle the austere forest life. He has surely come to take Her back."

The brothers left the hut to ascertain more facts. By now, the army was clearly visible on the foothills of the mountain. From their standpoint, they had an eagle-eye view of the entire army. They saw their father's royal elephant, as usual tugging right ahead of the army, but what was unusual was the missing royal canopy from its summit. The brothers looked at each other in apprehension immediately noting the change.

final summit

A large part of the army, occupying at least one and half *yojanas* of space, began settling down into makeshift tenements. Bharata's focus was the column of smoke ascending the sky. That column of smoke for him was a sacred temple dome under which the holy deity was housed. It definitely indicated the presence of His personal deity, Rama. Bharata felt that this whole trip from Ayodhya to Chitrakoot was a holy pilgrimage. And after reaching the holy spot, he was now climbing toward the deity he had been mentally worshiping for so many days; he would physically worship the same in a few moments and continue to worship[11] till the end of his life with a commitment to serve His instructions.

Close at heal was Shatrughna, and the brothers were flanked by Guha and Sumantra. Dozens of Guha's archers were guarding the four, forming a tightly knit semi-circle behind them. They walked with their heads turning in all directions, trying to survey the land for even the slightest sign of danger.

Bharata knew well that the most crucial influencers in this mission were Vasistha and the mothers; thus, he had already requested Vasistha to bring the mothers. As he trekked uphill, panting up the steep uneven climb, he loudly shared his state of mind with other trekkers. "I cannot become peaceful until I place my head at Rama's feet and uphold His claim to the throne of Ayodhya. He will be a king anywhere He goes. The animals and birds of Chitrakoot mountain are blessed that Rama resides on the crest of this mountain as King Indra does high in his heavenly abode."

He allowed his elbows to rest for a second on a tree trunk and was amazed to find the touch very soft. He looked up to find a deerskin on the tree trunk. Taking this as an indication, they continued moving ahead.

---

[11] Prayer is not about approaching God for temporary solutions but approaching Him with a permanent commitment.

Bharata continued sharing his mind: "When I reach Him, I will not mind if He rejects me assuming me to be an accomplice of my mother's evil plans. But I know that He won't. I am yet to see another person who has a greater ability to forgive than my brother does.

Whether He rejects me with anger or accepts me with love, kicks me or embraces me, my mood toward Him will remain the same. I will lie down on the dirty ground, grasp His lotus feet and wet them with my tears of repentance and love."

Mounted high on these noble thoughts, Bharata reached a flat terrain on the top of the mountain. The various markings of the animal skins on different trees, clearly pointed toward his destination.

brothers' reunion

In the loving embrace of many fig trees, *jambu*, mango and *tamala* stood a mega banyan tree that seemed to be the king of trees there. Amid these wonderful trees stood a leafy hut, which, though simple, had the elegance of a royal palace. From a distance, they could hear the Mandakini river's soft gurgling dance over the mountainous rocks. This had to be the place where Bharadwaja *muni* had directed them.

As they strained their eyes, they could see a heap of dry wood chopped to be used for cooking and sacrifices. Close by lay heaps of dried deer and buffalo dung used for providing heat at night.

The four of them began walking cautiously closer to the hut. The hut floor was covered with *kusa* grass. The front wall of the house displayed a heavy bow and two crisscrossed swords mounted on it. From a rafter nearby, hung a set of quivers with arrows.

As they edged closer, the sight transfixed them and they froze. Not even an eye blinked.

With a sacrificial fire blazing high, the room was splattered with a golden hue. Seated around the sacrificial fire were Sita, Rama and Lakshmana. Rama's face was clearly visible to them. Eyes closed in rapt attention, lips moving in prayer, hands deftly moving the ladle offering various ingredients into the fire, an erect back and head held high, Rama appeared like a wise sage. The combination of matted hair with antelope skin and tree bark wrapping caused the four to wince. What misfortune! A prince had been forced to turn into a recluse.

Bharata ran into the hut and fell at the feet of the seated Rama. The sheer force with which he fell at Rama's feet made everyone in the room flinch. He sobbed hysterically holding on to the feet of Rama, who stood up seeing his younger sibling. The next moment Shatrughna, too, fell at Rama's feet and cried.

It took a few moments for Rama to decipher that these were his brothers. Though He was expecting them both, He had not imagined them to be dressed as ascetics in bark and deerskin. Of course, it had been 12 long years that they had been staying with their grandparents far away from Ayodhya and Rama. And not just that, the brothers looked so weak that Rama could not recognize them.

Amid sobs Bharata said: "One accustomed to being honored by

a bench of sophisticated ministers now lives with crude animals! One draped in the softest of silks is now wrapped in bristly barks and skins. One whose body was anointed with the most fragrant sandalwood pulp is now smeared with dust."

Rama's sturdy arms reached down, picked up the crestfallen brothers and embraced them fondly, drawing them really close to His broad accommodating chest. He then pulled away and lovingly glanced at both of them, taking an inventory of their physical state. For Bharata and Shatrughna, this one glance was worth the whole effort of coming to Chitrakoot. They felt all their fatigue vanish and new energy infuse into their tired limbs. Rama sat them down and placed their heads on His lap and caressed them with His tender hands. As the brothers sat there, savoring their elder sibling's love, Sumantra, Guha and the others filed into the hut. Witnessing the love between the brothers, all eyes in the room turned moist.

Suddenly Rama began unleashing a barrage of questions. All lips were sealed. Tears dried up in an instant from the fear of not wanting to answer these with untruths and displeasing the very symbol of truth.

"Where is Our father? Why have you left him alone and come here? Did he manage to handle the pain of separation from Us gracefully? I hope there are no shortcomings in your service to Our father. Are you handling the herculean affairs of the kingdom efficiently despite your youthful inexperience?" No one was equipped to answer Rama's pointed questions at this point of time. They stood gaping at Him.

Almost as a much-needed breather, the natural king and leader in Rama began giving Bharata tips on effective management of the kingdom. By now, the ministers of Ayodhya had also gathered around.[12]

management mantras

Knowing well that Ayodhya's people were experiencing the pain of separation from Him, Rama chose not to begin the conversation on a negative note. Instead of discussing the problems in Ayodhya, He began offering solutions to many leadership problems of Ayodhya. He taught the world the most crucial lesson on leadership: *Vision-based action.*

Rama perceived that once the discussion began about the problems in Ayodhya, He would never be able to give Bharata tools to handle the kingdom; so before that discussion began, Rama handed over all the knowledge Bharata would need to rule for the next 14 years.

Rama revealed five management concepts a good leader has to adhere to. These five tenets form the most important limbs of a leader's portfolio.

1. RESPECT MANAGEMENT

The foundation of any leadership rests on respect management. A leader who respects his superiors, allows the flow of energy

---

[12] No one realized at that point in time, but these spontaneous utterings from Rama's mouth became the Rama sutras of effective management of the kingdom of Ayodhya for all times to come.

to descend into his life. With that in mind, Rama's questions to Bharata were:

a. Are you treating your preceptors respectfully?

b. Are you making sure mother Kaushalya and Sumitra are happy?

c. Is the venerable Keikeyi rejoicing?

d. Do you honor Sayujna, the son of Vasistha?

e. Are you respectful toward, *brahmanas*, teachers and ministers?

f. Are women respected and taken care of? Respect toward them is the root of all the good that happens in society and disrespect toward them is the root of all evil in society.

2. DECISION MANAGEMENT

Decision-making with discernment becomes an ornament that brings respect and appreciation from followers. Rama gave Bharata some crucial pointers:

• Do not deliberate either alone or with too many men.

• Your decisions should not be made public before being carried out.

• Neighboring kings should not understand your undertakings before execution.

• Your decisions should have maximum benefit at minimum cost.

• Do not delay decision-making.

- Do not falsely accuse, kill, or punish a noble man without appropriate inquiry. Remember that tears of victims falsely accused actually destroy justice givers.

- Do not release a thief for greed of wealth.

- Encourage your ministers to be impartial to both the rich and the poor.

3. REPUTATION MANAGEMENT

Reputation is like a glass ball. It has to be clean, but before that, it has to be in your grip. People see before they hear; they judge a leader on the basis of his actions before they get inspired by his words. The reputation of the leader imbibes confidence in the follower. Rama's suggestions to Bharata were:

a. Do not fall prey to excessive sleep and wake up at an appropriate hour.

b. Contemplate about the adroitness of your action in the second half of the night.

c. Dress royally. The regal appearance of a king gives confidence to the subjects.

d. Make yourself available to hear your subjects' grievances. First-hand interaction with the leader gives hope to the subjects.

e. Do not overindulge in wealth, religion or delights of the senses. Overindulgence or indulgence at the wrong time or place creates doubts in subjects.

f. Do not eat without sharing. Not sharing makes one hardhearted and others jealous.

g. Avoid incurring the wrath of *brahmanas* by falling into wrong habits.

h. Ensure that servants are not disrespectful toward you nor should they hasten away in fear on seeing you. Disrespect and fear are two extremes indicating barriers in connections between the leader and his subjects.

4. TEAM MANAGEMENT

Team management is to a leader what life management is to a doctor. When a team is managed with grace, the subjects are filled with gratefulness; the team becomes the solution to all problems a leader faces. Rama revealed these pearls of wisdom:

a. One wise man is better than a thousand stupid ones; one good minister can ensure the prosperity of a kingdom.

b. Assign tasks according to the level of intelligence, ability, skill, position and status of the employee.

c. Surround yourself with ministers who are not only incorruptible and full of integrity but also born and raised in a family that imbibes Vedic values and culture.

d. Train your ministers to avoid inflexible decisions that make the subjects fearful.

e. The army chief should be cheerful, wise, courageous, well-behaved, loved by his subordinates, efficient, born and raised in a family that imbibes Vedic values and culture.

f. Honor courageous warriors in public.

g. The army should be paid their salary and daily provisions on time. A delay in wages and maintenance causes the servants to become corrupt and infuriated with their master.

h. Select an ambassador who is knowledgeable, wise and skillful, has a presence of mind and knows how to speak to the point.

i. Through three spies, unacquainted with one another, collect all information about your important officers as well as those of your enemies. Do not place your trust on one spy.

j. Do not spy on your own ministers, your guru and the princes. Monitor their actions.

k. Do not house a physician who is an expert at aggravating a disease, a servant intent on bringing disgrace and a valiant warrior seeking kingly power. They can be the cause of your destruction.

5. Character Management

A leader should religiously avoid the 14 sins. By carefully avoiding these, the leader can suitably manage his character.

a. Giving the material world as much importance as spiritual world

b. Carelessness

c. Procrastination

d. Lack of appreciation of righteous people

e. Neglecting duties because of overindulgence in intoxicants

f. Overt attachment to sensory indulgences

g. Autocracy in decision making

h. Avoiding decisions already made

i. Dishonesty

j. Revealing confidential information

k. Demonstrating anger at a respectable mother, father, guru, wise men and the weak, even if they have committed a mistake

l. Indulging in discussions with people of adverse opinions and thus wasting valuable time

m. Invading enemies from all directions

n. Respecting bad people

wounds reopened

Everyone stood mesmerized by Rama's eloquence and His mastery over the psychology of leadership. When they began to praise Rama, He steered the direction of the discussion yet again toward the sensitive zone.

"I am still not clear why you have come dressed in barks and skins. How did our father and the ministry permit the king to wear this?" Rama now paused clearly indicating that He had spoken enough and that He now preferred to hear.

Aware that it was time to shatter three more hearts, Bharata said: "Which kingdom and which king? Which father and which son? The king is gone and the kingdom is bereaved. The father is gone and the sons are orphaned.

Remembering the son he loved the most and cursing the wife he hated the most, Our father went to the higher realm. Our father died a sad man. One moment of inattention on his part stripped him off all the reputation he had built over his lifetime, just as a single moment of inattention by the snake charmer is enough to strip him off his boastful skills. But, because he died remembering You, he has surely reached a higher realm. But my mother is hell-bound for her gross error.

Being the key person around whom revolves this entire treason strategy, I can only be saved from a similar destination as my mother is destined for if You return and rule the kingdom. This one act of Yours will grant me freedom, my mother pardon, joy to these thousands of people and grace to the city of sin, Ayodhya. I have come all the way from Ayodhya to speak just these words. Considering me to be Your disciple and servant, please grant me this.

I do not even know if the oblations that I offered for our father were accepted by him. Rama, I request You to offer oblations to our father. Because his last thoughts were of You, whatever You offer will surely reach him."

Rama, who had so far been guarding the dam of self-control, let it crumble and tears began gushing out of His eyes and intense loving emotions poured out of His mouth. Loving memories of His father hit Rama so intensely that He swooned and collapsed with a thud. Sita ran up to Him and sprinkled some water on His face.

Slowly opening His eyes, Rama said: "I have lost all reason to return to Ayodhya now. The city has lost its essence. Without the emperor, it's meaningless to reside there. How unfortunate am I that I did not have the chance to express My lifelong gratitude to him as he left this world. O Bharata, how fortunate you are to have been able to offer the last rites to him.

How miserable this is! Sita, Your father-in-law is dead and Lakhsmana, your father is dead."[13]

With Sita leading the way, the party walked up to the Mandakini river. Rama offered oblations of water in the name of Dasaratha and prayed for a higher destination for His father. Then with the help of Lakshmana, He offered *pinda*[14] made of flour mixed with edible herbs to Dasaratha and placed them under a tree. After the rituals,[15] everyone returned to the hut in a sober mood. No one spoke or cried. They were all contemplating the implications of what had just happened. Finally, Bharata looked at Rama's swollen face and broke down into heavy sobs. This acted as the trigger, and every person in the room began wailing uncontrollably. The wails became so loud that the troops on standby at the foothill of the mountain could hear the grieving.

They understood that the brothers had met and were lamenting the loss of their father and the pain within their hearts was reverberating across the mountain. Abandoning whatever they were doing, they raced up the mountain, cursing Manthara and Keikeyi for heaping such a mountain of sorrow on them.

---

[13] Why did Rama not say that His father was dead?

Because Rama found Dasaratha's presence in Lakshmana's caring attitude, Sita's love, Bharata's commitment, Guha's friendship and Bharadwaja *muni*'s blessings. But He felt that He was unable to give all this to Lakshmana and Sita, so naturally they must be missing him.

[14] *Pinda* is food offered to a dead ancestor.

[15] Rituals are like a plate and spoon used to serve a cake called prayer. The flour used in the cake is like faith, which constitutes the real substance of the cake. But the main ingredient of the cake is the sweetener, which is love. The plate of rituals offers the prayer of our love kneaded with faith in God.

Rituals can become empty plates if the ingredients of faith and love are missing from the cake.

relentless sorrow

On their way up, Vasistha and the mothers, too, could hear the cries of lamentation. They had reached the banks of Mandakini, where Rama, Lakshmana, and Sita had offered *pinda* to Dasaratha a while ago. The inferior quality of the offerings put everyone in discomfort. Mother Kaushalya dropped on her knees next to the offerings and began mourning. "Such poor offerings to the king of the world! How has destiny become so cruel to the Ikshvaku dynasty? Why does my son have to go through such humiliation? Why does my husband have to go through such insult?"

Sumitra helped her get up, and they proceeded ahead, finally reaching the hut. At the door, they heard Rama telling Bharata: "You cannot blame Our father for what has happened to Me nor can you blame mother Keikeyi. Neither can you blame yourself for all this. Destiny alone is solely responsible for everything in this world. Human beings are pawns at the hands of higher powers. My forest life, too, is destined by higher powers, *Daiva* (the hands of God). As far as the death of Our father is concerned, it is the act of time, *kala kritha*. When both destiny and time are not in Our hands, what purpose does blaming anyone serve?

When tiny humans set certain expectations from life and the higher powers that control both destiny and time have contrary plans, there is a disturbance. The disturbance is never in the plans of higher powers but always in our mental expectations. The frustrated human tends to thrust the blame for his failed hopes on people who are just instruments of destiny and time.

Bharata, don't blame your holy mother because of the frustration of your expectations. And definitely don't blame our respectable father for what has happened to Me. They are absolutely free to give any instruction for the welfare of their children. A son should neither analyze the orders of his parents nor criticize them. But more than anything else, never blame yourself. Align your expectations with higher plans.[16] Don't ask Me to commit the sin of disobedience to My parents by returning to the kingdom."

Hearing Rama's words, Bharata did not immediately align his expectations with higher plans, but he did align his head with the feet of Rama, who He felt was the highest person in his life. As soon as Bharata bent down to touch his head to the feet of Rama, the three mothers and Vasistha became visible to Rama at the doorway. The towering presence of Bharata was covering Rama's vision of the doorway.

Rama immediately stood up and folded His hands in veneration. He went forward and paid his respects to the three mothers and the *acharya*. The three mothers embraced Sita and cried seeing her emaciated condition. Rama asked His guru to be seated on an appropriate place and Himself sat at His feet. Soon all the ministers, mothers, the three brothers and Sita sat down, with the discussion veering toward the lost glory of Ayodhya.

Bharata's entire army had by now gathered around the hut and each could have a glimpse of Rama, Lakshmana and Sita in their forest clothes. Their emaciated look made the soldiers sad. Tears of sorrow fell from their eyes like melting wax in fire.

The saga continued all night long. Rest was on no one's mind.

---

[16] Before measuring the dimension of life, don't stitch the cloth of expectation. You will be left with loose-fitting disappointments and desires torn apart.

tug of love

With the rise of the sun, everyone performed their morning rituals and prayers. Yet again, they gathered together with determination. Bharata's troops were determined to convince the forest dwellers to shun the forest and return home. But the forest dwellers' determination was carved on stone.[17]

Right from the beginning of the conversation, Rama was grave-faced and Bharata was logical and well-planned. The previous day, both had a small taste of what was to come. Bharata realized that being sentimental with Rama was useless. The only possible way out was presenting logical arguments. He had by now contemplated sufficiently to accumulate a series of logical arguments. Rama had realized that these thousands of people had come to push Him into a corner with their emotions, logic, respect and intense love. He had decided not to budge an inch. Thus began the tug of war. Or should we say, tug of love!

With folded hands Bharata began: "My dear brother, tell me according to the codes of *dharma*, is one responsible for the sin that takes place in his absence? The fiasco in Ayodhya occurred when I was away. Is it not my duty to undo the wrong upon my return?

My mother has received the kingdom from the king and has handed it over to me. Now it is mine and I am free to do as I deem fit. If the kingdom is really mine and I decide to hand it over to You, why

---

[17] When fights create comfort to oneself and discomfort to others, it creates violence. But when fights create discomfort to oneself and comfort to others, it creates harmony.

should You decline it? This is not sin! Isn't there a legal provision for gifting one's property to another?

My dear master, Ayodhya is like a dam that has been repeatedly and violently slammed by the waves of adverse emotions. Very soon the dam will burst. No ordinary person can repair the damaged situation in Ayodhya. Just as a donkey cannot compete with a horse in a race, nor can a fledgling compete in a flight with a giant Garuda, a simpleton like me cannot match Your maturity and foresight. As much as a tall fruit-laden tree is useless to a dwarf, the richly endowed kingdom of Ayodhya is too lofty for a short-charactered person like me. The kingdom needs Your high-principled guidance.

We yearn to see You grace the kingdom mounted on a royal elephant!"

"Bravo! This is exactly how we feel!" chorused the crowd. Bharata smiled hearing many ratifying his desire in unison.

Rama's voice instantly quietened everyone. It wasn't booming, it was firm but soothing. He said: "Bharata, you speak as if everything ordained to happen, happens by your evaluation. Humans are merely destiny's puppets. Just as the puppet has the freedom to move as long as the string attached to it allows, a human being has the freedom to only choose a response to any situation that befalls him or her. Destiny, which is under the control of God, is the decider of good and bad fortune. But humans can choose how to react to the decisions made by God. He can never really change the decisions once made.[18]

---

[18] The rat cannot predict the appearance of a trap, a fish cannot foresee the dangling of a bait and a moth cannot guess when the fire will be lit.

The only permanent factor in this world is temporariness. Everything melts away in the course of time. Time is a deceptive magician with a sardonic sense of humor. Just as small children play with balls for enjoyment, time juggles with two balls, the sun and the moon. To the budding lotus of youth, time acts like the nightfall that closes it, and to the elephant of life span, it acts like a lion that reduces it.[19]

Except for *dharma*, everything else in this world is temporary. Just like the wind tosses away a dewdrop from a leaf, the winds of time throws away the temporary things of this world; therefore, Bharata, do not run after stability in temporary things. Look for holding on to the permanent stable things in life. Each day brings us closer to death, reminding us not to hold on to temporary things. Follow the directions of destiny and follow the path of *dharma* as laid down by Our father."[20]

Bharata excitedly argued with his brother, "I agree that everything is temporary and death is a leveler. But is it not also true that when a person comes close to death, he is bewildered and makes his greatest mistakes. But as for our father, not only was he close to his death when he made that awful decision, he was also infatuated with a woman who influenced his decision; therefore I say that his decision

---

But once the trap appears, it is the rat's choice whether to run into it; when the bait dangles, it is the fish's choice whether to grab it; and it is the moth's choice whether to plunge into the flickering flame.
The lesser the limitation of choice, the smaller is the circle of control.

[19] In every race where time is a participant, the award ceremony precedes the competition. Time always runs with a gold medal adorning its neck.

[20] Birds don't hold on to their feathers, rivers don't hold on to their drops, oceans don't hold on to their waves, the sky does not hold on to the sun and night does not hold on to the moon. Why do humans try holding on to transient objects that were never theirs' anyway?

was definitely faulty. Aren't children supposed to rectify the faults of their parents? Why should someone accept an insensible act blindly? Which sensible man would make such a decision, just to please a woman? A sensible son would never follow the unrighteous instruction of his father. Don't you want to save our father and mother from the terrible consequences awaiting them?"

Rama smiled mysteriously, "Not really Bharata! This decision was made when the king was in his senses and not under any influence. It was nowhere taken at the time of his death. In fact, this decision was taken many years before Our birth."

"What? How can this be?" Bharata was now confused and literally groping for words.

Sumantra frowned hearing this statement from Rama. Where was this heading? He was hoping that the conversation did not head the direction he saw it going.

"When he married mother Keikeyi, the king promised her father that he would appoint her son as the heir to the throne of Ayodhya. The marriage was sealed on this pact. No one knew this except king Dasaratha and king Ashwapati, your grandfather. Of course at that point in time, he had no son and only if he married Keikeyi would there have been a possibility of a son. But when we were born, the situation changed. That was precisely why he had wanted to coronate Me in such a hurry and that was why no invitation of My coronation was sent to your grandfather. But at the core of his heart, our father knew that the coronation would not occur, which is why he was so fearful from the day before the coronation. The two boons that he had given Keikeyi were not even part of his worries because he had made a much bigger promise before that to her father; therefore I say, my brother, the king had made the decision to coronate you when his sanity was intact."

Rama's words shocked Keikeyi. This was news to her. Why didn't her father tell her this? Why didn't Manthara know this? To a certain extent, the guilt she was bearing for so many days decreased a little. She was not completely wrong after all.

Sumantra was the most shocked. Of course he had known this story for long, and he had been guarding this little secret[21] with all his life. How did Rama know of it? How He knew did not matter, but He knew, that was what mattered. For Sumantra, there was no way now that Rama would accept the kingdom.

Rama continued addressing the shocked gathering, "The duty of children is to save their parents from hellish consequences that await those not fulfilling their promises. A son is called *putra* because he is supposed to save his parents from going to the hell named *Puta*. You fulfill the promises of Our father by becoming the king of Ayodhya and thus save him from hell. And I will for My part stay away from Ayodhya and fulfill the same promise. In addition, I will travel to Gaya and offer oblations for Our father.

Bharata, Our father's decision is perfectly just and balanced. He has given you the kingship of humans and has given Me the kingship of animals. The cities are meant for you to rule and the forests are meant for Me to rule. A white umbrella will shield your head and green umbrellas in the form of trees will shield mine. One of Sumitra's sons, Shatrughna, will assist you and the other, Lakshmana, will assist Me. I do not even see an iota of a glitch in

---

[21] Sumantra's duty was to bury the secrets in his heart and reveal them only when needed. He knew some day he would have to reveal this secret. But he was surprised when Rama revealed it instead. Sumantra realized that day, the deepest guarded secrets are known to Rama.

our father's division of property or of rulership.[22]

My dear brother, there are four gates to the door of perfection. Peace (*shanti*), introspection (*atma vichara*), satisfaction (*santosh*) and wise company (*satsang*). Desires locks the door called peace; ignorance locks the door called introspection; hankering locks the door called satisfaction; and misguidance locks the door called wise company. When these four locks are broken with determination, the door to perfection opens up. I urge you to introspect and accept whatever comes of its own accord into our lives with satisfaction and remain peaceful in the company of wise men. That's what I will do in the forest and that's what you should do in Ayodhya. If we retain this mood, then whether we stay in the forest or in Ayodhya, it won't make any difference."

Bharata had come prepared. Pat came his reply, "The qualities that You mention are apt for an ascetic to possess. You may be dressed like a hermit, but how can You abandon Your duties as a *kshatriya*? Giving up prosperity and wealth and living in the forest is meant for the third stage of life called *vanaprastha*. Which scripture recommends a *kshatriya* to abandon his duties and take up the duty of someone else? Don't the scriptures say that it is better to do one's own duty inefficiently rather than doing another's duty perfectly? The first duty of a *kshatriya* is to protect the citizens, physically from enemies, emotionally from disturbances, intellectually from weaknesses and spiritually from wrong habits. If You don't rule Ayodhya, thousands will have no such protection. If You really want to live a life of pain, why don't You take up the pain of protecting the citizens? This is far

---

[22] The art of forgiveness is about seeing balance in injustice, harmony in chaos and love in hatred.

greater pain than the pain of self-eliminating austerities.[23]

If You are not willing to give up the forest life to abide by our father's words, then we suggest that You stay in the forest and rule Ayodhya. We have got all the paraphernalia for installing You as the king. Vasistha and all the sages will install You in the presence of Your subjects as the king of Ayodhya. At least You should not have reservations about this proposal. But if even this is not agreeable to You, then hear Bharata's decision.

If You can be so insistent about Your *vrata* (vow), I too can be firm about mine. As long as You remain in the forest, I too shall remain. I never asked my father for the kingdom and neither did I tell my mother to conspire on my behalf. Why should I then rule the kingdom? If it is ordained that one of the sons of Dasaratha remain in the forest, let me be that son. I will replace You in the forest."[24]

Rama turned to Lakshmana who had by now turned purple with the shame and embarrassment of having doubted his brother's integrity. Lakshmana could not meet Rama's eyes but he continued staring at Bharata with tears of appreciation flowing down his cheeks.[25]

Rama turning to Bharata said: "As far as *kshatriya dharma* is concerned, where have I given it up? My mighty bow is always at

---

[23] The common link between working on self-growth and assisting in community growth is that self-growth is a by-product of assisting in community growth.

[24] Most people prefer to focus on their rights and prefer others to focus on their responsibilities.

Ayodhya is a model where everyone makes their responsibility their right and considers their rights as impediments.

[25] Most quick judgments turn into quicker embarrassments.

My side to protect the needy. I will continue ruling the forest and maintaining sanity and peace here. So, in essence, I am not really abandoning My duty. One does not always need position and power to perform duties.

As far as charity is concerned, once given, it cannot be reversed or changed. Then why speak of the charity of a person now deceased? King Dasaratha's charity was clear and had many witnesses. We are in no position to change or cancel it. There was no order from the king that Bharata should live in the forest. You cannot replace Me in the forest, neither can I replace you in Ayodhya. Any modifications to the king's order is *adharma*."[26]

Realizing Rama's steely resolve, the citizens lost heart. They were simultaneously sad and happy – sad that Rama would not return with them, but happy that they got to witness a unique kind of selflessness and extreme uprighteousness.

skepticism to belief

"Enough! Stop this madness! *Dharma*, duty, righteousness, hell, heaven… all this is nonsense. I am fed up of hearing all this rubbish." Everyone froze at these words spoken with intense anger. All heads turned toward the direction of the sound. Jabali was pushing his way ahead to stand in front of Rama and Lakshmana.

"Life is a constant journey." He continued, "In life's journey, two people may spend a night in the same village. Only fools consider

---

[26] Convenience is about changing the law to suit your life, but maturity is about changing your life to salute the law.

such time spent to mean eternal bonding. All relationships, including that of a father or mother, are transitory phases in this journey called life. The intelligent attach too much importance to the fleeting relationships of this world. Everyone is born alone and dies alone. Only a crazy fool gives more importance to relationships than one gives to a seat after a journey ends.

The only thing that matters is how to minimize discomforts and maximize pleasures to live happily. Life is just a combination of the sperm and the ovum. One shouldn't give any more importance to relationships than this. The king has gone, so have his dreams and aspirations. Now You have to live Your life with new dreams and new aspirations. Don't ignore the enjoyment that has walked into Your life through the kingdom.

I laugh at those who talk about the future consequences of present actions. Who has ever seen the future? Or who know what happens beyond death? What we can see is what we can experience with our senses here. Let us focus on enjoying the present and let thoughts about the future reside in the mind of clowns. What is in our perception is all there is to know.

The concepts of *dharma*, consequences, renunciation, austerities, charity are mere gimmicks of clever men to induce fear in the minds of people to fleece them. These clever men induce the fearing multitudes to offer food to their ancestors promising that it will reach them. Ha! Ha! And fools believe it to be true. How can a dead man eat? So much food is thrown on the ground only to be eaten by animals and birds. Of course, the priests do become fatter. A priest's burp of satisfaction – is that a sign that the ancestor is satisfied? If food offered here reaches another person elsewhere, why not use this technique to travel from here to elsewhere? Why don't we perform sacrifices for those who travel out of town?

The existence of another world is a myth. Reality is what exists before our eyes. I pity those who devote their life to religion and I appreciate those who live a life centered on pleasures. Don't take life so seriously. Lighten up. Accept the kingdom that Bharata is offering You and enjoy Your life to the fullest."

Every word Jabali spoke ignited Rama's anger. He respected the sage who was in His father's ministry, hence did not want to react harshly without hearing him out. By now things had reached a boiling point. Rama could no longer tolerate another word. "What you are speaking right now is nonsense! What you speak seems logical and sweet, but these are nothing but sugar-coated poison pills. What you think of as a life of enjoyment is simply a means to create a life of frustration.

Vedic concepts act as reins to direct the unruly mind. When one rejects the Vedic concepts, one whole-heartedly submits to the mind, a mind that always plots to drag you toward your lower nature. The Vedic concepts are not against enjoyment but against unmonitored and unprincipled enjoyment.

The intention behind a person's behavior is the actual measure of his strength. Great people have the ability to discern true behavior by zooming into the hidden intention rather than judging on the basis of appearance. Such sensible people lose respect for those that lead a hypocritical life. If as per your advice, I act just for the sake of enjoyment, then I will have to struggle with double standards: one standard to please myself and yet another standard to inspire the world to accept my leadership.

To facilitate my whims, I will have to be a noble person externally but a dishonest one actually, a person decked with good qualities externally but impure actually, well behaved externally but ill-behaved actually and appear righteous externally but care nothing for the rules of conduct in actuality.

When a leader plays such a double game, how can he expect his followers to be transparent and accountable to him? The standard of a leader has to be impeccable to generate genuine following. Will a leader be happy if his followers have double standards? Naturally not!

The basis of any governance is truth. One should fear an untruthful person more than a snake. Every good quality has its foundation in truth. If that be the case, why should I not be truthful about following the words of My father? I declare for everyone to hear, nothing can cause Me to abandon the bonds of morality. Not greed for more, not forgetfulness amid temptations and not pride in My abilities will make Me abandon the path of truth and morality.

Millions of exalted people in the past have abided by the Vedic concepts and have demonstrated perfection at a personal level and perfection at the governance level. And you have the audacity to say that all that is false. What is your qualification to claim to be better than all of them? Should I believe you, the one who has no credibility or them who have such high timeless reputation and respect? I do not blame you for all that you have said today, I believe that the court of Ayodhya has made an error by appointing you in the ministry. Your words of atheism are totally unworthy and people should stay away from you."

People were awestruck with Rama's ability to refute and strike down Jabali's arguments logically. But they were even more dumbstruck with Rama's angry outburst. This was perhaps a first in their lives. Now they knew that only one thing could trigger Rama's anger, and that was, atheism.

By now Jabali's confidence was replaced by shame. He fell at Rama's feet and said, "Rama, I am not an atheist. Bharata's struggle to convince You convinced me to take this measure. How long could I tolerate seeing the incessant tears in Your mother's eyes? How long can I tolerate seeing Your father's prosperous kingdom turn into a ghost town? Rama, my thought was that if being a theist was so painful, would not many want to be atheist? But after hearing Your strong message, I am convinced that no one can change Your decision. And I have understood the painful reality of You being a leader wanting to set the highest standard for the future well-being of the world. Glory be unto You and Your dynasty. Please forgive me for my audacity, it was only out of love for You and nothing else."[27]

To convince Rama further, Vasistha stood up and seconded Jabali, thus convincing Him regarding the genuineness of Jabali.

people decide

Both the parties were just as adamant as they were in the beginning. So much drama, yet no conclusion! It was time for the Big M to intervene. But will the Big M succeed in being conclusive this time?

Vasistha cleared his throat and addressed Rama with the authority of a guru. "From birth every person has three primary instructors,

---

[27] The root of the tree of love is intention and expression is its leaf. Jabali's interest in atheism was only an expression of his love, which was rooted, in the right intention.

But Rama rightly pointed out that most people have access only to the expression and can't see the intention; therefore, even if the intention is right, the expression should not be wrong, to result in healthy love.

the father, the mother and the teacher. The father gives life, but the teacher gives the wisdom to live life; therefore, the instructions of the teacher are considered by the great as more important.

I am not just Your guru, but also the guru of Your father. Naturally by following my instructions, You need not be worried about transgressing the codes of *dharma*. If I tell You to accept the kingdom, you will not just be fulfilling your duty toward me, but toward thousands of people. By following my instructions, you will be following your duty toward all these people who have taken this journey from such a distance. By following my instructions, you will not lack reverence toward your aging mother. And by following my instructions, you will not be cruel and neglectful toward an expectant brother. By satisfying so many people, how will you be transgressing principles of *dharma*, Rama?"

Hearing the spiritual master speak with the tone of authority, Rama folded his hands and kneeled. Balanced and yet firm, He spoke, "What you have said is indeed true. The instructions of guru, father and mother have all to be obeyed even with one's life. But often when the instructions contradict one another, the instructions must be followed in the order they were delivered. I will first follow the instruction of My father for 14 years and then will obey the instruction of My mother and My guru. Thus I will not be neglecting any instruction."

When Bharata heard this, he went berserk. In a final attempt to persuade his brother, he told Sumantra to lay *kusa* grass on the ground where he would perform *prayopavesa* (fasting avoiding food or water till death) till Rama agreed to return to Ayodhya. Sumantra looked at Rama without attempting to follow Bharata's orders, Bharata got a heap of *kusa* grass himself and spread it on the floor.

Rama was visibly annoyed with Bharata's adamant behavior. He said, "What wrong have I done to you that you take this step? *Prayopavesa* is a practice meant for the *brahmanas* in extreme cases of helplessness and for lack of any other option, but it is not to be attempted by rulers. Forget your mission and return to Ayodhya. Be assured that even if the moon loses its soothing light, the Himalayas shakes off its snow and the sea transgresses the shores, I will never falsify My father's promise."

Bharata was now helpless. He was not equipped to handle his brother's anger. Moreover, there was no way he could displease his brother. Feeling vulnerable, he ran out of the hut to the citizens of Ayodhya who had all accompanied him so bravely on this long arduous journey. "Citizens of Ayodhya! The tradition of the Ikshvaku dynasty has been to consult you before making important decisions. Our King Dasaratha did not consult you before taking the most important decision of banishing Rama. As a result, he went through so much suffering and so did you. You came with such enthusiasm to take Rama back with you, why don't you say something at least now? If you fail to speak up now, we will return empty-handed. Someone please say something!"

A senior citizen spoke up on behalf of the rest: "We know Rama well. And now that we have heard Him, He knows what He is doing and He knows what is right for us. Although what is right can also be painful for us! Let Rama keep the words of His father. We will not persuade Him any further."[28]

---

[28] Many have the fortune of knowing what is right, but few have the guts of doing what is right.

The courage to do what is right shudders at the pain in doing it.

Rama walked up to Bharata and lovingly touched his shoulders. "Reflect on what we spoke today and on what the citizens just concluded. Do not think impulsively,[29] think reflectively. Only then will you see reason. Rest assured, I will return after 14 years and rule the kingdom assisted by My virtuous brothers."

final say

As if taking a cue from Rama's words, a shower of flowers rained on the gathering. Glancing up, everyone saw an assembly of celestial sages who were eavesdropping on the conversation. The sages were highly impressed with the sincerity of both brothers. They considered Dasaratha fortunate for having such sons and the people of Ayodhya for having such illustrious rulers. They, too, felt fortunate to have had the opportunity to witness and hear this dialogue.

The celestial sages knew the purpose behind Rama's exile. To expedite that, they gave Bharata their opinion distinctively. One of them spoke for everyone: "Bharata, if you have any regard for your father, accept and abide by the words of Rama." Without giving him a chance to speak, they vanished into thin air.

The citizens of Ayodhya perceived that they had just witnessed something miraculous and that these were not ordinary sages.[30]

---

[29] Impulsive thinking prioritizes action before a thought. Reflective thinking prioritizes thought before an action.

[30] Greater miracles happen when human beings come together to perform the greatest miracle on earth – cooperate for a higher good.

With trembling limbs Bharata turned his attention toward Rama. Understanding his predicament, Rama spoke, "Dear brother, in your humility, you have often expressed your inability to rule Ayodhya, but I assure you that your humility is your strength. You are extremely competent to rule the country. Remember that character is better than competence. Use your humility to seek good council from wise personalities who are unbiased and selfless. Do not ever blame your mother for all that has happened. A mother is always to be sincerely respected."

All this while, Bharata was inconclusive and disturbed, but now there was clarity on his face. Yes, he was still disturbed, but had a clear direction. He turned around and clapped. In a moment an assistant came with a silver plate in his hands carrying something covered with a heavily embroidered silk cloth. To everyone's surprise, including Rama's, Bharata unveiled a pair of gold-studded wooden sandals. Lifting them up, he gently placed them close to Rama's feet and requested Him to wear it. Rama looked at Bharata quizzically.

Bharata explained humbly, "My Lord, I know for sure that You will not return for 14 years now. But if I sit on the throne, I will feel that I have cheated You. This dilemma can be solved only if I install Your footwear on the throne. The footwear will assure me that I am ruling the kingdom on Your behalf, and it will give the citizens confidence in the rule. Wherever Your lotus feet are, there is bound to be great gain and assured security."

The citizens of Ayodhya wept as they witnessed Lord Rama stepping into the sandals. Bharata, himself in tears, took a solemn vow: "I vow that for the next 14 years, I shall wear matted hair and dress in tree bark and deerskin. Eating only roots and fruits, I will live in the outskirts of Ayodhya. I will earnestly rule the country as Your humble representative. I also vow that if I do not see You on the day after the completion of the 14 years, I will jump into the pyre and end my existence."

Rama embraced Bharata to His heart's content and ruffled his hair in affection, promising him that He would return on time. He pulled Shatrughna, too, into His loving embrace and patted both their heads. Before pulling away from them, He whispered into their ears, "Do not be angry with mother Keikeyi. You both have a vow by Sita and Me never to disrespect her."

Bharata and Shatrughna went around Rama thrice and then Bharata, held the footwear on his head and began descending the mountain.

One by one, Rama greeted all who had come to Chitrakoot from Ayodhya. Rama greeted everyone according to their positions, age and their relationships with Him. After bidding farewell, Rama noticed the three mothers. He walked up to them and touched their feet one by one and embraced them. He especially showered more love on Keikeyi and soothingly removed all her embarrassment by that one gesture. He directed the three mothers toward their palanquins. Despite being seated in their palanquins, they kept staring at Rama, Lakshmana and Sita. Unable to speak or move, they kept shedding tears. Rama ended their embarrassment and predicament by entering into His hut, out of their vision. They had no choice but to leave.

sovereign sandals

On reaching downhill, Bharata placed the footwear on the royal elephant and mounted his chariot. They decided to circumambulate around the mountain, clearly indicating to the world and embedding in their mind that their life was centered on serving and worshipping Rama. After that the caravan commenced its return journey.[31]

On their way back, they stopped briefly at Bharadwaja *muni's* ashram and narrated the entire episode to him in great detail. He was naturally impressed with the natural nobility that flowed in the veins of Rama and Bharata. He compared the descent of nobility in the Ikshvaku clan to the natural propensity of water to flow downwards.

Moving ahead, they reached Ayodhya. Everyone was happy-sad that day. All homes were discussing the greatness of the Dasaratha family. Despair had turned into hope. Every home in Ayodhya marked Rama's date of return on their walls to remind them of the joy that was to come 14 years later.

For Bharata, the next 14 years were going to be mechanical. His body would surely function at its best in the service of Rama's footwear, but his mind was always rushing ahead of time and waiting for time and his body to catch up.

When someone asked him who was actually responsible for all that had happened in Ayodhya, Bharata said something that shocked everyone.

---

[31] For Bharata, the two sandals or *padukas* meant a lot. From one perspective, he considered the two like two watchmen entrusted with the duty of guarding the lives of people in Ayodhya.

From another, the *padukas* were like a pair of hands that assisted in the performance of good deeds or like a pair of eyes that showed the right path.

He also considered them his two jewel boxes that enshrined the two-jeweled syllables that he had –Ra and Ma.

Na mantarya na cha matarasya
doso na rajan na cha ragavasya
mad papa eva atra nimittam asit
vana pravase ragunandanasya

"Manthara is not to be blamed for what happened. She is a maid after all, what do you expect from her? Even Keikeyi is not to be blamed for this mishap. She is a mother after all, what do you expect from her? She has natural blind affection for her son. Even the king is not to be blamed. He had to keep his words after all, how can he be at fault? Nor can Rama be blamed for the whole catastrophe. He is an obedient son after all, with the burden of setting the right example for the world to follow. If you want to know who is actually at fault for Raghu nandana going to the forest, let me tell you, it is my sin that is at fault. Because of my sin, so many people had to suffer."[32]

The very next day Bharata and Shatrughna left Ayodhya to reside in the outskirts at a village known as Nandigram. This village faced the forest where Rama resided. He set up a small hut there and established a throne on which Rama's sandals were installed. For the next 14 years, Bharata conducted all his state affairs from that hut. While living a very austere life of prayer and repentance, he faithfully reported to the sandals every small and big contribution he made for the kingdom. He gave the sandal all updates to do with the affairs of the kingdom. The kingdom grew in size and prosperity reigned. The presence of nothing could replace the absence of Rama.[33]

---

[32] Accepting the blame for events that happen in our life is like sitting on fire. Remember that when plain corn sits on fire it becomes popcorn, an experienced and sweeter corn.

[33] Anything connected to the Lord becomes special. In fact, the *paduka*

Ayodhya seems to have become peaceful after the meeting with Rama. But was Chitrakoot peaceful after the arrival of Bharata? Could the ever-insecure forest, provide security to Rama, Sita and Lakshmana?

---

or footwear that sat at the feet of the Lord, became the ruler of Ayodhya. This is true for people, too. Anyone who sits at the Lord's feet becomes qualified to sit at the head of everyone; therefore, a king who is a great devotee is highly respected, as is a *guru* who has taken refuge in the Lord. An *acharya* analogizes the Rama–Bharata *milap* episode by comparing Rama to a lion, the *paduka* to a lioness, Bharata to a cub and Ravana to an elephant. The lion, lioness and the cub lived in a cave named Ayodhya. One day, the three came out of the cave. When the lion heard the trumpeting of a proud elephant, he jumped ahead to shatter his pride. The lioness on seeing her husband leaving a higher purpose, took her cub back into the cave.

Here, the *acharya* says that it is not Bharata who took the *paduka* back to Ayodhya, but it was the *paduka* that took Bharata back to Ayodhya. The *paduka* was directing Bharata.

CHAPTER 9

POWER OF THE POWERLESS

The four youngsters loved travel. But what they loved more was the possibility of thrill that every journey afforded them. Of late, they had begun experimenting with risky fun. The adrenaline rush these precarious exploits gave them was hard to resist. The kick they got from these was way better than even the best of intoxicants.

With each adventure, they hunted for more and more opportunities for that exhilarating high. What had triggered this craving, they couldn't figure out. If their fathers were to decide, they would have said, age. But the boys were beyond caring for their father's opinion now. With rippling muscles and advanced degrees in combat, the boys were confident they wouldn't ever run to their fathers like wimps. What came in particularly handy was Jayanta's shape-shifting ability. It always worked when nothing else did![1]

Their destination today was Chitrakoot mountain – the honeymoon hotspot on earth for celestial couples. Since the day Anasuya *devi*'s power forced Mandakini river to descend on earth, Chitrakoot, an

---

[1] The riskiest risk is the thrill of inconsequential fun paying the heavy cost of a gambled life.

otherwise obscure location, came into the limelight. Of course, today they were hoping that they wouldn't be spotted by any of their relatives or father's colleagues. But that itself was a risk, wasn't it?

As they discussed the possibility, they saw something that caught their attention instantly. An opportunity had presented itself! They hid behind rocks and waited for the right time.

a moment's rest

The past few days had been exhausting. Less physically, more emotionally! Meeting the ardent residents of Ayodhya had drained their energy. Every time Rama entered the house, He could visualize His teary-eyed mother standing in a corner of the room. Each time He crossed that room, He almost consciously avoided stepping on the spot Bharata had sat down to fast until death. He could no longer sit where His venerable *guru* Vasistha was seated a few days back.[2]

To make things worse, there was a daily stream of visitors from in and around Ayodhya; those unable to join the excursion with Bharata, ventured on their own unannounced. Finding the trio in Chitrakoot was no longer difficult. Rama suspected that maps had probably been made in Ayodhya with clear routes right up to their hut on the hill.

To clear His head a bit and to return to the frame of mind He was in before the arrival of Bharata and his army, Rama pulled Sita

---

[2] When one spends a dreamy night, there is more exhaustion than rejuvenation.

Conversely, an emotionally disturbed mind depletes a fully recharged body.

along with Him for a stroll in the scenic valley on the other side of the mountain. The army had successfully managed to destroy the serenity and beauty of the mountain on the front side. Appreciating nature's beauty and savoring Sita's unassuming and undemanding presence, He was soon transported to another world. Sita was happy to see this change in Rama. She knew that her role would be to help Him unwind the emotional knots He would probably become entangled in from time to time. She decided to flow with His mood.[3]

She allowed Him to choose the turns and stops. Under a huge banyan tree, Rama decided to rest for a while. Sita, sensing His mood, sat down leaning against the tree, with her legs extended, gently allowing His head to rest on her lap. With the tenderness of the breeze, her fingers began to run through His hair and occasionally caress His forehead. Within seconds, sleep had surrounded Rama.

an eye for a peck

High on the branch of a banyan tree, a crow nodded his head, his eyes riveted on the couple below, stealing an occasional glance at the three hidden boys who were directing him through gestures. Now! The sign was clear. The crow swooped down silently and perched on the ground.

His heart started pounding in anticipation. He was going to do something very dangerous, but exciting. The crow observed the

---

[3] An emotionally disturbed mind is like a river that flows zigzag through the mountains. It needs a friend like the fish to flow along with its ups and downs. It does not need a dam that questions its direction of flow and feeds it with conflicting ideas.

couple closely. From their attire, the pair seemed ordinary, like a hermit and his wife. But there was something in their demeanor that seemed to tell another tale, something a crow could not decipher, even if the crow happened to be none other than Jayanta, the son of the king of demigods, Indra.

The man resting on his wife's lap was definitely different from all the sages he had seen so far – he appeared too regal to be a sage. And, his wife was far more stunning than all the alluring damsels of the heavens. The deceptive appearance was what made this whole dare even more exciting and enticing for Jayanta. He had no clue about what he was going to do, but he was sure he was willing to go to any lengths. Especially so in this disguise; it was safe to do anything as a crow.[4]

The crow hopped thrice, inching away from the couple. The flapping of his wings caught Sita's attention. Instinctively, She stiffened. She opened Her eyes and saw the crow. She relaxed and thought, "Oh, it's only a crow." But the crow's strange stare made her uncomfortable. Weren't crows supposed to be afraid of humans? But this creature was glaring at Her. She glanced at Her husband sleeping peacefully on her lap, unaware of the world. She decided to ignore the bird.

The crow then slowly began shuffle closer to her. She realized that something was terribly wrong here. She began to wave and shoo off the crow, careful not to disturb Her husband. This was not worth ruining His sleep.

---

[4] A human mind dreads leaving evidence of a sin committed for the fear of the consequences of being recognized.

When a person becomes unrecognizable, his character also becomes alien.

A true spotless character should be governed by the conscience not by recognition.

She thought She saw the crow smirk and noticed devious excitement in his eyes. The crow lunged forward and touched Her shoulders and jumped back. She quivered. What was that! The crow jumped yet again, touched Her and returned to his position. Sita was confused between fear for Her safety and the need for Her husband's rest.

The crow's heartbeat became so loud that he could hear nothing else. He missed all the "stop and return" gestures his friends had been making. He decided to take things to another level and up the ante. Jayanta wanted to share his discovery with his friends later, confirmation of what they always doubted – the greater the risk, the greater the fun. But later. First things first!

The crow jumped and began flapping its wings and raised itself to the level of Sita's face. He then swooped down and clawed at Her chest. Sita was aghast at the crow's audacity. She tried to flap him away. But the crow dodged Her and pecked Her yet again. The ordeal was turning out to be extremely painful and embarrassing to Sita. By now She was bleeding profusely, but the crow hadn't had enough yet.

Rama suddenly opened His eyes when a drop of hot blood fell on His cheek. He instantly sat up. Aghast to see so much blood oozing from Sita's body and Her eyes filled with tears. He screamed, "Sita! What is this? Who had the audacity to do this to You?"

The foolish crow did not hear Rama, either because his heart was pounding too loud or because he was trying to decode his friends' gestures. But when he jumped toward Sita again, his eyes met with Rama's cold stare. He cawed and jumped away, landing a distance away from the couple.

Something about the way Rama picked up a blade of grass told him that everything was over. Holding the grass to His forehead,

Rama closed His eyes and murmured some *mantras*. Jayanta started backing off. With steely eyes filled with anger, Rama raised the blade of grass and threw it toward the crow. The crow saw the grass shine like the sun as it whizzed ahead. The bird panicked and prepared to escape. He flew over the three boys hidden behind the rock, but the blade of grass that seemed to turn into a *brahmastra* kept following him! The boys sat helpless, unable to help their friend.[5]

The crow flew helter-skelter, but the *brahmastra* kept the chase constant. Jayanta the crow knocked on the door of a sage in Chitrakoot. As soon as the sage opened the door, Jayanta fell at his feet shouting, "Shelter, shelter!" The sage considered Jayanta's tale with compassion, but when he realized that Rama's *brahmastra* was chasing him, the sage shooed him away.

Jayanta dodged the *brahmastra* and fluttered in vain. He finally reached the abode of his father, King Indra. Panting and explaining the details of his misadventure, he begged for protection. Indra told him that no one but Rama could protect anyone He decided to kill.

Realizing that his father was powerless and could not help him, he ran to Lord Brahma's abode. Wasn't *brahmastra* his weapon? Surely he could recall it! As he was rushing toward *Brahmaloka*, he made an important observation. From the time the *astra* had been chasing him, its speed varied depending on the direction he was facing. When he faced the direction of the earth, more specifically in the direction of Chitrakoot and most specifically in

---

[5] Fallible partnership is when one is ready to share the fun but not the repercussion.

Just like monkeys come together to enjoy a feast but scatter away at the first hint of trouble, fallible friends come together to enjoy cheap thrills and wither at the first hint of sharing responsibility.

the direction of Rama, its speed reduced drastically. When he faced away, the speed increased. Was it programmed to slow down when one turned toward Rama? But he brushed aside that thought and skidded toward Brahma's feet.

"Sorry, though this *astra* is definitely mine, I have no power to stop it. There is only one person who can help you and that is Rama." Saying this Brahma comfortably closed his eyes, as if nothing happened. Even Shiva had the same opinion and answer. Jayanta was now at his wit's end and his energy had waned. There was only one logical thing to do now: become shameless![6]

Jayanta decided to do what his pride would have never otherwise allowed him to. With a thud, he fell at the feet of Rama. Rama and Sita looked at each other. The *brahmastra* was hovering close by, waiting for clear directions from Rama. Rama had since taken care of Sita's wounds. The crow was panting and had almost lost consciousness.

When Sita saw the plight of the crow, compassion filled Her heart. She noticed that though the crow had surrendered to Rama, but he really did not know how to actually surrender. His head was away from Rama's and his back toward Him. This was perhaps the first time the crow had surrendered to anyone. Sita compassionately touched the crow's head and pushed it toward Rama's feet. The crow felt the motherly touch of Sita. It almost felt as if mother Sachi was touching his head. Instantly shame covered his heart with sincere repentance of the blinded folly of brutally attacking this saintly lady.

---

[6] If committing a mistake is a higher act of shamelessness than accepting the mistake, then why does one feel ashamed while accepting and excited while committing?

Rama knew that Sita was indicating that He forgive the crow. His law always bowed before Sita's love. He silently decided any act of punishment would be delivered only in the absence of Sita. Her kind of compassion would compel Him to forgive everyone.

He looked at the crow and at the *brahmastra* and then at Sita who was slowly nodding Her head suggesting that He forgive. He said, "The *brahmastra* cannot go in vain. It has to act in some way. But your compassion cannot go in vain either. Since You have touched his head, I cannot even cut it off. So let the *astra* destroy only the right eye of the bird as punishment."[7]

In a flash, the crow was blinded in its right eye. An eye lost for a lesson learned. What an adventure it was! Jayanta returned more mature than his age and an eye less but with better vision.[8]

time to shift base

Under the starry sky, Rama, Sita and Lakshmana sat around a fire lit by Lakshmana. Rama shared with Them the conversation He had that afternoon with the leader of the community of sages in

---

[7] When law dominates love, punishment is given prominence over forgiveness. When love dominates law, compassion is given prominence over violence.

When there is a balance between law and love, the seed of repentance is planted in the soil of love and under the scrutiny of the hot sun of penance.

[8] It is believed that from this day on, crows see at a time with only one eye (either left or right), for crows have divided vision, which means each eye sees differently, independent of the other. This story teaches us to depend less on our eyes and more on our vision.

Chitrakoot. He revealed that some hidden fear reigned among the sages and that they were thinking of quitting Chitrakuta and traveling to another destination.

Rama said, "Initially I presumed they were unhappy with Our behavior or Our service. But they clearly said that their fear stems from the recent frequent visits of demons to Chitrakoot. They had been carefully suppressing this information to avoid disturbing Us. But now, matters have come to a head as they have decided to shift base after being subjected to enough and more abuse at the hands of the demons. Of course they have offered to let Us join them if we so wished."

As Sita and Lakshmana sat silently contemplating, Rama continued, "I have decided that we will travel with them. Not so much because of the demons, but because this place has become a repository of so many memories of our loved ones. It is no longer an appropriate place to reside. Besides, if people from Ayodhya visit us so frequently with valuable gifts, where is the question of leading a life of anchorites?"

Sita and Lakshmana nodded Their heads in agreement. The three of Them felt sorry for having to abandon the place They had been living here for the past year or so. Sita lovingly touched the walls of the hut Lakshmana had so painstakingly built for them. She recollected Valmiki's words. Was there a call for Them from somewhere? Was that why They had to leave so hastily? But She had not heard any, or did She actually hear a hidden call of some urgency elsewhere in Rama's words.

374 • Shattered Dreams

wonder women

The trio followed the band of sages trekking along the Mandakini river. They seemed excited about the 16-mile trek to the *ashram* they were gushing about.

The elderly sage who owned that *ashram* was nothing short of a hero. But surprisingly they spoke in the same tone and in fact more enthusiastically about the greatness of his wife. This old sagely couple had some fascinating adventures that attributed them with super-human persona.

What really surprised Rama was that Sita already knew about the sage's wife! In fact, she narrated tale after tale revealing how enterprising a person she was.

"This holy river that we have bathed in all these days is thanks to Anasuya." Sita said pointing to the river to their left.

"Really!" Rama exclaimed, revealing His enthusiasm to hear the story from Sita's mouth. "And how did that happen?"

Encouraged by Her eager audience, Sita spoke animatedly. "Long ago, there was a great drought in this land and there were no rains for 10 years at a stretch. The sages in this area were dying of thirst and the flora and fauna of this region had wilted away. Anasuya took it upon herself to restore the prosperity of this region. Thus began a long, intense series of austerities resulting in the demigods being pleased enough to permit her to bring the heavenly Mandakini river to Chitrakoot. With the descent of Mandakini in this land, prosperity reigned and it became a hotspot for the sages to perfect their lives. After this episode, the rest of the sages became aficionados of *Atri* and *Anasuya* devi."[9]

Rama absorbed Sita's stories. Sita continued charged by Her husband's interest, "She may be famous in Chitrakoot because of that, but something else she did earned her universal fame and also envy."

"And what could have been more fascinating than getting the heavenly Mandakini to descend to earth? It took my ancestors almost four generations to succeed in getting the Ganga to descend, that too after such herculean efforts. What can be more heroic than this?" Rama was clearly excited to hear more.

"Anasuya was exceptionally compassionate like her parents, Kardama *muni* and Devahuti. She jumped at every opportunity to serve the world selflessly. Once the world was haunted by an enigma that Lord Brahma himself was unable to resolve. But Anasuya's enterprising spirit and her loyalty to each of her commitments, gave her the strength to resolve a calamity of such magnitude." When they heard what Sita said, the brothers and the sages stopped walking, waiting for Her to continue.

"A sage named Ugrasravas, also known as Kaushik, lived in a place called Prathishthaan. Shilavati was his chaste and loving wife. Though Ugrasravas lived a life of a sage, he could not control his mind. Every now and then his base instincts got the better of him. By constantly abusing his body, the effect of his hypocritical lifestyle began to take its toll. He contracted a deadly form of leprosy and his

---

[9] Anasuya teaches us the art of winning others' hearts.

When you do at least one thing that they can't do for themselves and for which you don't get paid, the result is a pleased heart.

limbs melted away because of it. Yet his urge for pleasure only grew.[10]

With genuine love and affection, Shilavati continued to serve her ailing husband. Her affection for her husband and commitment toward him grew daily as his desire to visit a courtesan. Incapable of bringing himself to the house of courtesan, he shamelessly begged his wife, Shilavati, to help him in his endeavor. Shilavati steadied her mind and decided to serve her husband this way, too. She reasoned that she wanted to remain committed to her duty as wife irrespective of how much her husband neglected and abused his role. In such a trying circumstance, she sought relief and direction in her mother's words about how a wife can actually control the universe purely through her chastity. Though disgusted with his request, she wasn't willing to give up on him. She propped him up and silently began helping him wobble out of their house toward the courtesan's house beyond the forest path. They had no idea that something awaited them in the middle of the forest.[11]

Standing on one leg, hands in the air, an austere sage named Mandavya *muni* was performing intense *tapasya* outside his *ashram*. Nearby, a group of dacoits had dodged the king's soldiers after looting the royal treasury. They chose the silent *ashram* of Mandavya *muni* as the ideal hiding place for their loot. The soldiers followed the thieves to the *ashram* and without bothering about the meditation posture of the *muni*, they began interrogating him.

---

[10] Lifestyle is not so much about habits as much as it is about mindsets. Imitating habits is easy, but emulating mindsets is difficult.

The value of imitation jewelry is not estimated by its shape but by its worth.

[11] Infatuation and reasoning are two swords that cannot be housed in the same sheath. Infatuation cuts reasoning and reasoning punctures infatuation.

A search of the *ashram* revealed the treasure and the innocent sage was considered an accomplice to the theft. The thieves were apprehended and presented at the scene. The king thoughtlessly ordered all the thieves including the sage to be speared to death. Within moments, all the thieves died, but the sage did not. The king's retinue departed, leaving the sage to deal with his slow death. Then Lord Shiva appeared and blessed the sage with longevity, although he chose not to interfere with the spear that had impaled his body. Cursing everyone around, Mandavya *muni* remained helplessly wedged onto the spear.

Not too far away, placing his complete weight on Shilavati's shoulders, Ugrasrava wobbled along. With sunset, not only did light leave the forest, it also obscured Ugrasrava's mind. This resulted in Ugrasrava tripping over the limp body of Mandavya *muni* that was supported on a spear. The sudden jerk caused a new jolt of pain to rush through the weak sage's spine. A string of fiery words followed an ear-splitting cry. 'You rascal! Let sunrise mark your death!' Shilavati was struggling to support her husband who had lost his balance by tripping over. When she heard the curse of the angry sage, she froze. But she was aghast when she saw the predicament he was in. But wouldn't a woman without her husband be exactly like this helpless sage, plunged into sorrow? She did something that had never been done before. She closed her eyes and summoned all her energies and spoke. Her voice boomed across the forest. Even her husband could not recognize the voice. 'If I have been chaste to my husband and have not deviated in my fidelity toward him even for a second, let the sun not rise.' While Mandavya *muni* could not believe his ears, her husband trembled in fear, unable to recognize the sudden power emanating from his wife. 'Did she really mean what she said? Was it really possible for a mere mortal to prevent the sun from rising?'

Shilavati bent to pick her husband up and cast a sidelong glance at Mandavya *muni* in contempt. The sheer anger in her eyes made the *muni* uncomfortable. He looked at the spear in his body. Of the two, the piercing pain of the spear seemed more bearable than piercing rage in the eyes of this angry wife. As she picked up her husband, she looked straight into his eyes. Her husband meekly requested her to take him back home. The courtesan was long forgotten. Silently, the pair returned.

The *muni* waited for her words to be proven wrong and for his curse to have effect. The wait seemed just too long. Animals had begun to crawl around although it was still dark. Other sages, his friends, who had transformed themselves into birds, hovered over the *muni*. It soon became evident that the sun would not rise. An intensely chaotic period began in the world with the sun just unable to rise. Demigods soon realized the catastrophe the absence of sunrise would bring. After a long conference with Lord Brahma, they returned to their abodes when the creator agreed to set things right.

A thorn can be removed only by another thorn. A poison can nullify another poison. Similarly, words of a pious chaste woman can only be undone by the words of another such woman. So Brahma approached Anasuya *devi* at Atri *muni*'s ashram. On understanding the unusual predicament and the need for immediate action, Anasuya reached Shilavati's house. Shilavati immediately agreed to allow the sun to rise provided her husband's life was spared. She did not need anything more than the nod of assurance from another virtuous lady. Soon the sun rose, and the world rejoiced. Ugrasrava had to die because of Mandavya *muni*'s curse, though. But keeping her word, Anasuya offered prayers, and with the power of her purity brought Shilavati's husband back to life.

The most content was Lord Brahma. He was happy to see two

women of his creation, live such spotless lives. But he was happier to see that the laws of this universe made by him had bent to the discretion of these pure women. He became sure that there is no higher power than duty and purity of love and devotion to God. He blessed the savior Anasuya for her motherly affection toward the world; he himself would take birth as her son to experience her motherly love."[12]

Anasuya *devi*'s tales delighted Rama and Lakshmana. Every time They heard the greatness of any woman, Their respect and veneration for women increased manifold.

The group literally glided into the *ashram* of Atri muni. Eager to see the heroes of Sita's stories, Rama, Lakshmana and Sita entered the

---

[12] Madavya *muni*, however, continued to remain wedged on that spear for many days. One day the king heard about the story of Lord Shiva blessing him and also about the fact that the sage was still mysteriously alive. Realizing his folly, the king unsuccessfully attempted to extricate the spear.

The only option was to cut it resulting in the sharp tip (*ani*) of the spear to stay stuck in his abdomen. From that day onward his name was prefixed with Ani (which means the tip) and he was known as Ani-Mandavya *muni*.

After many years of wandering with the tip of the spear in his body, Ani-Mandavya once happened to meet Dharmaraj or the god of death. On being upset with the injustice he suffered, Ani-Mandavya asked for an explanation for his predicament. The god of death explained that in his childhood Ani-Mandavya had pierced helpless birds with sharp grass reeds and his present suffering was a reaction to those.

Ani-Mandavya *muni* felt that this explanation was unreasonable and that the actions of boys below age 12 should not be considered for such cruel reactions under the laws of karma. In extreme anger, he cursed the god of death that he would be born on earth and go through an insulting experience just like he was going through now. The god of death graciously accepted the curse and was born as Vidura, in Hastinapura and played an important role in the Mahabharata as the uncle of the Pandavas and Kauravas.

silent *ashram*. Sita had ignited respect in Their hearts toward these revered personalities. They now wanted to hear more from them directly. The trio saw a frail elderly figure standing at the door of the hermitage to receive them. Rama, Lakshmana and Sita paid Their respects to the venerable sage, while he welcomed them with great reverence and honor. Having them seated comfortably inside the hermitage, Atri *muni* called out to his wife.

Dressed in the simple clothes of a forest dweller, hair white with age and waking stick in hand, a grand old lady entered trembling like a frail plantain leaf in the wind. Rama, Lakshmana and Sita stood up in utter respect. They could clearly see that although her limbs had wrinkled, her face radiated a brilliance clearly indicating that her determination and purity had not waned. All three of them instantly fell in love with this peerless couple. What surprised them further was the amount of respect they both had for one another![13]

Anasuya looked at the three of them lovingly and then broke into a broad smile. She held out her hand to Sita and gestured Her to come closer. Sita coyly walked toward Anasuya. Anasuya held Her hands and took Her into the inner chamber.

when givers beg

"There is great power in simplicity. Our lives are a glaring proof of this fact. Otherwise why would the universal administrators

---

[13] A hero is not one who tries to surpass others, but one who strives to solve the knots in others' lives at the cost of personal sacrifices.

A hero is not one who usurps the legacy of fame but one who lives behind the inheritance of a great example.

constantly approach us for help? The non-enviousness and whole-hearted dedication of Anasuya and my self-control unaffected by the three modes of nature, this combination has made us powerful in the eyes of the world. Look at us, Rama! Do we look powerful at all?" Rama glanced at Atri who was speaking these words with confidence and yet humility. He was definitely making a point.[14]

Power should never be sought in physical strength, but in mental strength." Rama answered. "You may not have physical powers, but the lifestyle of dependence that you have led has made you mentally powerful. Nothing is impossible for people like you."

Atri was impressed by Rama's analysis. "That's precisely right, Rama. The confidence helped Anasuya tackle a test that the universal administrators tricked her into. Do you want to hear that story?"

"Of course, the more I hear about simple people achieving amazing feats, the more I consider Myself fortunate to have the opportunity to spend these years amid people like you. Respected sage, My greatest joy would be to lap up every word you speak. Only to hear tales like this, have I given up My opulent kingdom. Please go ahead! Explain every detail."[15]

Atri cleared his throat and spoke, "Greatness not only attracts appreciation, but also envy and doubt. Once the wives of Lord Brahma, Lord Shiva and Lord Vishnu met to discuss what they had

---

[14] *Anasuya* means non-enviousness and *Atri* means one unaffected by the three modes of nature – passion, ignorance and goodness. *Atri* refers to the one who has self-control.

Wherever there is a combination of *Anasuya* and *Atri*, there exists the confidence to handle the most complicated problems.

[15] The complexity of simplicity is that it makes your life seem like a specialty.

heard about Anasuya's feats. They were simultaneously happy and doubtful. They doubted that one could accrue so much power just by being chaste to one's husband and performing one's prescribed duties. They literally forced their reluctant husbands to test Anasuya properly so that the world knew the secret of her reality.[16]

The holy trinity stood in front of this very house in the form of three illustrious sages. Anasuya was surprised when the sages made a bizarre charity request. They wanted her to feed them while she was naked. She was in a fix; she had to do her duty of serving her guests, but at the same time, she had to be the dutiful, chaste wife and defend her purity. She did something she thought was best– pray for direction. Her prayer was answered in the form of a wise idea.[17]

She smilingly called them inside and had them seated. She took a pot of holy water and silently chanted some *mantras*. Along with the *mantras*, she silently prayed that if she had been really loyal and really pure, then this water must fulfill her desire. Pouring the power of her purity into the water, she opened her eyes. She walked up to the three sages who sat clueless about her actions. She sprinkled the water on the three of them and instantly the three sages became innocent toddlers. They had lost all their cognizance of life and began frolicking about carelessly. My intelligent wife shed her clothes and served the toddlers food. By this time, she had fallen in love with the babies so much that she decided not to turn them back into adults. Since we were bereft of children, when she showed me the three lovely babies, I consented happily.[18]

---

[16] Saraswati, Parvati and Lakshmi wanted to use doubt as a medium to reveal the true glory of Anasuya to the world.

[17] Pray, when there is no other way.

[18] *Jnana* means knowledge and *vijnana* means application of knowledge.

At that point, we did not realize that this decision of ours had caused an upheaval in the universe. The wives of the trinity had gone berserk. They had wanted to test Anasuya, but it was she who ended up testing them. They approached the wise sage Narada *muni* for a solution. He advised that a problem that began with begging had to end with begging. The husbands started the problem by begging with a hidden agenda and the wives have to end the problem by begging without any agenda. Soon the consorts of the most powerful of celestial beings were at our doorstep. Seeing Lakshmi, Saraswati and Parvati together Anasuya was awestruck and paid her respects to them and besieged them for blessings.

But she was surprised to see the three of them stand with palms open, begging her. She was taken aback. The givers were asking today. What did such powerful women need from a simpleton like her?

When they revealed to Anasuya that the three sages that had come to her house were their celebrated husbands, Anasuya was embarrassed and in fact ashamed that she had treated such powerful beings so casually. She hastily brought the three children in front of the goddesses. The goddesses were pleasantly surprised to see for once their powerful and formidable husbands look so helpless. They were sweetly attracted to this form of their Lords. Anasuya chanted some *mantras* and sprinkled holy water on the children and their were back to being Lord Brahma, Lord Vishnu and Lord Shiva. Anasuya and I paid respects to these holy deities and worshipped them with all honor.

Acquiring *jnana* is in one's hand. But *vijnana* is the product of grace. When there is *anasuya* (non-enviousness) it is possible to easily distill *vijnana* (application of knowledge) from *jnana* (knowledge).

Being pleased with the purity of Anasuya and with our simplicity, the three divine couples offered us a boon of our choice. We looked at each other and without a single word of discussion, together we spoke from our hearts. We requested for three children who would each be expansions of Brahma, Vishnu and Shiva. Gladly the gods consented and we were soon blessed with three illustrious children. Our first child, Chandra (the moon god) was an expansion of Lord Brahma, Durvasa was an expansion of Lord Shiva and Dattatreya was an expansion of Lord Vishnu. Our children now continue our legacy of serving the world with their simplicity and purity.[19]

gifts of wisdom

"I was always fascinated by the story of Your marriage with Rama. I had heard so many versions of the story. Now that I have heard it directly from Your mouth, I am completely blissful. Though I may be so much older than You are, when I look at You, I remember my younger days and my adventurous spirits. I am sure You will have a hundred more adventures than I." Anasuya shared her thoughts with Sita in the inner chamber.

"When I heard that you had left the comforts of your home to accompany your husband to the forest, I derived more joy than I did when I heard the story of your marriage. You know why?" Without waiting for an answer from Sita, Anasuya continued speaking. "For a woman her husband is her best friend and well-wisher. Through thick and thin, if husband and wife live together, the bond that

---

[19] Service becomes a legacy when your needs are replaced by others' needs. Service becomes a burden when others' needs bother your needs.

they form cannot be cut even by death. Rather than looking for comforts, the couple should actually be looking for the comfort of being together. For both, there cannot be a greater comfort than that."[20]

Hearing her words Sita spoke frankly, "Yes mother Anasuya. I have heard the virtue of being close to the husband sufficiently from both My mothers. I am indeed fortunate that I have a husband who is love personified and takes care of Me with the tenderness of a mother and prudence of a father. That being the case, why should I not give more than My best to Rama who is the most virtuous and sensitive person on earth just because He has lost His fortune? And when I have such an illustrious example in you in front of Me, why would I even doubt the efficacy of executing one's prescribed duties?"

Anasuya was very pleased with Sita's attitude and sweet demeanor. She kissed Sita's forehead. She gushed, "Sita I am impressed with Your virtue and piety. I want to grant You a boon. Ask me anything You wish for."

Sita said, "With My husband by My side, what needs do I have? Your blessings are sufficient for this life."

The answer floored Anasuya totally. "Your answer has brought more joy to me than anything I have experienced in the past. You have proved that for You nothing matters more than pleasing Rama and being with Rama. Sita, be assured, as long as You keep this mood alive You are absolutely safe. The day You forget this and desire anything else other than Rama that day will prove to be the worst

---

[20] Joys and sorrows through thick and thin are two pieces of wood bonded together by the gum of resilient commitment.

day of Your life.[21] Let me now give You something that will help You please Rama even more."

As Sita was mentally pondering over Anasuya's words, Anasuya brought out an ornately carved wooden box studded with valuable gems. She handed over each item from the box to Sita explaining to Her how to use them. A garland that would never fade and would create a heavenly smell when worn; special apparels and ornaments that looked simple but enhanced beauty unlimitedly when worn; unique scented cosmetics and body creams, which when applied would also enhance beauty even if Sita were exhausted and tired.

Sita accepted the gifts of love from this elderly sagacious woman and embraced her with gratitude and love.

On Anasuya's request, Sita adorned herself with those apparels, ornaments and cosmetics and appeared in front of Rama. Rama had never seen His wife in such splendor. He was impressed with Sita's new look. Anasuya smiled with satisfaction as Sita showed Rama the various gifts that She had received.

With the passing of the night, passed an important phase of Rama's journey. The easy phase! Dawn marked the beginning of an epic adventure that none could imagine. With gratitude in Their eyes, insightful stories in Their mind, gifts in Their hands and love in Their hearts, Rama, Sita and Lakshmana left the abode of Atri *muni* and Anasuya *devi*.

---

[21] Was this a forewarning to Sita to be better prepared for the upcoming sequence of events?

The sages led Them southward. The Dandakaranya jungles were awaiting them and so were the inmates of the jungle.

What has Dandakaranya in store for the trio? Are They going there voluntarily or are They being sucked by some unknown force? Was Anasuya actually predicting the future or was she telling Sita that She could change it by Her decisions?

Author Profile

Shubha Vilas, a spiritual seeker and a motivational speaker, holds a degree in engineering and law with a specialization in patent law.

His leadership seminars are popular with top-level management in corporate houses. He addresses their crucial needs through thought-provoking seminars on themes, such as 'Secrets of Lasting Relationships', 'Soul Curry to Stop Worry' and 'Work–Life Balance' to name a few.

He believes that a good teacher, no matter how knowledgeable, always sees the process of learning and teaching simultaneously as an inherent aspect of personal and spiritual growth.

Shubha Vilas periodically interacts with the youth in premier institutes across the world, inspiring them to live a life based on deeper human values. Close to his heart is his role as a guide and teacher to school children, teaching foundational values through masterful storytelling.

Traveling across the globe and meeting people from all walks of life, he teaches the importance of being governed by *dharmic* principles, meting out spiritual lifestyle tips and contemporary wisdom to deal with modern-day life situations.

Ramayana.shubhvilas@gmail.com
www.facebook.com/shubhavilas
twitter – @shubhavilas

Watch out for the next book in
Ramayana – the Game of Life series:

SHIFTING TIDES

Covering the *Aranya Kanda* of Valmiki's original, Book III – *Shifting Tides* narrates the delightful stories of Rama, Sita and Lakshmana as they travel southward across the land. Set deep in the Danadakaranya forest, the book is filled with wise and wondrous meetings with rishis and teachers, such as Sharabhanga and Suteekshna. Here, too, is the gripping saga of the mighty sage Agastya.

Shifting Tides promises action right from page one. The divine three are menaced at each step by demon-kind, which holds Dandakaranya in its vice-like grip. The tale meanders from carnivorous deer that harass the sages to mystical lakes that produce musical sounds and single-handed combat with 14,000 demons. The brothers' capture by humongous Viradha; a horrific nose-ear disfigurement; Sita's abduction by Ravana; and the last stand of the loyal vulture Jatayu are all a part of this thrilling narrative.

Coming soon in 2015, *Shifting Tides* is a treat for bookworms and spiritual seekers alike. Read Shubha Vilas's portrayal of this shifting balance of power from good to evil and find out how our heroic trio will persevere!